WALMART IN CHINA

EDITED BY ANITA CHAN

ILR PRESS
an imprint of
CORNELL UNIVERSITY PRESS
Ithaca & London

First published 2011 by Cornell University Press
First printing, Cornell Paperbacks, 2011

Printed in the United States of America

Library of Congress Cataloging-in-Publication Data

Walmart in China / edited by Anita Chan.
    p. cm.
    Includes bibliographical references and index.
    ISBN 978-0-8014-7731-7 (pbk. : alk. paper)
    ISBN 978-0-8014-5020-4 (cloth : alk. paper)
    1. Wal-Mart (Firm)   2. Discount houses (Retail trade)—China.   3. Discount houses (Retail trade)—United States.   4. Business enterprises, Foreign—China.
I. Chan, Anita.   II. Title.
    HF5429.215.C6W35   2011
    381'.1490951—dc23   2011021221

Cornell University Press strives to use environmentally responsible suppliers and materials to the fullest extent possible in the publishing of its books. Such materials include vegetable-based, low-VOC inks and acid-free papers that are recycled, totally chlorine-free, or partly composed of nonwood fibers. For further information, visit our website at www.cornellpress.cornell.edu.

Cloth printing   10 9 8 7 6 5 4 3 2 1
Paperback printing   10 9 8 7 6 5 4 3 2 1

CONTENTS

v

ABBREVIATIONS

ACFTU	All-Chinese Federation of Trade Unions
ADGM	assistant deputy general manager
AFL-CIO	American Federation of Labor and Congress of Industrial Organizations
ANROAV	Asia Network for the Rights of Occupational Accident Victims
CBA	community benefits agreement
CEO	chief executive officer
CSM	customer service manager
CSR	corporate social responsibility
ES	Employee Standards program
ILGWU	International Ladies' Garment Workers Union
MNC	multinational corporation
NBC	National Broadcasting Corporation
NGO	nongovernmental organization
NMWF	Nien Made Windows Fashions Company Limited
OEM	original equipment manufacturer
P&G	Procter & Gamble
POS	point of sale
PREL	Pacific Resources Export Limited
RFID	radio frequency identification
RHW	regular hourly wage
SACOM	Students and Scholars against Corporate Misbehaviour
SEIU	Service Employees International Union
UFCW	United Food and Commercial Workers Union
UPS	universal product code
WTO	World Trade Organization

WALMART IN CHINA

INTRODUCTION

When the World's Largest Company
Encounters the World's Biggest Country

Anita Chan

Many books have been published about Walmart, not least because it is the biggest corporation in the world.[1] Walmart's colossal size enables it to affect the agenda of world production and trade. Walmart's market impact within America is reflected in a catchy book title, *The United States of Wal-Mart*.[2] Though such books tend to touch on Walmart's reach beyond the United States, and in at least one case even contains a chapter on Walmart's reach in China,[3] there has not yet been a book devoted to Walmart's significant presence in China. China today is the source of the great majority of the merchandise Walmart sells. China has also emerged as one of Walmart's largest and fastest growing retail markets, with close to two hundred giant Walmart stores spread across China's provinces.

What happens when the world's largest corporation encounters the world's biggest country? There are two areas of special interest—the impact of the Walmart supply chain, including the impact on the Chinese workers who manufacture Walmart products; and separately, Walmart's retail business and its brand of management practices when imported across cultures into the Walmart supercenters inside China. In both respects, has Walmart succeeded in a Walmartization of China?

WALMARTIZATION

The impact of Walmart on retail business in the United States and beyond has been so enormous in the past few decades that a new expression, "Walmartization," has entered the English lexicon. Anything can be "Walmartized": from "wal-martization of the U.S. economy," "wal-martization of organics," "wal-martization of education," "wal-martization of health," to "wal-martization of embyros," and the list goes on.[4] Originally, "Walmartization" was a pejorative phrase used to describe the economic impact of large outer-suburb shopping outlets and big box stores on small commercial districts and locally owned businesses.[5] Economies of scale allowed Walmart to buy cheap and sell cheap so that it could honor its "everyday low price" promise to consumers. Any similar kind of big-eats-small phenomenon of mass marketing earned that pejorative label of Walmartization.

A second pejorative meaning of the term has been from the perspective of labor—the charge that Walmart undercut local stores' wages and provided little or no benefits such as health insurance, coupled to a well-organized antiunionization policy that has been so successful that in a period of several decades, not one out of the more than four thousand Walmart stores in the United States has been obliged to recognize a union presence. Of course, Walmart is not the only company that is antiunion. But Walmart has set the standard for other retailers and industrialists. For this, Walmart has gained the wrath of the American trade union movement.[6] As described by two academic labor sociologists, "Wal-Mart represents an employment and industrial relations model far removed from the Fordist consensus of the postwar period (in which General Motors set the standards: relatively stable employment, secure benefits, and rising wages in exchange for productivity increases and protracted periods of labor peace)."[7]

The term *Walmartization* has been used in a third sense: that Walmart's great size and bargaining power as a purchaser has changed the manufacturing system from being producer-driven to retailer-driven. It has been argued that producers today have had to bow to a retailer with a dominant market share in order to acquire sufficient orders to sustain production. When manufacturers could not meet Walmart's low-price demands, Walmart looked abroad for cheap production sites—in particular, in China.

Which brings us to our initial questions: As China became the most sought after manufacturing region, and as Walmart started sourcing a very high percentage of its products there, has this in any way Walmartized China? Have Walmart's pricing strategies put pressures on Chinese suppliers and in turn adversely affected Chinese workers' work conditions or wages? Have Walmart's employment policies at its Chinese stores positively or adversely affected the retail workers' circumstances? Has Walmart succeeded in keeping Chinese unions at arm's length?

The chapter authors are all well qualified to write on these and other related issues. The great majority are experienced academic researchers on industrial and commercial practices. Most have previously engaged in research inside China, and all but one of the contributors are fluent in Chinese. Several of us initially came together because of our shared research interests and decided to concentrate on the different aspects of Walmart's operations in China because of its scale and its importance to the new shape of global manufacturing and retailing. When funding became available, we were able to begin field research and contacted others who had been conducting research on Walmart to join in a cooperative international effort.[8] The contributors to this book are spread around the world, with six located in the United States, four in Australia, two in Hong Kong, and one in China.

There has been a lot of interest within China about Walmart's large presence there, with numerous Chinese press reports this past decade about Chinese-based production of Walmart merchandise and Walmart's rapid entry into the Chinese retail market.[9] As a result, part way through our research and writing, we held a conference at Beijing University in July 2007,[10] so that we could share our initial findings with specialists from within China and obtain their feedback. Some sixty Chinese academics and trade-union staff members participated in the conference, and it became obvious that their belief in the importance of conducting research on Walmart's massive operations in China was as great as our own.

WALMARTIZING THE GLOBAL PRODUCTION CHAIN IN CHINA

Nelson Lichtenstein's chapter provides a background on Walmart's origins in the rural heartland of Arkansas and its growth in past decades, its domestic sourcing policy, its innovative corporate policy of low prices, its unique corporate culture, and its strategies to beat out major competitors. Lichtenstein also discusses how, when domestic sources could no longer meet Walmart's low-price policy, Walmart turned principally to sourcing overseas, mainly from Asia.

Walmart was not the only multinational of the developed North to turn to sourcing heavily from the developing world. Back in the 1970s this relocation of the world's manufacturing site of intensive labor production to Asia had nurtured the growth of the Four Little Dragons (South Korea, Taiwan, Hong Kong, and Singapore). When China began to open up to foreign investment in the early 1980s, offering vast stretches of greenfield sites and an abundance of labor far cheaper than the Dragons, another wave of regional manufacturing relocation was set in motion. Brand-name companies like Nike at that time encouraged and helped its main Taiwanese manufacturing partners to move their factories to China. So massive was this relocation of Asian supplier companies that the majority of the so-called Chinese manufacturing suppliers today are actually Four Little Dragon companies that have set up assembly plants in China. In the past decade, local Chinese capital also has increasingly been drawn into the supply chain.

Walmart reportedly sources some 70 percent of its merchandise from China. So rapid and massive was this shift to goods manufactured in China that by the middle of the first decade of this century Walmart alone imported more from China than many nations did. It became China's sixth largest export market—just behind Germany—in 2004, buying some $18 billion worth of goods.[11] When the two giants Walmart and China established a stable symbiotic relationship at the turn of the millennium, and as Walmartization of the supply chain took root on Chinese soil, Walmart's competitors had to use the same sourcing techniques to survive.

Once sourcing from China became a bandwagon, Walmart contributed, as observed in chapter 2 by Xue Hong, in driving down the wages in supplier factories. While brand-name companies like Nike have their reputations to protect against high-end consumers' concerns that their purchases might be made by exploited labor, a retailer like Walmart does not build its reputation around a brand-name product that needs protection. Selling relatively low-end merchandise, with an ability to place massive orders, it largely strives to use this advantage to source more cheaply than its competitors. Xue Hong's chapter describes in detail how Walmart places orders and squeezes suppliers in China, who face pressures to go along. In the process, migrant workers in the supplier factories bear the brunt of the pressure to cut costs. Each tier of suppliers in the supply chain places price pressures on its own suppliers and subcontracting manufacturers, and Xue Hong shows that the greater the number of tiers and the longer the production chain, the lower the wages in the bottom rung of this pecking order of companies.

The chapter by Yu Xiaomin and Pun Ngai, which focuses on two toy factories as case studies, observes how Walmart took over from Toys "R" Us as the world's biggest toy retailer. They provide details on how this happened, how Walmart exercises its sourcing practices and low wage policy, and how workers at the two factories were pressed to work very long hours for low wages.

As China gradually became the world's manufacturing workshop, the wages in China's export sector competitively affected wages and labor standards throughout the Global South.[12] As multinationals increased their sourcing from factories located in the poor nations of the South, an antisweatshop movement consisting of American university students, trade unions, NGOs (nongovernmental organizations), and church groups emerged seeking to halt the downward drive of wages and work conditions. Both Xue Hong's and Pun and Yu's chapters discuss how the antisweatshop movement instigated the global proliferation of corporate codes of conduct. Eager to join the club, Walmart drew up its own corporate code of ethical standards and hired monitors to audit suppliers' factories in China. Both chapters demonstrate the difficulties Walmart faced in implementing this and the ineffectiveness of the monitoring exercise.[13] The irony is Pun and Yu's discovery that at the two Walmart supplier factories they studied, the factory that experienced repeated monitoring nonetheless continued to impose worse conditions on its workers than the one that was not monitored.

In the past two decades a large number of reports from academics and labor NGOs have documented poor work conditions and low pay among China's export-industry workers who make products for multinationals like Walmart, but the data have been anecdotal. Anita Chan and Kaxton Siu's chapter goes beyond this narrative level by conducting a statistical survey of workers from nine Walmart supplier factories (four garment and five toy factories). In analyzing wages and work hours, they show that the piece rates used in the garment industry result not only in a lower hourly wage rate than the time rates used in the toy industry but also that the more hours garment workers work each month, the lower their hourly wage. Analyzing workers' attitudinal responses, they compute what they call workers' "tolerance level" for exhaustion when subjected to excessive overtime. They argue that today's global production chain produces a "sweating" condition that is a throwback to the days of the industrial revolution of the eighteenth and nineteenth centuries in the West.

The several book chapters on Walmart's supply chain and its suppliers in China warrant Pun and Yu using the expression "Walmartization." The technique of squeezing suppliers has been popularized in the corporate world, though no other corporation can do it on the same scale as Walmart. The new elaborate logistics technology first used by Walmart is fast becoming standard practice. The factories studied in these three chapters all have multiple buyers, since the supplier companies try to ensure they do not become totally dependent on Walmart. But the workers in these factories toil today under the same conditions and wages regardless of whether the products they make are destined for Walmart or for other buyers.

There is a perpetual search for localities that can offer lower production costs. Thus the symbiotic relationship between Walmart and China is changeable. In 2007, for instance, the world's largest manufacturer of socks, Langsha, refused to take Walmart orders because it claimed the price offered by Walmart was too low for the Chinese company to make any profit. Chinese labor costs were rising, and Walmart began looking more intensively for procurements elsewhere. Walmart was also mindful of protectionist pressures within America against China. That same year, Lee Scott, Walmart's CEO, observed that even if Walmart reduced sourcing from China, labor-intensive jobs would never return to the United States: "Even with the economic nationalism that's emerging today, the anti-China kind of thing, much of the product, if it moves out of China because of tariffs, is going to move to Indonesia, or Vietnam or Cambodia."[14] If another regional labor-intensive manufacturing relocation was needed, this would only mean another wave of Walmartization in another part of the world.

For the time being the situation is still relatively stable and most of Walmart's merchandise continues to flow from Chinese-based factories, but Walmart is also hedging its bets by diversifying. In 2010 Walmart announced that it had decided to source garments from Bangladesh in a big way. Knitwear and woven garment exports make up 75 percent of this poor country's exports, and 30 percent of Bangladesh's garment exports to the United States already went to Walmart. In February 2010 the Bangladesh Garment Manufacturers and Exporters Association revealed after a visit by Walmart International's CEO that Walmart plans to double its purchases to $2 billion a year and would source 20 percent of its garments from Bangladesh. At a meeting in Dhaka with the association, the CEO strongly urged that a comprehensive garment industrial zone be established.[15] Notably, such zones are exempted from Bangladesh's national labor laws and trade unions are prohibited.[16] In China, Walmart does not take the initiative to reshape the landscape in the same way as in Bangladesh. Walmart adjusts its protocol in accordance with the strength of the state it deals with.

WALMARTIZING WALMART STORES IN CHINA

As the middle-class in urban China began expanding rapidly Walmart moved into the People's Republic beginning in the late 1990s to capture a share of their spending, and by 2010 it had close to 200 giant stores across China. Unlike in the United States, where Walmart is a low-end retailer, Walmart in

China largely serves the rising middle-class. Some of the stores in China feature large parking lots to accommodate the new auto-owning urbanites.

Walmart cannot Walmartize its China-based Taiwanese, Korean, and Hong Kong-owned manufacturing suppliers by injecting into them the Walmart corporate culture and management methods. But Walmart can do so at its stores in China, where Walmart has direct management control over employees. In the first of the four chapters on Walmart's retail operations, David Davies analyzes the Walmart corporate culture in one of the Walmart stores. A second chapter, by Davies and Taylor Seeman, tells the story of a Walmart store general manager, Edward. The third chapter contains diary entries of a low-level supervisor named Li Shan. The fourth discusses the working conditions of a cashier at a Walmart store. Together their stories provide a glimpse into the world of Walmart retail employees at different levels. A question is: What occurred to Walmart management culture when it was transferred to China? How does it differ from the corporate culture back in America, and how do different levels of Chinese employees adapt to, reject, or live with this culture? Has Walmartization succeeded in inculcating some fifty thousand Chinese store employees into embracing the company culture that Nelson Lichtenstein discusses in chapter 1? These chapters show that the answer is not black and white.

To begin with, what are the essential elements of Walmart's corporate culture that was created by Sam Walton in the early days of Walmart? As Lichtenstein describes it, Walmart culture bears the hallmark of the rural American Bible Belt of the 1950s and preaches the virtues of frugality, self-cultivation, obedience, and diligence. Walmart's corporate culture was also characterized by a personality cult exalting Sam Walton, bombarding employees with slogans and teachings of the great leader, extolling workplace paternalism, didacticism, communitarianism, and collectivism. By happenstance, as David Davies points out, these share much in common with Maoist and Confucian teachings. The culture and institutional methods of implementation are not that alien to the Chinese populace.

There is also a hierarchic dimension in these three case studies of employees: the higher the rank, the easier it is for the employee to accept the Walmart culture, in part because it is his/her role to impart this culture to the charges. Davies has coined the term *corporate cadres,* "because management is held to standards and expectations that discipline their behavior even as they must rely upon it to discipline others as they manage day-to-day work at stores." Li Shan, a lower-level supervisor, never believed in the Walmart culture to the same extent as the store manager Edward. It was not his job to preach that culture, being on the receiving end. He was keen to learn the success of business management techniques from the world's biggest corporation, but to him the culture was an instrumental vehicle, a management tool.

Lihua, Eileen Otis's research assistant, became a participant observer at a Walmart store by working there as a cashier. Her research role required her to be "objective," to observe the culture from the outside. But in her description of the induction of the other new lower-level employees by the store's management, the Walmart culture did not seem to have been inculcated in the new recruits either. This could be seen in the extremely high turnover rate of ordinary workers. Out of thirty new recruits, after two months only three remained. The efforts to instill a corporate culture of loyalty, to raise morale, and to dangle carrots did not compensate for the high intensity of the work (especially for cashiers), a "techno-despotic" labor regime (a term coined by Otis), low pay, pressure to work harder and faster, and surveillance by supervisors and customers. In a manual job where a daily concern to eke out a living takes precedence, the Walmart culture leaves little impact. In all of these case studies of employees, the Walmart cheer that Walton invented after being inspired by what he saw in Korea did not seem effective. It was at best a ritual that employees had to go through under the watchful eyes of supervisors.

Edward was surprised to learn when he went for training in Bentonville, Arkansas, that many aspects of the Walmart corporate culture in the United States did not survive Sam Walton. Today in the back rooms of American Walmart stores there are barely any displays of the Walmart cultural paraphernalia, whereas in Chinese stores, as described in great detail by David Davies, the displays at the front and in the back rooms of the stores are elaborate and dominating, with Sam Walton staring you in the face. No employee can escape them. The Walmart culture and its moralizing permeate the stores as constant didactic reminders. Perhaps only in China, where slogan displays still prevail throughout the urban landscape, do employees so easily accept the bombardment. Walmartizing the original U.S. Walmart culture can, at least superficially, claim some success in China, if not among the rank and file then among managers.

WALMART, THE CHINESE UNIONS, AND THE CHINESE STATE

In July 2006 the All-Chinese Federation of Trade Unions (ACFTU) declared the establishment of a union branch in one of the stores, taking Walmart by surprise. Today, all Walmart stores in China have union branches. Chapter 9 explores why and how the Walmart store unions were set up, and why they have been accepted by Walmart. It will be seen that when the largest corporation in the world had to deal with a strong state, it had to capitulate, but secured provisions to do so on its own terms.

One aspect that should be noted was the lack of knowledge of trade unionism among lower-level union officials and workers. As will be seen in chapter 10, the only union model that local Chinese union officials know is the Maoist corporatist model of working closely with management. The role of a union branch at a state factory under Mao was to organize social events and provide nonwage benefits on behalf of management. As interviews conducted for chapter 10 also show, Walmart store workers from the countryside are likely not even to have previously heard of the word *union* and were unsure what it is supposed to do. Even a store manager like Edward had never had any contact with trade unions until he was suddenly told one existed at his store. (Neither do labor NGOs in China that work closely with factory workers have much understanding of trade unions.) Walmart accepted union representation at the workplace in circumstances where at most stores there was no knowledge among potential participants of what this might entail and where Walmart could control events without opposition.

This book, in sum, examines Walmart's operations in China from a number of important angles. It examines how and why Walmart turned to China as the main source of its merchandise. It examines Walmart's relations with the many thousands of manufacturers based in China who supply the huge retailer with the bulk of its products. And it penetrates a number of factories there that produce Walmart goods and investigates shop-floor work conditions and labor standards. Other chapters reach inside the giant Walmart stores that have sprung up across China. They explore the nature of Walmart's corporate culture within the stores and how it has been shaped to fit Chinese employees. In three chapters, the work situations and views of employees are examined from the perspective of a store manager, of a lower-level supervisor, and of check-out cashiers. And finally, the unionization of Walmart's retail operations is examined—one of the few instances around the world where Walmart has accepted a union. China looms large in the operations of the world's largest corporation, and through extensive, rigorous research this book illuminates its various aspects.

PART ONE

The Walmart Supply Chain

1 WALMART'S LONG MARCH TO CHINA

How a Mid-American Retailer Came to Stake
Its Future on the Chinese Economy

Nelson Lichtenstein

A globalized world of commerce and labor has existed for centuries, but today's globalization differs radically from that of even a few decades past because of the contemporary role played by the corporate kingmakers of our day—the big box retail chains that now occupy the strategic heights once so well garrisoned by the great manufacturing firms of the Fordist era. At the crux of the global supply chains stand the Walmarts, the Home Depots, and the Carrefours. They make the markets, set the prices, and determine the worldwide distribution of labor for that gigantic stream of commodities that now flows across their counters. The deindustrialization of Detroit, Pittsburgh, and Cleveland entailed not just the destruction of a particular set of industries and communities, but the shift of power within the structures of world capitalism from manufacturing to a retail sector that today commands the supply chains which girdle the earth and directs the labor power of a working class whose condition replicates much that we once thought characteristic of only the most desperate, early stages of capitalism.

FROM BENTONVILLE TO GUANGDONG

All this is graphically evident on a visit to the two most dynamic nodes of today's transnational capitalism—Bentonville and China's Pearl River Delta. It is easy to get to Bentonville, Arkansas, where Walmart has its world headquarters in an unimpressive, low-slung building close by the company's original warehouse. There are lots of direct flights from Denver,

Chicago, La Guardia, and Los Angeles to this once-remote Arkansas town. Bentonville itself has a population of just twenty-five thousand, but the parking lots are full, the streets crowded, and there is new construction everywhere. Most important, Bentonville and the rest of northwest Arkansas is now home to at least 750 branch offices of the largest Walmart "vendors." They have planted their corporate flag here in the hope that they can maintain or increase their sales to the world's largest buyer of consumer products. Procter & Gamble (P&G), which in 1987 may well have been the first company to put an office in this part of Arkansas, now has a staff of more than two hundred there; likewise Sanyo, Levi Strauss, Nestlé, Johnson & Johnson, Eastman Kodak, Mattel, and Kraft Foods maintain large offices in what the locals sometimes call "Vendorville." Walt Disney's large retail business has its headquarters, not in Los Angeles, but in Rogers, Arkansas, right next door to Bentonville. These Walmart suppliers are a who's who of American and international business, staffed by ambitious young executives who have come to see a posting to once-remote Bentonville as the crucial step that can make or break a corporate career.[1] If they can meet Walmart's exacting price and performance standards, their products will be sucked into the stream of commodities that flow through the world's largest and most efficient supply chain. For any manufacturer, it is the brass ring of American salesmanship; this explains why all those New York, Hong Kong, and Los Angeles sophisticates are dining at the surprisingly large number of gourmet restaurants that have sprung up in northwest Arkansas.

If Bentonville represents one nerve center of capitalism's global supply network, Guangdong Province is the other. Located in coastal south China, it constitutes the raw entrepreneurial engine that links a vast new proletariat to the American retailers who are putting billions of Chinese-made products on a million U.S. discount-store shelves every day. With 15 million migrant workers, tens of thousands of export-oriented factories, and new cities like Shenzhen, which has mushroomed to more than 7 million people in just a quarter of a century, Guangdong lays an arguable claim to being the contemporary "workshop of the world," following in the footsteps of nineteenth-century Manchester and early twentieth-century Detroit. This was my thought when we taxied across Dongguan, a gritty, smoggy, sprawling landscape located on the east side of the Pearl River between Guangzhou and skyscraper-etched Shenzhen. We drove for more than an hour late one Sunday afternoon, along broad but heavily trafficked streets continuously bordered by bustling stores, welding shops, warehouses, small manufacturers, and the occasional large factory complex.

The Chinese government in Beijing chose Shenzhen as a special economic zone in 1979 because of its proximity to Hong Kong. A few years later the entire Pearl River Delta became part of the zone, with low corporate taxes, few environmental or urban-planning regulations, and the increasingly free movement of capital and profits. The results were spectacular. Gross domestic product in the Pearl River region leaped from US$8 billion in 1980 to US$351 billion in 2006. Shenzhen's population rose twentyfold. Guangdong Province itself produces a third of China's total exports, and almost 10 percent of all that finds its way to Walmart's U.S. shelves.[2]

Although Walmart owns no factories outright, its presence is unmistakable. Its world buying headquarters is now in Shenzhen, and it has already opened more than three hundred stores all over China, with others to come. It is feared and respected by everyone involved with any aspect of the export trade, which is why the executives at the Yantian International Container Terminal in Shenzhen, now the fourth largest port in the world, give top priority to cargoes bound for Walmart.

When Walmart first made the decision to source such a high proportion of its products in China, it did so not merely because goods were cheap and wages low but because, for Walmart and other multinational companies doing business there, a sound currency, excellent infrastructure, political stability, and a compliant workforce were nearly as important as low costs. Governments at both the provincial and national level were making huge infrastructure investments, and similarly tens of thousands of foreign investors from Taiwan, Hong Kong, South Korea, Japan, and the United States were building production facilities of increasing complexity and capacity. This made it possible to transform raw materials into containerized consumer goods in just a few weeks. Nike managers at the huge Yue Yuen factory complex in Dongguan bragged that they could fill an order from the United States in just two months. Container ships were loaded in half the time it took in Los Angeles.[3] It took four days for exports to clear customs in Guangzhou, eight days in Calcutta, and more than two weeks in Karachi. Likewise, the proportion of total production lost to power outages totaled 2 percent in Guangzhou, but 6 percent in Calcutta and Karachi.[4]

A decade ago such stability and efficiency seemed overwhelming compared to other East Asian manufacturing venues. As Andrew Tsuei, then managing director of Walmart's global procurement center in Shenzhen recognized, there were other countries where products could actually be sourced more cheaply. But as he argued, "If we have to look at a country that's not politically stable, you might not get your order on time. If you deal in a country where the currency fluctuates every day, there is a lot of risk. China happens to have the right mix."[5] But as this essay and others in this volume make clear, such stability and predictability no longer characterize the procurement operations of Walmart and other global retailers in China. Labor unrest, wage increases, and an unpredictable exchange rate have generated much tension within the global supply chains dominated by Walmart and the other retailers. To evaluate these growing contradictions, a historical understanding of this new socioeconomic phenomenon is essential.

POWER AND PLACE IN THE RETAIL SUPPLY CHAIN

Neither Bentonville nor Guangdong, these anchors of the trans-Pacific supply chain, are the product of some abstract process of globalization; rather, both were constructed by a set of political and policy choices, in the United States and throughout the globe, that have shifted power from manufacturing to retail distribution, and from an economy in which the interests of relatively high-wage men played a central role to one in which the flexible, low-wage labor of women is increasingly crucial.

For most of the twenty-first century, Walmart has occupied the number-one spot on the Fortune 500 list of the largest American companies. With nearly 2 million employees worldwide and sales of more than US$375 billion in 2008, it is undoubtedly the largest private enterprise on the globe. However, size alone is not what makes Walmart and the other great retailers of our day, such as Tesco, Carrefour, Home Depot, and Sears Holdings, so important. Rather, it is the power that they command in the world economy, the leverage that they exert throughout the supply chains that channel the commodities from manufacturer to merchant, and from Asia to North America and Europe.

This is not the first time that the merchants have been on top. Retail hegemony in the twenty-first century echoes the mercantile regime once presided over by the great seventeenth- and eighteenth-century merchant and banking houses of Amsterdam, Hamburg, and the City of London. By the early nineteenth century, the merchants and traders of Philadelphia, New York, and Boston had moved to the fore. In a society in which production was highly decentralized and largely that of agricultural commodities, the power of these wholesalers, jobbers, and traders to make a market and manipulate it for their own purposes put them at the center of commerce, politics, and culture. They owned the clipper ships and railroads that extended the supply chains of their day across a continent and around the world.[6]

In the United States, the Civil War ended this first era of merchant power. For more than a century thereafter, until the 1980s, manufacturers set the price and determined the market for much of what they sold: the retailers, even when combined into large chains, had to take whatever prices and products they were offered.[7] Today, the merchants again stand at the apex of the world's supply chains. Indeed, the very phrase *supply chain* did not even exist twenty years ago. Historians and sociologists such as Emmanuel Wallerstein had first developed the idea of a "commodity chain" as part of a world systems schema. Then, in the 1980s, business consultants like Bain and Company coined the phrase *value chain management* or *supplier rationalization* to describe how components and materials were purchased and transformed into saleable goods. Frederick Abernathy and John Dunlop used the phrase *commodity channels* as recently as 1999 to describe the way apparel moved from Asian and Central American suppliers to North American retailers. In the twenty-first century, however, "supply chain," with its hard linkages and connotation of domination and subordination, has become the artful phrase. Theorists such as Gary Gereffi and Gary Hamilton have emphasized the market-making potential of the contemporary buyer-driven supply networks in order more clearly to evaluate the hierarchy of power and profitability that characterizes contemporary global trade.[8]

Much of the global economy is now driven by the supply chains that have their nerve centers in Bentonville, Atlanta (Home Depot), Minneapolis (Target), Troy, Michigan (K-Mart), Paris (Carrefour), Stockholm (Ikea), and Issaquah, Washington (Costco). The goal of these megaretailers is to contract for only those goods that consumers will actually buy in a given time frame, not what a set of once-powerful supply firms found it convenient and profitable to ship. Like Ford's first assembly line, which soon made obsolete so many traditional skills and processes in the metal-bending core of the U.S. economy, these supply-chain innovations have superseded virtually all other configurations in the manufacturer–distributor–retailer nexus.

Using a wide variety of new information technologies, the big box retailers of our day collect point-of-sale (POS) data and relay it electronically through their supply chain to initiate replenishment orders almost instantaneously. Thus when Walmart sells a tube of toothpaste in Memphis that information flashes straight through to Bentonville, then on to the P&G headquarters office in Cincinnati, the Ohio home-product manufacturer, which then immediately sends the electronic impulse directly to an offshore toothpaste factory, which adjusts its production schedule accordingly. In the days when products were made in the United States, P&G had long used its market power and sophisticated research on consumer buying habits to secure an outsized share of shelf space from traditional retailers. Today, Walmart has turned this power relationship on its head. The retailer's superior point-of-sale data collection system enabled Walmart to know more about the consumers of P&G products than did the manufacturer, which is one reason that P&G moved its main sales office to Bentonville in the 1980s. By the mid-1990s, Walmart was P&G's largest customer, generating more than US$3 billion in sales, or about 20 percent of P&G's total revenue. But P&G executives were well aware that their good fortune turned on Walmart's sufferance, which explains why they bought Gillette in 2005. The US$57 billion deal was designed to transform P&G into an even larger supply firm that could challenge Walmart's pricing power and its private label brands, but even this megamerger was not enough. "If you want to service Walmart you have got to be more efficient," asserted the retail consultant Howard Davidowitz. "The power will stay with Walmart."[9]

This is "lean retailing." To make it all work, the supply firms and the discount retailers have to be functionally linked. The giant retailers of our day, Walmart first among them, "pull" production out of their far-flung network of vendors, depending on the market. The manufacturers can no longer "push" product onto the retailer or the consumer. Constant and unpredictable changes in sales patterns must be met by just-in-time delivery systems. "Supply Chain Management"—that is the new business school buzz phrase—is the "science" of getting this to happen in the most efficient and cost-effective way.[10]

WALMART'S RURAL ORIGINS

Walmart's history exemplifies this transmutation, but with a distinctive Arkansas accent. The company had its origins and began its stupendous growth in what might well seem a highly unlikely place. For most of its history, the Ozark plateau of northwest Arkansas and southern Missouri has been poor, white, and rural. Neither the New Deal nor the civil rights revolution had really come to the region when Sam Walton began to assemble his chain of small-town stores in the 1950s and 1960s. At this time the agricultural revolution of the early postwar era was in full swing, depopulating the farms and sending tens of thousands of white women and men in search of their first real paycheck. Some left for California or the industrial cities of the Great Lakes, but most were anxious to remain, near family, friends and small towns they knew so well.[11]

Walton took full advantage of these circumstances. He could pay rock-bottom wages and find a ready supply of grateful workers, especially women, who were delighted to exchange the grinding life on a subsistence farm for the sociable world of a small-town discount store. Walton's folksy paternalism was not a new management style, but he carried it off with brio, expressing a barely veiled contempt for the federal laws and bureaucratically structured Yankee business practices that sought to reshape Southern commerce. Like so many other employers of his time and region, Walton played fast and loose with minimum-wage regulations and overtime standards, not to mention the new laws governing race and gender equality in the workplace. And, of course, Walton and his growing army of store managers were bitter foes of any union effort to organize the workers in his company. State-level "right-to-work" laws, which deprived trade unions of the contractual right to insist that all workers in a firm covered by a collective bargaining contract join and pay dues, had been passed by the ultraconservatives who dominated most Southern legislatures in the 1940s and 1950s. This weakened existing labor organizations, made it more difficult to organize new ones, and created an antiunion business climate that speeded the migration of hundreds of labor-intensive industrial firms from the high-wage North to the small towns and rural areas of a still desperately poor South. With other Southern firms—in textiles, apparel, and food processing—Walmart therefore seized the opportunity to pioneer the union avoidance and union-breaking tactics that have become so characteristic of American management in recent years.[12]

At the same time, Walmart has projected a corporate culture that has celebrated family, community, and a faux-egalitarianism, uniting ten-dollar-an-hour sales clerks with the millionaires who work out of the Bentonville corporate headquarters. Although Sam Walton died in 1992, the company's communitarian ethos has long been identified with the founder's persona. As early as 1985, *Forbes* magazine calculated that Walton was then the richest man in the United States, but he still projected a sense of populist egalitarianism. Walton derided computer-age expertise and ostentatious displays of wealth, instead celebrating hard work, steadfast loyalty, and the mythos of small-town America as the key that unlocked success both for the corporation and the individuals employed in its many stores and warehouses.

Although his company avidly adopted the latest telecommunications and inventory-control technologies, the founder deemphasized the centrality of all that hardware. "We are no tech; not high tech or low tech," Walton told thousands of admirers who attended his last shareholder meeting in 1991.[13]

Walton and other executives institutionalized this imaginary social construction through an adroit shift in the linguistic landscape. They labeled all employees "associates," routinely used first names in conversation and on identification badges, and renamed the personnel department the Walmart "people division." Associates who perform below par are not disciplined but rather "coached" to achieve their potential.[14] Symbolic leveling of this sort often takes on a Carnivalesque flavor at the corporation's stadium-size annual meeting, where top executives are put through skits, songs, and vaudeville-like routines that embarrass them before thousands of raucous associates.[15] Even more important than this faux classlessness is the Walmart culture of country, faith, and entrepreneurial achievement. Don Soderquist, Walmart's chief operating officer during the early years of the company's overseas expansion, has taken it on himself to be the foremost articulator of the Walmart culture. He wrote in his 2005 memoir, *The Wal-Mart Way*, "I'm not saying that Wal-Mart is a Christian company, but I can unequivocally say that Sam founded the company on the Judeo-Christian principles found in the Bible."[16]

Soderquist is right to emphasize the extent to which Walmart exists within a particular kind of Protestant cultural universe, even if corporate officers refrain from declaring this evangelical sensibility to be an overt component of the Walmart culture. Arising out of an American South that spawned so many megachurches and TV evangelists, Walmart is immersed in a Christian ethos that links personal salvation to entrepreneurial success and social service to free enterprise.[17] Walmart publications are full of stories of hard-pressed associates, once down on their luck, who find redemption (economic and spiritual) through dedication to the company. Selfless service, to the customer, the community, and to Walmart, will soon reap its own reward. Thus a 1991 *Associate Handbook* declared that Walmart "believes management's responsibility is to provide leadership that serves the associate. Managers must support, encourage and provide opportunities for associates to be successful. Mr. Sam calls this 'Servant Leadership.'"[18] That phrase, which has gathered a subtle Christian connotation though secular in its first use, has appeared with increasing frequency in Walmart publications and also among a growing number of company vendors.[19]

It is one thing to have formulated a distinctive corporate culture; it is quite another to have preserved and reproduced that set of ideological and organizational structures when building stores and distribution centers outside the home territory, but Walmart has succeeded. In the 1970s and 1980s the company did not leap across into the rich but culturally alien suburban markets, but instead spread through tier after tier of rural counties where many small towns and distant suburbs welcomed the big-box stores. Although Walmart was opening or acquiring hundreds of stores, in the late 1970s the average distance of a new store from Bentonville was only 273 miles. For years Walmart recruited executive talent almost exclusively from the south-central states, and when Walmart did put its stores beyond a hard drive from northwest Arkansas, its high degree of centralization ensured that the Bentonville ethos would not be diluted.[20] Walmart's large fleet of corporate jets enables many regional managers to live in Bentonville, even while administering a far-flung retail territory. The company's famous Saturday morning meetings, during which sales reports are interspersed with appearances by country singers or athlete celebrities, put the top brass, scores of middle managers, and a selected group of lesser folk together in a ritualized setting that may be "quaint and hokey" but which a visiting *Fortune* reporter avers "makes the world's largest enterprise continue to feel as small and folksy as Bentonville. And what ever makes Wal-Mart feel smaller and folksier only makes it stronger. Or scarier."[21]

Logistics and Procurement: At Home and Abroad

During the company's years of dramatic growth in the last three decades of the twentieth century, a distinctive corporate culture gave Walmart managers a powerful sense of élan, but that alone could not account for the company's revolutionary transformation of American retailing. Dramatic innovations in logistics and procurement represent an equally important contribution to Walmart's rapid growth and high profits during the three decades after 1970. Because the company was focused initially on establishing stores in such remote and rural locations, distribution costs were very high and deliveries unpredictable. Walton had to do his own warehousing and build his own trucking and communications network to service his ever-expanding set of stores.

This required large capital investment, but it gave Walmart the lowest distribution costs in retail. Indeed, Walmart is a company driven far more by "operations" than by "merchandising." Purchasing, warehousing, distribution, trucking—what we today call "logistics"—have become the corporation's core competencies. Before the 1980s, "logistics," the task of scheduling production, storage, transportation, and delivery, was a purely military term.[22] The Vietnam War, though a humiliating U.S. military defeat, turned into a triumph of supply chain logistics when civilian-run container ships proved enormously efficient on the trans-Pacific run between Oakland and Cam Ranh Bay. A decade later, Japanese "just-in-time" production methods, initially in automobile and electronic production, demonstrated that inventory and labor costs could be slashed if subcontractors were kept on a tight leash by the firm that stood at the apex of the manufacturing supply chain.[23]

Walmart has deployed its hyper-efficient operational arm, not in upmarket product design, but to move the mountain of goods that flow across its shelves to put a conventional basket of branded consumer goods before the public at a consistently low price. At the core of the Walmart system stand more than a hundred huge distribution centers. A typical "DC" sprawls over 1.2 million square feet, about the size of a dozen Walmart stores all put together. Two or three hundred trucks arrive each day, either from the company's suppliers or ready to pick up a load for one or more of the stores. Each truck nestles into one of the hundred or more bays that penetrate every side of the mile-long exterior wall. Boxes large and small are quickly fed up one of the many small conveyors—there are more than twenty miles of them in all—that reach into the interior from each loading dock. These riverlike streams of boxes soon consolidate themselves into four larger tributaries at a "merge center" from which the torrent of boxes, each carefully labeled and assigned, stream into a mechanized sorting area. There, electric arms reach out and guide the boxes ordered by particular Walmart stores off the main river and down into one of the facility's one hundred chutes, which lead onto a waiting truck, all at the rate of two hundred cartons per minute, seven days a week, twenty-four hours a day.[24]

Given the Walmart drive for efficiency and cost-cutting, Sam Walton and his successors were determined to cut out the middlemen. Even before his company built its first DC, Walton hated jobbers and salesmen. He resented the expense, the overhead, the time, the meeting and greeting that had long been part of the American merchandise-buying system. Out-of-town buyers visiting New York City on their annual or semiannual sojourn had long mixed business with pleasure. After a day on Seventh Avenue buying blouses and underwear, stockings and bras, there would be plenty of time for a good meal, a play or concert, and then a restful night in a nice hotel. But not for Sam Walton's crew. Gary Reinboth, an early store manager who doubled as a buyer, remembered:

"Sam was always trying to instill in us that you just didn't go to New York and roll with the flow. We always walked everywhere. We never took cabs. And Sam had an equation for the trips: our expenses should never exceed 1 percent of our purchases, so we would all crowd in these little hotel rooms somewhere down around Madison Square Garden.... We never finished up until about twelve-thirty at night, and we'd all go out for a beer except Mr. Walton. He'd say, 'I'll meet you at six o'clock.'"[25]

Such frugality did not cease once Walmart became large enough to buy 20 or 30 percent of everything that a single manufacturer turned out. By the 1980s much of the purchasing was taking place via computer-assisted transactions; thus the 5 percent commission charged by wholesalers and manufacturing representatives seemed to Walton like wasted cash, charged to Walmart's ticket. Indeed, Walton inculcated an outright hostility to the hail-fellow-well-met culture that had long characterized the retail/wholesale buying relationship, either in New York, Chicago, or out in the hinterland. The friendships, lunches, and kickbacks were over. "All the normal mating rituals are verboten," a marketing vice president for a major Walmart vendor told *Fortune* in 1988. "Their highest priority is making sure everybody at all times in all cases knows who's in charge, and it's Walmart. They talk softly, but they have piranha hearts, and if you aren't totally prepared when you go in there, you'll have your ass handed to you."[26]

As early as 1972, Walmart began getting rid of the manufacturing representatives, the middlemen who visited every store, took orders, and stocked shelves. Those who sold sparkplugs, windshield wipers, and other automotive supplies were the first to go. By eliminating this wholesaling service, which cost Walmart 10 or 15 percent on the base price of its automotive merchandise, it could buy direct from the manufacturer.[27] It took a few years, but by 1986 Walmart had eliminated all the reps who handled auto parts and accessories. Next came an across-the-board edict, promulgated by Walmart in November 1991. In a letter to all its vendors, CEO David Glass declared that henceforth Walmart would no longer negotiate purchasing contracts with anyone except top executives employed directly by the manufacturing firm in question.[28]

Walmart also moved quickly to cut out as many middlemen as possible in its overseas buying operations. Pacific Rim logistical innovations were assimilated into the retail supply chains when, in the 1970s and 1980s, Sears,

K-Mart, and numerous U.S. apparel makers began to take advantage of the cheap labor and growing sophistication of the export manufacturers fueling the rapid growth of the Asian tiger economies, especially Hong Kong, Taiwan, and South Korea. At first this was largely through contract manufacturing, whereby U.S. retailers directly sourced batches of differentiated goods specially ordered for sale in niche American markets. The bulk of the importing was done by the manufacturers selling goods to Walmart and other mass merchandisers. However, why should the company buy goods through the New York import houses when it could purchase children's apparel directly from Central America, shoes from Korea, and electronics goods from Taiwan? A Walmart purchasing office was therefore set up in Hong Kong in 1981 and in Taipei in 1983, with five regional offices on Taiwan in just five more years. By 1989 there were ninety staffers in what Walmart called "the Orient." These operations were kept on a tight leash from Bentonville because all purchasing decisions were made at the Arkansas home office. There buyers would take a look at sample goods brought by salesmen and then ask Hong Kong or Taipei to find a direct supplier.[29]

Staffers at the Asian offices searched out manufacturers, negotiated prices and production schedules, and monitored quality. When orders were finally in production, shipments went directly to Walmart storage warehouses located in Edmond, Oklahoma and Macon, Georgia. Of course, direct imports by Walmart and other discounters only made up a small share of all the imported goods they sold in the United States; in the mid-1980s, Sam Walton estimated that his company's direct imports accounted for only 5.8 percent of its total sales. But if one counts as Walmart imports all the Asian-made products and components that its U.S.-based vendors incorporated into their merchandise, then the proportion of all Walmart sales derived from Far Eastern exports pushes that proportion far higher, to perhaps as much as 40 percent of Walmart sales in that decade alone.

Until about 1985, the supply chains that led from East Asia to the United States were loosely linked and relatively unstable. In that year, or shortly thereafter, production began a decisive shift to mainland China because a 40 percent revaluation of most East Asian currencies negotiated between the United States, Japan, and the Asian "tigers" in September 1985 at the Plaza Hotel crippled the export advantage long enjoyed by these Pacific Rim economies. Combined with rapidly rising real wages in South Korea and Hong Kong, the so-called Plaza Accords set off a scramble for a new set of export platforms, chiefly in Guangdong and other sites in coastal China.

This production shift was rapid but not difficult. Some pioneering Taiwanese and Hong Kong contractors manufacturing in China had already begun to supply the American retailers.[30] Walmart buyers also became directly involved in this production shift, training mainland Chinese how to make goods that would sell in the United States, tightening up the retail supply chains, and giving the big box stores even more leverage against their vendors, both foreign and domestic.

THE "BUY AMERICAN" ROAD TO CHINA

Walmart led the way in squeezing labor costs out of its vendors both at home and abroad, and ironically the company's famed "Buy American" campaign of the late 1980s proved most useful here. The origins of the program lay in a confluence of political and economic factors. Beginning in the late 1970s, international competition had hit U.S. workers hard, not just from high-profile durables like Japanese cars, German cameras, and electronics manufactured throughout the Far East but also in those items that discount stores like Walmart sold in such abundance: children's clothing, women's apparel, underwear, footwear, hardware, small kitchen appliances, radios, television sets, and the first generation of electronic calculators, watches, and toys. In the apparel industry, imports accounted for 31 percent of U.S. sales in 1976, shooting up to 57.5 percent in 1987. More than 250 domestic garment factories closed between 1980 and 1985.[31]

The unions, which still had a good deal of clout in Washington, complained loudly. The AFL-CIO had been free-trade militants all during the Cold War, but this changed in the 1970s, as their members lost jobs and income trying to compete with countries where workers took home wages that were but a small fraction of even the lowest paid U.S. employee. Since democratic rights and independent trade unionism were often absent within the working class of the new Asian and Central American export nations, U.S. labor often found a large and vocal set of allies at home. Free-trade opponents of the labor movement called the union strategy "protectionism," but labor partisans continued to fight for what they saw as a "level playing field" that eliminated tax incentives for U.S. corporations operating abroad, prohibited the low-wage "dumping" of surplus product in the American market, and even raised tariff and quota barriers to some foreign goods. To this end, the unions played the nationalist card: the International Ladies' Garment

Workers Union [ILGWU] spent millions on a campaign designed to fuse the call to "Buy Union" with a new and forthright "Buy American" imperative.[32] The iconic Buy American image of the next decade consisted of an angry group of unemployed auto workers wielding a sledgehammer to smash a Toyota at a union picnic. Since then thousands of workers slapped on bumper stickers that proclaimed "Buy American: The Job You Save May Be Your Own."

Although the poor working conditions that he witnessed when he visited Central American garment factories in 1984 may have offended Sam Walton, he was aware in the early 1980s that the company was now so big and so involved in Central American and Far Eastern sourcing that any successful legislative effort designed to curb imports would have an immediate impact on its competitiveness. In 1983, in an early Washington foray, Walmart had made clear its opposition to import quotas on foreign-made apparel. However, something had to be done. The closure of several Arkansas firms had led to an outcry against the import practices of big retailers, and Governor Bill Clinton was among many state officials who appealed to Walton to reconfigure his purchasing program in order to keep more production at home.

In 1984, Clinton learned that Phillips-Van Heusen was moving its production offshore to meet demands from Sears and Penney for lower prices. Arkansas had been hit hard by the recession of the early 1980s which wiped out more than 1.6 million blue collar jobs nationwide. At Brinkley, a small manufacturing and cotton-processing town deep in the heart of the Mississippi Delta, ninety jobs, held by a workforce largely composed of African-American women, were at stake. Clinton got on the phone to David Glass, then head of Walmart stores, and asked whether the Bentonville merchant could send some business to the locally owned firm. Sam Walton immediately called up Ferris Burroughs, president of Ferris Fashions, a producer of plaid work shirts, and invited him to Bentonville to see if his plant could be converted to produce a shirt that Walmart had previously imported from abroad. Thus, in early 1985 Ferris Fashions signed a contract for production of nearly a quarter of a million cotton flannel shirts. Clinton helped get the company a $300,000 economic development loan and Walton touted Ferris Fashions as a prime example of a product "conversion" that could "Bring it Home to the USA." At a press conference announcing the Ferris Fashions deal, Clinton pronounced Walmart's Buy American program "an act of patriotism and it makes good economic sense in the long run."[33]

Discount Store News' rueful remark that Walmart's "Buy American" program proved "a public relations coup historic in its dimensions" reflected the chagrin of the Bentonville retailer's competitors.[34] Walmart buyers referred to "conversions," in which products once purchased abroad were "converted" for manufacture in the United States. Since the company asked state economic development agencies to help find U.S. manufacturers for these conversions, Walmart won extravagant praise from governors and other political officials around the country.[35] However, Walmart never released any firm figures on the proportion of its product costs that came from overseas. In fact, Asian procurement rose steadily all during the heyday of the Buy American program as the corporate buying staff resident in East Asia more than doubled in size.[36] Sam Walton did not deny that Asian imports were still rising, but he sought to distance the company from this uncomfortable fact, especially following the brutal suppression of the Chinese democracy movement in Tiananmen Square in 1989.

One way to avoid this potential public relations problem was to create a buffer—a middleman or a buying agency that would purchase Asian products without showing Walmart's hand. "The decision was to set up an exclusive buying agency," remembered a Walmart buyer closely involved with the decision. "The main reason for going into [the deal] was not to be exposed as going into Communist China."[37] Walton turned to a close friend and tennis partner, George Billingsley, to serve as head of the operation. Billingsley knew little about retail or procurement, but he held Walton's absolute confidence, which was the key thing in a multi-billion-dollar business that might well come under a barrage of media scrutiny. To run this import business, Walmart brought in Charles Wong, a seasoned Walmart vendor who would run the day-to-day operation out of Hong Kong. Within two years, Billingsley and Wong had set up Pacific Resources Export Limited (PREL), actually a shadow organization, as Walmart's exclusive buying agent, and PREL shifted onto its payroll virtually the entire Walmart buying staff in Asia. PREL soon had twenty-nine offices throughout Asia, from Dhaka to Seoul. With a staff of more than seven hundred, it was the largest commissioned buying agent in the world.

Billingsley served Walmart well. He kept PREL's overheads low enough to satisfy Bentonville's relentless cost squeezers. Equally important, Billingsley presided over Walmart's first factory inspection regime. Because Filipinos knew English and were prepared to travel widely, PREL hired Filipino inspectors, not Chinese or U.S. nationals, to make annual visits to some of the five thousand factories from which Walmart sourced its products.

They had a checklist, covering both product quality and factory working conditions. On occasion, PREL pulled a contract from a vendor whose hazardous conditions posed a threat, either to the workers themselves or to Walmart's reputation. For example, PREL dropped a factory in Shenzhen two years before a fire there killed thirty-nine people. An inspector had noted that four exits were blocked. If the factory had still been a Walmart vendor, Billingsley told a reporter in 2001, the story on the front page of the *New York Times* would have read "39 Dead at Walmart factory in China."[38]

Walmart's Buy American campaign and its increasing reliance on Asian imports were inexorably linked. Walmart would increase domestic purchasing, but use the prospect of such procurement to drive down supplier costs, including wages and profits, and transform these vendors into Bentonville pawns.[39] The company knew that U.S. labor costs were much higher than in Central America or East Asia, but it sought to make up the difference by freezing wages and forcing logistic and production "efficiencies" on its suppliers.[40] As a result, vendors saw their gross sales skyrocket and their net profits plunge. Indeed, a packaged goods vendor told *Discount Store News,* "Walmart's highly proactive approach to product development may, unintentionally, be making American business less competitive." Because Walmart now set the parameters of product development, companies like his were "no longer manufacturers" but were becoming sources that "produce only the products that Walmart has decided it wants to sell, which in turn make R&D and introduction of new products redundant and unprofitable."[41]

Such was the case with Ferris Fashions; after the 1984 deal with Walmart, the shirt manufacturer was now Walmart's creature. The big retailer designed the shirts, sold them under its "American Edition" label, found a Taiwanese supplier from which it purchased the flannel in huge bulk, and bought the entire factory output. Employment soon rose to three hundred, but the jobs were poorly paid, without health insurance, and often subject to chaotic and inequitable piece-rate variations. Walmart's pressure for lower production costs never slackened. Pointedly, the company continued to import a nearly identical shirt sporting Walmart's "Ozark Trail" label from Turkey, Pakistan, and Kenya. When Ferris Fashions workers signed up with the Amalgamated Clothing and Textile Workers Union in 1990, Ferris Burroughs told them "to stop messing around with the union" because Sam Walton "wouldn't buy union goods." Since the company was now dependent on Walmart for the vast majority of its sales, it had neither the money nor the freedom to develop new products or diversify its customers.

When consumer demand for its distinctive plaid product declined after the turn of the millennium, the company's fortunes plunged. In October 2005, the factory joined the line of abandoned stores and gas stations on Brinkley's desolate main street.[42]

A report from the U.S.-based Economic Policy Institute calculates that, between 2001 and 2006, Walmart, which then accounted for 9.3 percent of total U.S. imports from China, had alone been responsible for job losses amounting to almost 200,000 American workers, largely in consumer-goods manufacturing. Since Walmart and the other big box retailers export almost nothing to China, the United States sustains a giant trade deficit, which China has funded by purchasing more than $1 trillion in U.S Treasury bills and other government securities.[43]

By this point, of course, Walmart had long since abandoned its Buy American program. Imports from Asia had begun to soar in the mid-1990s after China devalued the yuan almost 40 percent against the dollar. In 2006 the company bought about US$27 billion worth of Chinese-made goods, up from US$22 billion the previous year and US$9.5 billion in 2001, the year before Walmart and China consummated a qualitatively closer connection. That was the first year in which China was a full-fledged member of the World Trade Organization. Walmart, no longer fearing an import backlash in the United States, abandoned PREL and brought its vast buying and inspection apparatus under direct company control. Walmart moved several hundred staffers to Shenzhen where they occupied three floors of a nondescript glass office tower. Within a year of the move, Walmart made the Shenzhen office its global purchasing headquarters, an emphatic declaration of China's central importance to the company's fortunes. By 2006, about 80 percent of the six thousand foreign factories in Walmart's supplier database were located in China.[44]

Walmart did not own any of these vendor factories, but in many ways the company had become a de facto manufacturing enterprise, with skilled buyers who helped vendors develop and design products according to the tastes and proclivities of its customers, as analyzed by the "data mining" made possible by Walmart's sophisticated Information Technology department in Bentonville, not to mention a computer data facility said to be second in size only to that of the National Security Agency. Because Walmart has an intimate understanding of the manufacturing process and because its purchasing power is so immense, the Bentonville company was able to transform its five thousand Chinese suppliers into powerless price-takers, rather than partners, deal makers, or oligopolistic price administrators.[45]

After a devastating 1992 NBC exposé that documented abusive child labor practices in Bangladesh, Walmart drew up an elaborate factory certification program. Since then, Walmart has replicated many of the features found in the factory inspection and certification programs that have been supported by branded companies like Nike and Liz Claiborne. At least once each year Walmart audits the fifty-three hundred factories from which it purchases directly. The company's Ethical Standards Department employs more than two hundred, half in China. It has established an elaborate green–yellow–red "traffic light" system that categorizes factories according to their adherence to Walmart's labor and environmental code; 1 percent of all factories are dropped from the Walmart supply network after failing the inspection.[46]

None of this has enabled Walmart to escape a barrage of criticism, however. The AFL-CIO has proved an early and persistent critic, focusing on the use of prison labor by Walmart suppliers in China. Then in 1995, when Kathie Lee Gifford was confronted with evidence that the factories producing her clothing line, marketed at Walmart, employed children in Honduras sweatshops, she broke into tears on national television, thereby adding a bit of glitz, and a satisfying victory, to anti-Walmart campaigners. In more recent years the drumbeat of criticism has been almost constant. In 2001, KLD, the largest mutual fund aimed at social responsibility, said that it had sold its shares of Walmart and removed it from the Domini 400 Social Index because Walmart wasn't doing enough to prevent sweatshop abuses. Five years later, the Norwegian government also divested its shares. Meanwhile, Walmart has refused to join the Fair Labor Association, a monitoring group endorsed by many companies in the apparel and shoe industry. In 2005 the International Labor Rights Fund inaugurated a lawsuit against Walmart on the grounds that it fails systematically to enforce labor standards in its corporate code of conduct, and then lies about it to the American public.[47] Thus Walmart is the "dirty king" of South China, as one of our NGO informants told us; the "the lowest of the low," as a Reebok executive observed.[48]

Why is Walmart's record so poor? There are three reasons. First, there is an absolute conflict between Walmart's drive for low prices and its attempt to enforce a code of conduct, as discussed in detail in the chapter by Xue Hong. The Chinese vendors are prepared to take a loss on a first Walmart contract in the hope that they will eventually recoup their fixed costs.

However, given Walmart's enormous appetite, and its bias toward large suppliers, the vendors must subcontract, as must the subcontractors.[49] No one can effectively police the complex network of contractors, subcontractors, and family workshops.

Second, contributing to this price and production pressure is the telecommunications infrastructure that has so integrated the trans-Pacific supply chain. Walmart was the first to install the system. These instantaneous links between Bentonville and Shenzhen put relentless pressure on the Chinese vendors to meet production and shipping deadlines. A quarter of a century ago, the time-frame for inaugurating or increasing an overseas order was close to a year. Goods shipped from Hong Kong moved to warehouses in Oklahoma or Georgia, after which they were shipped on to the Walmart stores when managers noted that stocks had begun to run low. Such "out of stocks" represented a huge lose of sales, especially when demand for a hot item really spiked. By the 1990s, however, the perfection of Walmart's inventory control system meant that Bentonville could now measure all sales continuously. Because Walmart can so accurately forecast its inventory needs, and change procurement orders almost instantly, it now expects the same kind of flexibility from its manufacturers. A "spike" in the sale of a particular item in the United States, usually in apparel or electronics, is now instantly translated into a production "spike" at a factory in China or Bangladesh.[50] Hence the stop and start nature of work in so many Chinese factories, the heavy overtime required to meet an unexpected demand for product, punctuated by short work weeks and unpaid vacations.

Third, although Walmart itself is a "brand" in a way, few of the products it now sells depend on the kind of brand reputation so carefully nurtured by Nike, Levi-Strauss, or some of the fashion apparel makers. Originally, Walton and his key executives had built their Every Day Low Price strategy not on selling off-brand merchandise but on making well-known national brands available at highly competitive prices. However, in the early 1990s, as Walmart accelerated sourcing from China, Goldman Sachs analyst George Strachan released a study concluding that Walmart was in the midst of "a major strategic merchandising revolution... breaking from a history of almost exclusive commitment to national-brand products, expanding and improving its private-label offerings... and marketing them more aggressively than ever before." For most Americans low-prices trumped brand loyalty, so Walmart ramped up its unbranded productions. This surge in the sale of Walmart house brands proved a watershed.[51] By the early years of the new millennium, Walmart was sourcing about a quarter of its goods from branded manufacturers and the rest directly out of Chinese factories.[52]

All this made Walmart far less vulnerable to consumer pressures targeted at a well-known product.[53] The commodities that Walmart sells are interchangeable. The advantages of all this were driven home to us when Tiger Wu, a production manager at Nike, drove us over to the local Walmart to inspect the shoe department. Nike does not sell its shoes to Walmart, in either China or the United States, but it has recently purchased the nonbrand "Starter" line, which Yue Yuen now produces in increasingly large quantities.[54] At the Dongguan Walmart the shelves were full of cheap Starter athletic shoes. Mr. Wu was contemptuous of their workmanship, but even more so of their invisibility as an attractive "brand."[55] From Walmart's perspective, though, this is highly advantageous; it has no investment in the brand reputation, so it can easily and rapidly shift production from one Chinese source to another. The work of Pun Ngai and Yu Xiaomin in this volume further emphasize the propensity of big retailers like Walmart to source private-label products. As they point out, such lines give retailers more control of product development, pricing, and the production process, and also better profit margins.

Walmart's Troubled Future

Walmart and its defenders emphasize the extent to which the company and its emulators have been in the vanguard of a revolution that has squeezed billions of dollars out of a once-bloated system of manufacture, transport, distribution, and sales, thus contributing decisively to a cheaper market basket for millions of hard-pressed shoppers.[56] But not everyone is persuaded that this Walmart bargain is either beneficial or long for our world. When Walmart locates one of its grocery-selling Supercenters in metropolitan America, it asserts the legitimacy and power of a brand of capitalism that is antithetical to the regulated marketplace and the high-wage nation that was built by reformers and unionists during the middle decades of the twentieth century. The company is therefore constantly defending itself against a set of class-action lawsuits—some involving race and gender discrimination, others charging company violation of state and federal laws governing overtime pay, lunch breaks, and health and safety standards—filed by those who seek not only compensation for their clients, but reform of Walmart's internal pay and promotion practices.

Likewise, Walmart finds itself in the midst of a permanent political campaign, promoting its expansion plans for retail outlets before scores of zoning commissions, city councils, and county supervisory boards all across the United States. Here local merchants, environmentalists, liberal activists, and labor partisans have drawn the line against Walmart's effort to impose its alien business model on their home turf. As U.S. politics becomes increasingly polarized, it is certain that Walmart and every other employer of low-wage labor will become embroiled in a fierce political battle over the cost of an expanded health insurance system, an increase in the minimum wage, the definition of free trade, and the effort to unionize the retail sector. Walmart's omnipresence in commerce and culture has therefore drawn a new set of fault lines within American politics, creating the conditions for a day of reckoning, both at home and abroad, that is likely to transform almost every aspect of its far-flung operations.

As for manufacturing, the evisceration of U.S. consumer goods production has been largely completed, but the fate of the hundreds of thousands of entrepreneurs and the tens of millions of workers in Central America and East Asia is hardly settled. The commodities produced by this vast new working class are the lifeblood of the retail revolution, but it would be a mistake to count forever on this torrent of cheap and sweated products. As the Chinese yuan is revalued upward, and as the pay of East Asian workers continues to rise, so too will the cost of imported shoes and other consumer goods inch higher.[57] China, the most dynamic economy in the world, is also an exceedingly unstable place, plagued and energized by strikes, protests, marches, and demonstrations each year.

The market-minded Chinese government still in control of that meganation vacillates between repression and accommodation, while Western investors have jacked up both wages and prices, at the same time that they search for new lands and new hands with which to fill the insatiable supply chains that feed the big box universe. History teaches us that rapid industrialization cannot be sustained for long on the backs of an impoverished and unfree working class. From the mines and mills of Victorian Britain to the shipyards and shoe factories of contemporary East Asia, the search for a higher standard of living and a more democratic society in China seems to be beginning in earnest in the heartland of the industrial South. The revolt of the Chinese migrant workers may yet represent an insoluble challenge to the world Sam Walton built.

2 OUTSOURCING IN CHINA

Walmart and Chinese Manufacturers

Xue Hong

On July 17, 2007, Langsha Group, the largest sock maker in China, announced that it would end its three-year partnership with Walmart because of its unacceptably low prices for purchase orders.[1] Doing business with the world's largest retailer did not make it much money, with only a 2 to 5 percent profit margin in 2005 and 2006. In 2007, Walmart insisted on paying the same low price in spite of higher production costs. Langsha calculated that it would now be making a loss, and it rejected Walmart's order.[2]

This was not the first time that a Chinese manufacturer had declined to do business with Walmart, and some have started to criticize its price-setting practices publicly. However, the news made headlines and prompted public discussion about the relationship between Walmart and its Chinese suppliers.[3] In an Internet survey run by the largest Chinese-language infotainment web portal, more than 92 percent supported Langsha and 87 percent thought that Walmart was squeezing too much from Chinese manufacturers.[4] As Walmart has grown to become the world's largest retailer, it has developed a much closer trading relationship with China—more than 80 percent of its thousands of global suppliers are China based.[5] Many firms benefited initially from Walmart's huge orders, but the relationship between Chinese manufacturers and Walmart has soured. The retailer's incessant drive to keep down prices, which decreased profit margins and sparked fierce competition between factories, has shown Walmart to be a ruthless business partner.

The Langsha story developed in a surprising way. Walmart was unwilling to lose it as a supplier, so it finally compromised on pricing. Their new agreement is that from now on the sock manufacturer will become a

34

supplier of medium- and high-priced products for Walmart.[6] Not all Chinese suppliers have such bargaining power, however. Langsha is a giant, one of the largest sock manufacturers in the world, producing 1 million pairs per day, while most of Walmart's suppliers in China are small factories producing low-quality products. They have to accept Walmart's demands in order to survive in a competitive market.

This chapter will elaborate on three aspects of the relationship between Walmart and its Chinese suppliers: (1) Walmart's sourcing in China; (2) the business strategies that it adopts with its Chinese suppliers; and (3) the implementation of Walmart's ethical standards code in China, in particular the various subterfuges adopted by Walmart's suppliers and manufacturers when the retailer carries out its inspections of factory working conditions. The chapter emphasizes that the failure of Walmart's ethical standards code in China is an inevitable result of its "always low prices" sourcing strategies in the global market.

The information is based on interviews with suppliers and workers; factory tours between 2005 and 2006 with the help of a labor NGO based in Hong Kong;[7] and documents, news articles, and Internet forum discussions.[8] The interviews with workers in factories manufacturing for Walmart were conducted near the factories and in the workers' communities.[9] I contacted the suppliers during factory visits, at trade fairs, and at supplier conferences. I also had some follow-up interactions with the suppliers by telephone or e-mail. Most of them have regular business dealings with Walmart, although some have had only brief contacts and have not entered into a regular business relationship.

Walmart's Outsourcing in China

Low-Price Strategy and "Buy Chinese"

Walmart purchases merchandise from tens of thousands of global suppliers located in more than sixty countries. "Always low prices" has not only been a Walmart slogan for its customers but also has been its unstated motto when it seeks suppliers from the time it was established: Walmart forces its suppliers to offer an everyday "lower" price.[10] Since the 1980s, it has increasingly relied on low-cost Asian imports to stock its stores while forcing its U.S. suppliers to go offshore. Walmart has progressively used suppliers from Hong Kong, South Korea, and Taiwan, finally arriving in China in the early 1990s.

The "joint-venture of Walmart and China,"[11] as it has jokingly been called, is a result of the interplay between Walmart's "always low prices" strategy in global outsourcing and the size of China's vast pool of cheap labor. After three decades of market reform, China has become a "factory to the world." To encourage the development of export-oriented industrialization, Chinese central and local governments have provided many incentives for foreign capital to manufacture in China. Cheap labor is seen as its most important advantage. Millions of migrant workers from rural villages and poor provinces have flooded the labor-intensive manufacturing industries in southeast coastal areas. Meanwhile, collusion between local officials and investors and the powerlessness or total absence of labor unions in these factories mean that China is failing to implement its own labor law effectively, reducing labor standards for the sake of economic development.[12] This environment has become a heaven for manufacturers pursuing low-cost production, luring them from all over the world. Many of Walmart's global suppliers have shut down their plants at home or migrated from other countries in East Asia in the rush to set up new factories in China.

From 1997 to 2003, Walmart doubled its imports from China to US$12 billion. Today, 80 percent of its thousands of global suppliers are based in China and 70 percent of the merchandise sold in Walmart stores is assembled from China. As shown in the previous chapter by Nelson Lichtenstein, "Buy Chinese" is now the company's de facto strategy, rather than its previously proclaimed "Buy American" policy.[13]

Who Are Walmart's Suppliers in China?

In the United States, Walmart purchases products from two channels. In the first channel, Walmart sources merchandise directly from overseas and also takes responsibilty for customs clearance of those imports. These overseas suppliers usually work closely with Walmart's global procurement field offices, from placing orders down to shipment. The second channel is through Walmart buying from American domestic suppliers, which either manufacture in the United States or import from overseas. Such American domestic suppliers include brand multinationals such as Procter & Gamble and Mattel.

Walmart's Chinese suppliers either are owned by multinational corporations from the United States, Canada, Taiwan, Hong Kong, Korea, and other countries, or are joint-venture companies owned by Chinese entrepreneurs and foreign investors, or Chinese trading companies and factories owned by local capital. The manufacturers also vary hugely in terms of quality and size. Some are large companies listed on stock exchanges, while others are no more than family workshops; some are large factory complexes with a labor force of more than ten thousand workers, while others are small processing factories with just a couple of dozen workers. Langsha is only one of Walmart's many sock suppliers, but with five thousand workers it is the biggest sock manufacturer in China. TCL, one of Walmart's major TV suppliers,[14] has fifty thousand employees and is a leading Chinese consumer-electronics manufacturer. However, many small underground factories also manufacture products for Walmart, meaning Walmart merchandise could be made by factories that do not even have an operating license certified by local authorities.[15]

During my field work in south China, I came across eight factories manufacturing toys for Walmart.[16] The largest of them, in Shenzhen, Guangdong Province, is a manufacturing center for a Korean multinational corporation. It has a workforce of six thousand to seven thousand workers and can manufacture about 24 million stuffed plush toys every year.[17] At the other end of the spectrum, the smallest, owned by private capital in Chenghai, Guangdong, has only a hundred workers and depends on subcontracting orders from larger factories. Many of Walmart's Chinese suppliers are merely contractors and subcontractors, and most are not included in its list of official suppliers. Obviously, the trade channels and business strategies by which these different suppliers deal with the giant retailer vary greatly.

How to Get Purchase Orders from Walmart

As discussed in the chapter by Nelson Lichtenstein, in its drive for efficiency and profits, Walmart has been cutting out as many middlemen as possible in its overseas buying operations for more than two decades. It began to bypass wholesalers in the United States in the 1970s, established regional offices and exclusive buying agents in the Pacific Rim countries to expand direct imports in the 1980s, and set up its global procurement headquarters in China in the early 2000s. However, it is impossible for Walmart to eliminate all of the middlemen and buying agents in its global supply chain. Actually, many manufacturing factories in China still depend on intermediary organizations when doing business with Walmart.

Today manufacturers in China get purchase orders from Walmart in two ways: through middlemen/agents or by directly selling to Walmart. From the 1990s until the early 2000s, to secure Walmart orders almost all of the manufacturers in China depended on tiers of middlemen, including Walmart's American domestic suppliers (e.g., wholesalers, trade companies, and manufacturers), or international buyers or trading agents in Hong Kong and Taiwan, and Chinese trading companies and large supplier factories. A range of trade fairs in China, Hong Kong, and America helped overseas buyers, trading companies, and manufacturers build the necessary business relationships—in 2007, annual turnover from spring and autumn trade fairs in China exceeded US$73 billion.[18] The Canton Fair in Guangzhou, Guangdong, the largest trade fair in China, has been regarded as the most important channel for sourcing Chinese commodities. During every Canton Fair, one hundred thousand overseas buyers from more than two hundred countries and ten thousand of China's domestic trade companies and manufacturers gather to try to do business. Walmart's buyers, suppliers, and manufacturers have also been active at the fair.

Since Walmart moved its global outsourcing headquarters from Hong Kong to Shenzhen in 2002, it has further developed its relationship with China's manufacturers by buying directly from them instead of going through agents. Recently, some large Chinese manufacturers have opened sales offices in Bentonville, Arkansas, Walmart's world headquarters, in order to establish even more direct relations.[19] Theoretically, doing business directly should be good for both Walmart and its suppliers, since it eliminates reliance on middlemen.

However, trading agents and middlemen continue to play a significant role in Walmart's sourcing and cannot easily be bypassed for three main reasons:

1. When orders are placed, Walmart lays down strict requirements for high productivity, efficient logistics, and compliance with its code of corporate social responsibility, which can be met more easily by large and brand factories such as TCL. Medium- and small-sized factories find it difficult to satisfy these demands. To secure orders, they usually have to depend on subcontracting from trading companies or larger manufacturers.[20]

2. Trading companies or agents can help manufacturers manage matters such as customs clearance or Walmart's audit, arrange logistics and shipments, and share the business risks. By using trading companies, manufacturers can concentrate most of their energies on production.

3. Many small factories also need financial support from trading companies to tide them over because of Walmart's payment period. In most cases, Walmart, like many buyers, prefers to settle all its payments with its suppliers within sixty days or ninety days rather than paying the moment the products arrive.[21] So trading companies usually provide advances to the supplier to buy raw materials and maintain day-to-day operations.[22]

For these reasons, although Walmart would like to expand its direct-purchase policy, much of its product sourcing in China still depends on many kinds of middlemen. Indeed, quite a few Chinese factories have even refused Walmart's offer to buy directly from them because they need some buffers to share risks when doing business with the global retailer.[23]

Walmart's Low-End Goods

Although Walmart publicizes its "strict" policies on quality control and carries out sample tests, shipment tests, in-store tests, and so on, it is actually unable to implement effective quality control. With the profit margin so low, Walmart's manufacturers are forced to reduce the cost of production by seeking cheap, lower-quality raw materials. High product volume also makes it difficult for Walmart to control quality. Cindy Hu,[24] who worked at a large garment trade company in Nanjing, Jiangsu Province,[25] and did business with Walmart for more than five years, commented:

> Superficially, Walmart imposes demands for high quality, but from many years' business experience with the large retailer, we know that its quality control is not as strict as its requirements would suggest. For instance, in our garment industry, we are supposed to check for broken needles hidden in the clothes. Some buyers, especially the Japanese, require that their goods pass the check machine individually. However, in our company, Walmart's goods have never been scrutinized like that. The size of a Walmart order is much larger than the Japanese ones, by at least 10 and even 100 times. What can Walmart do with tens of thousands of items? During the Walmart quality audit, only a small proportion of the goods are selected for checking.[26]

Chinese manufacturers and traders regard Walmart orders as low-end products, so sometimes manufacturers making higher value-added products think it would damage their reputation if they were known to be connected with Walmart. On my first day at the Canton Fair in April 2005, I asked the manager of a toy trading company if it manufactured for Walmart. He heatedly denied it: "Our products are well-designed and of high quality. They are not for Walmart! My company has no relationship with Walmart." He explained:

> In the early 1990s, if a supplier mentioned Walmart it meant that it had some business experience with large multinational companies,

and it really did help the supplier get more production orders from other foreign buyers. However, now the situation is changing. Chinese trading companies and manufacturers have more choices. Of course, we like high-priced purchase orders which give more profits. My company's main buyers are from European countries, as well as some brand-name toy companies in the United States. Walmart's goods are cheap and have been labeled as of low quality and low technology. You know, any factory in China, even a family workshop, can do an order for Walmart. A close relationship with Walmart has no advantage for quality manufacturers.[27]

Thus in terms of the quality of Walmart merchandise, while Walmart makes some efforts to have strict requirements on quality control, its reputation for inexpensive merchandise means that it must often purchase lower-quality products.

Chinese Suppliers' Business Strategies with Walmart

The Unbalanced Power Relationship between Walmart and Its Suppliers

For the 2007 fiscal year, Walmart had US$374 billion in sales at its more than 6,800 outlets around the world (4,000 in the United States and 2,800 worldwide). More than 180 million customers per week visit Walmart stores, including 127 million per week in the United States.[28] Clearly, Walmart has a strong position in the world market for consumer products.[29] Its use of efficient logistics via high-tech information technology, from barcodes with UPC (universal product code) to RFID (radio frequency identification), gives it a tight grip on its supply chain, delivering the goods on time to the right place.[30]

Walmart's size makes its relationship with its suppliers very unequal. Although becoming a Walmart vendor means an opportunity to enter a large global consumer market, it is also a great gamble. Dealing with Walmart means that suppliers have to give up control over product development, branding, and pricing, and must accept the retailer's insistence on low prices, rapid turnover, and high sales volume. The inequality is further exacerbated by Walmart's global expansion: its increasing size in the consumer market leaves less space for suppliers to maneuver.

Walmart's Chinese Manufacturers' Struggles for Survival

"Low prices" and "high volumes" are the principle issues that Walmart suppliers have to contend with. "High volumes" is attractive but the "low prices" is a headache.

Mr. Hua, an employer from a garment factory in Nantong, Jiangsu Province, remarked:

> The biggest incentive for us to accept a Walmart order is high volume. In the garment industry, large quantities can reduce production costs per item. Walmart usually orders more than ten thousand dozen T-shirts of a particular size and style, while the Japanese buyers only order several hundred dozen. However, it's hard to make money from Walmart. The retailer sets a very low price. We only get a profit margin of 10 to 15 percent from Walmart, while we can get 40 to 50 percent from Japanese companies. Because of its size, a Walmart order can help factories keep running, but it cannot make them rich.[31]

Mr. Liu, from a trading company for craftworks in Guangzhou, made a similar comment:

> A Walmart order gives a very low profit, even when compared with other large American retailers; for example, it is usually 10 percent lower than Target, but the size of a Walmart order is at least five times that of a Target order. It is the large volume that makes it worth dealing with Walmart. Walmart really exploits our company, though. Usually, the price of our products in Walmart stores in the U.S. is at least six times what Walmart pays us.[32]

However, long experience has taught manufacturers in China how to survive Walmart's squeeze. Both companies have found means to increase their profit margins. Mr. Hua told me that he actually got the Walmart order from an American company when he went to a trade fair in Las Vegas, rather than through a Hong Kong agent. Eliminating a Hong Kong middleman gave his business a higher margin than many Chinese domestic factories are able to make. For his part, Mr. Liu emphasized that his company can make money from Walmart mainly because Walmart was less familiar with the production costs in the handicraft industry than in garment manufacturing. If Walmart had known more about his company's products, his profit margins would be squeezed tighter. In fact, many Walmart's suppliers are not as lucky as Mr. Hua and Mr. Liu. Quite a few manufacturers achieve a margin of less than 5 percent and some even temporarily produce at a loss when the cost of inputs increases, especially with China's recent higher exchange rate to the U.S. dollar.[33]

Walmart pressures its manufacturers to ensure rapid turnover and delivery of the right amount of product at the right time to the right place. A supplier from the garment industry in Fujian Province complained:

> A Walmart order usually requires a forty-five-day delivery. It takes us about fifteen days to get in the raw materials, but we dare not make preparations in advance, because the volume of the order is very large and we are not guaranteed it until the last minute. Yet if there is a hitch, Walmart won't accept any explanation; you have to pay fines and may even face sudden cancellation of the order.[34]

How can the suppliers and producers lighten this pressure? Mr. Hua, for instance, said that the most important thing is to "digest all the details of Walmart's rules and regulations"; by this he meant understanding Walmart's requirements on everything, and then finding ways to deal with them.

> Doing business with Walmart is like a battle. If you want to win, you have to know your enemy very well. Sometimes you have to obey Walmart's rules, but sometimes you don't have to comply with all of them. Walmart's number-one rule is low price; that one you have to satisfy. I don't think its requirements on labor rights are very important. Of course, you have to trick Walmart to make higher profits.[35]

As workers' wages in China's coastal cities have risen in the last two years, many suppliers reduce their labor costs by seeking cheap subcontractors in the hinterland. Some larger Asian companies are even considering opening new factories in other countries such as Vietnam, Bangladesh, and Cambodia to reduce labor costs and avoid the risk that China's currency may appreciate.[36]

Some suppliers also seek to keep the proportion of Walmart orders at an appropriate level to avoid becoming too dependent on them. However, there is no end to the retailer's pressure. Every year, according to some suppliers, the Walmart price gets lower and lower, to the point where some factories are even pushed to the verge of bankruptcy.[37]

Walmart's Suppliers' Subcontracting Chain

Subcontracting is very widespread among Walmart's suppliers for a number of reasons. Historically, in the early years of export-oriented industrialization the Chinese government placed strict controls on export licenses for manufacturing suppliers. Without an export license or similar authorization,[38] suppliers were not qualified to take any overseas orders. Licensed suppliers could take orders, but might not have the capacity to produce in sufficiently large volumes; they therefore had to subcontract some production orders to unlicensed companies. For a very long time, only trading companies and a few large factories in China had export licenses, and they had control of the supply chain. Things have now changed, and for many factories an export license is no longer a problem, but this history means that there are still a large number of subcontractors.

Second, Walmart's products are mostly labor-intensive, low-quality consumer goods that do not require sophisticated facilities to produce, so many small factories have the ability to manufacture them. In terms of quality, subcontracting is not a problem.

Third, subcontracting allows large suppliers to fill large orders within a tight timeframe. Generally, as soon as trading companies or large manufacturers get Walmart orders, they immediately distribute them to their contractors and subcontractors, who in turn farm them out to the next tier of subcontracting factories. The subcontracting factories are usually located close to Walmart's official suppliers. Many of these factories, some very small indeed, manufacture goods for Walmart as subcontractors without Walmart Factory Certification.

At the Canton Fair, Mr. Wang, an employer from a small privately owned toy factory of one hundred workers, remarked:

> Our city, Chenghai (in Guangdong Province) is famous as a manufacturing center for toys; it's known as the City of Toys and Gifts in China. There are many hundreds of toy factories, and most of them are small factories like mine. Orders are important to them for survival and development. Walmart is our industrial zone's biggest buyer. I can state that almost all the toy factories here work for Walmart in peak seasons. However, most of them have no licenses.[39]

More than 2,800 toy and gift subcontracting factories, employing more than 100,000 workers, cluster in Chenghai City.[40] Similarly, in Datang in Zhuji, Zhejiang Province, the world's largest sock-manufacturing center, there are more than 10,000 sock factories in a small town covering an area of 53.8 square kilometers, with an annual productivity of 11.8 billion pairs of socks per year, one-third of the world's annual sock output. Most of them are small, nonbrand factories depending on subcontracting orders. They take orders from Walmart through trading companies and large manufacturers like the Langsha Group.[41]

It is obvious that such large-scale subcontracting must create difficulties for quality control and social compliance. These subcontractors at the bottom end of the supply chain usually have the smallest profit margin and the worst working conditions. Walmart is not supposed to know about these small subcontractors, so they do not get monitored. But how about the bigger suppliers that are monitored? How effective is the monitoring in enforcing Walmart's Ethical Standards code?

WALMART'S ETHICAL STANDARDS IN CHINA: THE SQUEEZE ON LABOR

Walmart's Ethical Standards Program

Walmart established its Ethical Standards (ES) program in 1992 to monitor working conditions in its supplier factories. "Standards for Suppliers," also called Walmart's code of conduct, is the essence of the program. The program covers a factory's compliance with local and national laws and regulations, compensation, hours of labor, no forced/prison labor, no underage labor, no discrimination, freedom of association and collective bargaining, health and safety, environment, and the right to audit by Walmart. Factory inspections are the main auditing methods. Auditors are usually sent from the regional Walmart Ethical Office or by an approved third party.[42] Each inspection includes a meeting during which the auditors present a brief introduction to the factory management, followed by a factory documentation review, a factory tour, worker interviews, and then a closing meeting.

As Walmart's largest manufacturing center, China was one of the first targets of the Ethical Standards program in 1992. After one and a half decades of operation has this program been effective in improving labor standards for Walmart's manufacturers?

The answer is no. Instead, stories of Walmart sweatshops in China have continued to emerge in recent years. For example:

1. In 2000, the National Labor Committee showed that workers in Qinshi Handbag Factory in Zhongshan City earned three cents an hour working fourteen-hour shifts, seven days a week, thirty days a month.[43]

2. In February 2004, the *Washington Post* reported that in a factory in Shenzhen City men and women were working in terrible conditions among noisy machinery and clouds of sawdust, without adequate protection.[44]

3. In December 2005, China Labor Watch and the National Labor Committee revealed serious human-rights violations at Walmart toy sweatshops in South China: mandatory overtime work, work-related injuries, excessive quotas, use of underage workers, etc.[45]

4. In December 2006, China Labor Watch said that a survey showed that fifteen Walmart suppliers failed to pay the legally required wages or provide health insurance.[46]

These incidents were not isolated. My research fieldwork from 2005 to 2006 confirm the authenticity of these reports. I conducted interviews with workers and investigated labor conditions in dozens of factories in Shenzhen and Dongguan in south China that produce toys, telephones, garments, blankets, and baby buggies for Walmart, and I came to the conclusion that there is a huge contradiction between real working conditions and Walmart's proclaimed standards. Similarly, the next chapter in this book, by Pun Ngai and Yu Xiaoming, documents the many violations of labor rights in Walmart's supplier factories in the toy industry. Our findings call into question the effectiveness of the ES program.

WALMART AND THE CSR MONITORING INDUSTRY IN CHINA

Since the mid-1990s, many transnational corporations have launched codes of conduct programs specifying labor rights and labor standards while pursuing low-cost global production. Rather than effectively improving workers' rights, the implementation of corporate social responsibility (CSR) auditing in China has instead given rise to a profitable monitoring industry, as discussed in the next chapter by Pun and Yu. When one googles "factory audits" in Chinese in the Internet, a vast list of CSR websites appears, offering information, training courses on CSR monitoring, and even well-designed software in how to design fake authentic-looking certificates. There are a lot of companies, ranging from very large international consulting firms to small local ones engaging in the CSR business, claiming to provide "professional" consulting services in factory audits. The CSR industry has become a cat-and-mouse game between suppliers and their buyers.[47]

Walmart, as the world's largest retailer, is a major client of these CSR businesses. Thousands of supplier factories are interested in learning the experience of how to deal with Walmart. The company is an extremely popular topic in Internet discussion forums among suppliers.[48]

Second, Walmart has a bad global reputation on labor issues. The establishment and development of Walmart's Ethical Standards are specific reactions to the continuing pressures from international antisweatshop NGOs and anti-Walmart campaigns in the United States. In 1992, Walmart was exposed for using child labor in Bangladesh by the NBC News program *Dateline,* which is what instigated Walmart to establish the ES program. Since then, more and more violations in sweatshops supplying Walmart have been reported by labor NGOs.[49] The chapters by Pun and Yu and by Chan and Siu provide evidence of the low labor standards in Walmart's supplier factories in China.

Third, unlike other transnational corporations such as Nike, Reebok, Adidas, and Levi Strauss, which also implement CSR programs, Walmart does not have to protect consumer loyalty to an established brand-name product, and the retailer's low prices trump its customers' concerns.

Fourth, Walmart's self-policing CSR model transfers the main responsibility to eliminate labor abuses to its suppliers and manufacturers. Given this, Walmart's ES program is essentially a business strategy to improve its public relations rather than a tool to raise the labor standards of its global suppliers.

Below is a description of how Walmart puts its standards of suppliers in China into practice. It uncovers the myth of Walmart's ES program.

Maneuvering by Walmart's Suppliers

Over the fifteen years of the ES program's operations in China, Chinese manufacturers have become adept at pleasing Walmart auditors and concealing abuses.[50] During factory inspections, suppliers and manufacturers pursue the following strategies.

Model Factories for Auditors. To pass Walmart's audit, some suppliers, especially trading companies, set up model factories that have better workplace environments and labor conditions on audit day,[51] as it is simple to improve factory conditions for one day. When the audit is done and the orders are in hand, the suppliers redistribute the orders to other factories and to subcontractors. Although Walmart requires all its suppliers to disclose their subcontractors, demanding that orders be placed only with subcontractors who have also passed an audit, many subcontractors still slip under Walmart's radar.[52] Suppliers sometimes conduct factory inspections on their contractors and subcontractors, but they usually inspect only equipment and facilities (e.g., the fire alarm system) to avoid potential disasters that may attract public attention.

I was once involved in a workers' training program initiated by a multinational toy corporation and made eight visits to a toy factory in 2005 and 2006. The factory had been set up in 1997 in Shenzhen by a Taiwanese company and was an authorized Walmart supplier.[53] Within the factory walls there were two factory buildings with two different names. According to the workers, when auditors came to their factory, the boss only showed them the plant with better working conditions. Although the plant beside it was also producing toys for Walmart, the auditors had no interest in inspecting that one.

Creating Authentic-Looking Documents. Reviewing factory documentation is a key component of factory inspections. Documentation usually covers working hours, compensation, personnel data, production information. and records of the factory's audit history. Suppliers have learned that presenting authentic-looking documents is the best way to pass the audit, so they spend a lot of time on this and may even ask commercial agents to concoct factory documents to meet Walmart's requirements. After all, it is much easier and cheaper to fix their *documented* working conditions than to improve the *real* ones. A case study by Pun Ngai of a supplier factory points out that "creating paperwork" has become supplier factories' core activity in the corporate code implementation.[54]

The most important of all documents are the hiring records. The ES program is sensitive to age violations and noncompliance with labor laws, but factories commonly hire underage workers who use other people's ID cards. In summer, some factories even recruit temporary student workers from vocational schools and high schools,[55] and may not have signed labor contracts or bought social insurance for the workers. The personnel documents thus are cleansed of information on workers younger than eighteen and temporary workers recruited in peak seasons. On the day of the audit, these "unqualified" workers are told to have a day off.

Excessive overtime and illegally low wages are two major labor violations in Walmart's supplier factories, as noted in the the next two chapters. But how could such sweated factories pass Walmart's factory audits? Double book-keeping is the answer. Many factories record working hours using two different systems. In the books audited by Walmart, there is usually a set sixty-hour working week with an eight-hour regular workday and 2.5 hours of overtime work per day and one day off per week, to comply with Walmart's standards.[56] Under the system used for the factory's own bookkeeping, however, workers are not allowed, for example, to punch their time cards if the overtime is beyond either the legal limit or Walmart's standard. Their extra overtime records are kept only by line supervisors for in-house use.[57]

Some factories also manipulate workers' wages, especially basic wages and overtime payments. The workers' basic wage is usually set to match the local government's legal minimum wage to pass the audit. In practice, though, the factories pay less than the minimum wage because meals and an accommodation charge are generally deducted from the workers' pay packets even if workers do not eat at the staff canteen nor live in the factory dormitories.

Coaching Workers on How to Lie. During Walmart's factory inspections, auditors are required to conduct interviews with workers. However, factories coach workers by preparing handouts of standard questions and answers based on Walmart's code, holding training sessions or posting up the right answers on the shop floor. To ensure the effectiveness of these preparations, some factories even have a mechanism for rewards and punishment: workers who provide "good" answers in a Walmart interview get a bonus but may be fined or even fired if they tell the truth. Managers also impress on the workers that lying to the auditors will help the factory to secure large orders, while telling the truth will lose orders, which will lead to lower pay and even layoffs. Such "training" naturally influences many workers to lie and thus forfeit the chance to improve their working conditions.

A worker in a factory in Dongguan, Guangdong, that produces baby buggies for Walmart explained:

We usually have one-hour training sessions for several consecutive nights before buyers' factory inspections. It is not bad because the training is counted as overtime work and is paid. When one is selected for the interview and gives the right answers he or she will get a 50-yuan bonus. Before, the bonus was 100 yuan for each worker, but now, because the inspections are more frequent and more and more workers are interviewed, it has been reduced to 50 yuan. That is about two days' wage. In our factory, workers' daily basic wage is 16.5 yuan, and the overtime wage is 2 yuan per hour including weekends, and 3 yuan after 10:00 p.m., so our wage depends heavily on overtime work....I was once selected for the interview. I told them that my basic wage was 700 yuan per month. Why? It was not for the bonus at all. Really I was afraid that if our factory lost orders we would have less overtime and, as a result, lower wages.[58]

In some factories, underage workers are told to say that they are eighteen if they are questioned by strangers outside the factory gate. In December 2005, I tried to interview workers from a large toy factory producing for Walmart in Shenzhen. During a lunch break, I met a pretty young worker near the factory. After introducing myself, I asked:

Q: How old are you?
A: I am eighteen years old.
Q: Really? You look so young!
A: Yes, I am really eighteen years old.

I chatted with her for a while about her working experience, then asked:

Q: When were you born?
A: Oh, I was born in November 1990.

When I pressed her, the girl admitted that she had lied at first. She was only fifteen years old, and she said that there were several even younger girls in her department. All the underage workers had been instructed to tell any strangers that they were eighteen years old. Obviously such worker interviews cannot provide Walmart auditors with a true picture of working conditions inside factories.

Is Walmart Fooled?

Few suppliers regard their stratagems as cheating, as they believe that Walmart is well aware of working conditions in its supplier factories. Some have pointed out that no more than 10 percent of Walmart factories in China could reach the declared standards.[59] Walmart too admits that such situations exist. Its 2005 *Report on Ethical Sourcing* states that serious violations were consistently found. These included problems with payment of over-time compensation, coaching of workers for worker interviews, and the use of "double-books" to hide the true numbers of hours worked or wages/benefits paid.[60] Walmart explained these problems away as deficiencies of factory management and lack of local government enforcement rather than as consequences of fundamental flaws in its ES program.[61] The practical problems in the program's implementation include:

1. As noted, the widespread use of subcontracting means that the major-ity of manufacturers in Walmart's layered supply chain are not even over-seen by the program.

2. The program is not implemented consistently, and the suppliers know this. They know that Walmart's priorities are low price and prompt delivery and that business interests override other considerations.

3. The audit usually involves only a one-day visit, which is too brief. Moreover, in most cases the suppliers are notified beforehand, giving time for the factories to clean up their act. Walmart's official report indicates that there was an increase in high-risk violations from 35.6 percent in 2004 to 52.3 percent in 2005, after an increase in unannounced audits from 8 percent to 20 percent.[62]

4. The linkage of the audit to the award of purchase orders gives great power to the auditors conducting the inspection, making corruption a side effect of the system. Although before the inspection begins managers and auditors have to sign the Walmart Gifts and Gratuity Policy forbidding any offer or receipt of gifts or bribes, the use of the "red packet" (i.e., money put in a small red envelope) is no secret. The amount is usually in propor-tion to the volume of the order. Some suppliers find it annoying that they have to pay and yet still sign the document affirming that the auditors did not receive anything from their factory.[63]

5. Although some suppliers meet local minimum wage and legal overtime payment requirements because of Walmart's pressure, they offset this by, for example, increasing production quotas and speeding up the pace of the work. Workers who cannot finish the tasks in the specified time are penalized by not being paid for the additional overtime needed to finish the tasks.[64] However, Walmart has not noted this as a problem in the ES program.

6. A serious problem is that Walmart's standards do not involve the work-ers or take the workers' perspective into account. Most workers have no chance to get any training on the standards and have little idea about the ES program. Although Walmart asks its suppliers to post a copy of Standards for Suppliers publicly in their factories, in most cases the factories merely put a

copy up on the shop floor on the day of the audit and remove it after the auditors leave. Workers have no opportunity to read the poster carefully.[65] The only opportunity that they have to talk about their working conditions is when they were interviewed by auditors. But as we have seen, they are afraid to tell the truth for fear of losing their jobs or being punished by employers. Walmart has ignored workers' considerations and has not provided more practical channels for workers to express their ideas to auditors such as meeting auditors privately instead of in a group, training workers in the Ethical Standards, and setting up a grievance procedure. Walmart's 2006 *Report on Ethical Sourcing* mentioned that auditors provided factory workers a channel for complaints with a local helpline number and an e-mail address. However, according to Walmart's own report, only 150 workers used the hotline after more than 16,700 audits in 8,873 factories in 2006.[66]

Instead of improving working conditions, the ES program in reality has become a tool allowing Walmart to offload responsibilities onto its suppliers. Walmart's suppliers have to accept the audit unconditionally, and Walmart can heap most of the responsibility for labor abuses onto them. Its annual *Report on Ethical Sourcing* emphasizes that the company works proactively to improve working conditions globally, yet problems abound at the factory level. Further, the program is purchase-order-oriented, giving Walmart all the leverage. Walmart requires suppliers to read and sign the Supplier Agreement before it will sign a contract with them. Only if the factories pass the initial audit will they get the purchase orders. On audit day, therefore, suppliers naturally try to make working conditions in their factories appear better than they really are.

The business strategy of everyday low prices is the root cause of Walmart's failure to implement its ES program effectively. Squeezed financially by Walmart, suppliers and manufacturers pass its audit by using dodgy stratagems rather than by enhancing labor standards. The many subcontractors slip beneath its radar. Importantly, the program actually blocks out the workers' voices, and workers know little or nothing about the program, although it is sold to the world as being intended to improve their working conditions.

CONCLUSION: THE NEW CHALLENGES FACING WALMART AND ITS CHINESE SUPPLIERS

In the early 1990s, becoming a supplier to the giant retailer seemed to many Chinese manufacturers to provide a wonderful opportunity to enter the global market, to make money, and to expand their business. However, doing business with Walmart over many years has subjected them to extreme pressures in terms of low purchase prices, high volume, and rapid turnover. Some manufacturers have begun to walk away from the world's largest retailer. Many other suppliers have coped by squeezing workers in order to maintain low-cost production and by outsourcing to small contractors. The implementation of Walmart's Ethical Standards in China has exacerbated the imbalance in the retailer–supplier power relationship, shifting the main responsibility for compliance with labor standards to the factories. With time, manufacturers have learned how best to conceal labor abuses from auditors.

As the rising cost of labor and raw materials and the appreciation of China's currency lead to increased production costs, export-processing manufacturers are forced to raise the prices of their merchandise, placing the relationship between Walmart and its Chinese suppliers under new pressures. Although China remains one of Walmart's biggest trading partners, Walmart has not ceased to push its low prices strategy, by reducing procurement orders in China and transferring them to countries such as India or Vietnam.[67] Chinese suppliers who have geared up for large Walmart orders face disaster when the deal falls through and they are unable to find an alternative buyer. Although the company has in some cases made concessions to large brand-name manufacturers, it is still squeezing most manufacturers with excessively low-priced procurement demands. To survive, many small factories reduce production costs by sacrificing quality and workers' conditions.

The global financial crisis during 2008 and 2009 exacerbated the situation of China's export-oriented manufacturing industry. Thousands of manufacturers, particularly small- and middle-size ones, including many Walmart's suppliers, went into bankruptcy. In March 2008, Jinwoniu Company, Walmart's largest supplier of barbecue equipment, had to shut down. Walmart was Jinwoniu's major customer, accounting for 60 percent of the factory's production orders. Cooperation with Walmart had once contributed to the success of Jinwoniu, but when times were hard Walmart did little to prevent the bankruptcy of the company.[68]

The closure of Jinwoniu alarmed others among Walmart's manufacturers in China. To avoid suffering the same fate as Jinwoniu, some of them are trying to shift out of Walmartization, characterized by low prices, high volumes, rapid turnovers, and low-end products. Nien Made Windows Fashions (NMWF) has cooperated with Walmart for more than twenty years. It is succeeding in de-Walmartizing while still doing business with Walmart:[69]

1. It emphasizes upgrading rather than competing to get more production orders from Walmart.

2. It focuses on improving efficiency on the shop floor rather than further sacrificing workers' conditions. By introducing lean production and technology innovation, NMWF has gradually reduced its labor force by 20 percent yet is still able to increase output by 30 percent.

3. It is careful in keeping the proportion of Walmart orders at an appropriate level to avoid over-dependence on one major customer. NMWF had succeeded because of Walmart's large orders in the 1990s and has become one of Walmart's only two window suppliers in China. But today, Walmart's orders only account for 10 percent of NMWF's production. NMWF provides an example of how some Chinese manufacturers are learning to cope with Walmart.

During the global economic recession, the bankruptcy of many of the small suppliers has led to a growing concentration of Walmart's orders with large Chinese manufacturers, which might potentially threaten Walmart's bargaining power. The retail giant is afraid that more and more large suppliers like the Langsha Group will ask for higher purchase prices. Meanwhile, due to the economic downturn in the United States, Walmart has been eager to source ever cheaper products. For example, Walmart's 2009 theme was to pursue further price reductions.[70] This only further exacerbates conflicts between Walmart and its Chinese suppliers.

In early 2010, Walmart decided to change its global sourcing strategy. This strategy involves the creation of Global Merchandising Centers (GMCs), a change in leadership and structure, and a strategic alliance with Li & Fung, a gigantic Hong Kong-based global sourcing company.[71] Through its GMCs, Walmart wants to increase direct sourcing for its private brands, while through Li & Fung it tries to consolidate part of its sourcing portfolio. The new strategy is intended to enhance efficiencies and increase savings in Walmart's supply chain. However, it will definitely restructure the relationship between Walmart and its suppliers. Walmart's efforts to reduce the cost of products manufactured in China are unending.

3 WALMARTIZATION, CORPORATE SOCIAL RESPONSIBILITY, AND THE LABOR STANDARDS OF TOY FACTORIES IN SOUTH CHINA

Yu Xiaomin and Pun Ngai

This chapter uses the toy industry as a case study of Walmart's global production chain because today China is the largest producer and exporter of toys in the world and Walmart is one of the big buyers. China has more than eight thousand manufacturing companies employing more than 3.5 million workers, producing almost 75 percent of the toys in global trade.[1] The United States and the European Union countries are key markets for China's toy exports, accounting in 2005 for 47.7 percent and 22.4 percent respectively of the country's total toy exports.[2] China's share of total U.S. toy imports increased from 41.4 percent in 1992 to 90.6 percent in 2008 (see figure 3.1).

More than 95 percent of China's toy production in 2005 was located in six coastal provinces: Guangdong, Jiangsu, Shanghai, Zhejiang, Shandong, and Fujian.[3] Guangdong is the largest contributor, accounting for 69.3 percent of China's toy exports,[4] the majority of the province's toy factories being owned by Hong Kong toy manufacturers. In 2006, Hong Kong manufacturers owned more than four thousand of the nearly five thousand toy factories located in Guangdong.[5] Moreover, a large proportion of China's toys are exported through entrepôt trade via Hong Kong. Between 1983 and 2000, Hong Kong's entrepôt trade value of toys and sports goods increased from HK$8.9 billion (US$1.1 billion) to HK$103.1 billion (US$13.2 billion).[6] Most Chinese toy firms, whether owned by Hong Kong or Chinese investors, are original equipment manufacturers (OEMs), producing brand-name products for overseas manufacturers or retailers and relying heavily on them for manufacturing techniques, design, and distribution.

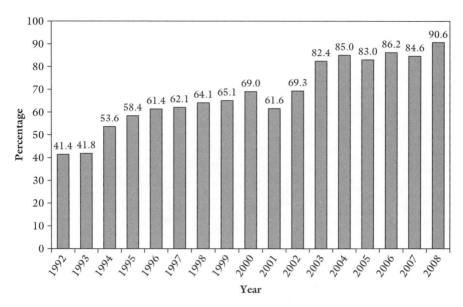

Figure 3.1. China's share of U.S. total toy imports, 1992–2008. *Sources*: The International Trade Administration of the U.S. Department of Commerce, "Top 25 Import Sources for All Toys, Games, and Dolls SIC 3942, 3944: Customs Value," http://www.ita.doc. gov/td/ocg/imp3942_44.htm, and http://www.ita.doc.gov/td/ocg/archive/aimp3942_44. htm; U.S. Department of Commerce, "Dolls, Toys, Games, and Children's Vehicles NAICS Code 33993," http://www.ita.doc.gov/td/ocg/toyoutlook_09.pdf.

The competitiveness of China's toy industry is based on a low-price strategy made possible by cheap land, energy, materials, and labor at the expense of workers' rights and interests. Since the mid-1980s, sweatshop labor abuses in China's export-oriented, labor-intensive industries have been extensively documented and criticized by journalists and labor rights advocacy groups. These critics argue that, in addition to global "race to the bottom" production strategy, the rampant labor abuses in China's export-oriented, labor-intensive industries are rooted in the Chinese government's lax enforcement of labor laws and haphazard implementation social security policies, and in the weakness of the Chinese trade unions in representing the migrant workers who are the main workforce of China's labor-intensive industries.[7] Just as salient has been the fact that labor rights abuses are also closely related to competitive trends in the global marketplace and the business practices of the multinationals that dominate the global consumer goods supply chains—firms such as Walmart, Nike, Levi Strauss, and Mattel.

The antisweatshop movement grew in the middle and late 1990s and pressured brand-name merchandisers and retailers sourcing production in low-wage developing countries like China to take social responsibility and uphold labor standards in their overseas supplier factories.[8] The toy industry was one of the industries receiving the most damning criticisms of sweatshop abuses. In response, leading toy merchandisers and retailers such as Mattel, Hasbro, Walmart, and Toys "R" Us felt pressured to adopt codes of conduct and to require their overseas suppliers to comply with them.[9]

In the past decade the number of kinds of codes of conduct has grown rapidly in the global toy industry and has caused the establishment of monitoring systems for code compliance ranging from internal monitoring to external and independent monitoring as discussed in Xue Hong's chapter. As the world's factory, China has become possibly the most-monitored country with regard to code compliance.

This study investigates how, and to what extent, Walmart's low-price-driven business model has redefined the competitive landscape of the whole industry and whether or not this has resulted in a "race to the bottom" in labor standards. Second, it examines the dynamics of corporate social responsibility (CSR) in the toy industry with regard to the adoption and monitoring of codes of conduct. Finally, this chapter presents our empirical findings on the nature and characteristics of Walmart's "legal-minimalist-driven," "self-policing-centered," and "punishment-oriented" CSR model, and examines its impact on workplace labor standards in its supplier factories in China.

The empirical research was conducted from June 2005 to January 2006 at two of Walmart's toy supplier factories located in Shenzhen, a city in south China. In this chapter, the factories are referred to as T_1 and T_2. Data were collected through in-depth interviews with workers and also by reviewing relevant documents. Production workers with staff cards and/or in uniform were approached outside the plants for interviews. By the snowball sampling method, twelve workers from different departments were interviewed on overall working conditions in the two factories: five from T_1 and seven from T_2. Through semistructured interviews, the workers shared their satisfactions and frustrations with workplace labor conditions in their factories as regards working hours, wages, dormitory conditions, food, social security schemes, and trade union activities. The documents reviewed included company documents (e.g. Walmart annual reports and CSR reports), online databases (LexisNexis, Chinainfobank, etc.) and websites (of toy industry associations and NGOs).

The Global Toy Industry

During the past four decades, the toy industry has become a US$60 billion global business. Historically, the industry was dominated by several American manufacturers, but in the early 1950s, to decrease production costs, American toy manufacturers began to outsource low-value-added production to low-wage countries such as Japan, Taiwan, Hong Kong, and more recently, China. The former manufacturers increasingly became toy "merchandisers," focusing more on high-value-added activities such as toy development, design, and marketing. In 2001, 67.1 percent of global retail toy sales (US$69.5 billion) took place in North America and Europe while 75 percent of internationally traded toys were manufactured in China.[10]

One of the most remarkable features of today's toy industry is the dominance of big corporations. Industry consolidation can be traced back to the 1980s. Of the top companies that existed in 1976, eleven went out of business by 1995 and twelve were taken over by Mattel and Hasbro, today's two largest toy merchandisers.[11] Between 1984 and 1999, the share of the U.S. toy market held by these two industry leaders increased from 21 percent to 33 percent.[12] The relentless competition has polarized the toy industry: Mattel and Hasbro manage a collection of familiar brands that dominate the market, while a host of small companies struggle to live on a single unique toy idea or theme (though these latter tend to be the ones driving product innovation and diversification). The big players enjoy competitive advantages ranging from economies of scale and brand recognition to resources for advertising and licensing agreements.[13]

At the same time, there has also been consolidation in the retail market. Globally, toys are sold through a distribution channel consisting of mass merchandisers, discount stores, toy specialists, department stores, and mail-order businesses.[14] During the past two decades, in the U.S. toy market, which is the world's largest, department stores have continuously lost market share to discounters such as Walmart, K-Mart, and Target, and to national toy chains such as Toys "R" Us. Today, the mass merchandisers and discount stores are the primary retail channel for toys, accounting for more than 50 percent of all U.S. toy sales in 2004.[15]

Walmartization of the Global Toy Industry

Surpassing Toys "R" Us in 2000, Walmart has since become the largest toy retailer in the U.S. market. In recent years, Walmart's status as the number-one retailer of toys has grown continuously, leading to a 34 percent share of the $31.6 billion U.S. toy business in 2006 (see figure 3.2). Being the world's largest toy retailer, Walmart is more powerful than any corporation has ever been in terms of its market clout, its dominance of the global supply chain, and its influence on the pattern of competition in the global toy industry. In the words of an industry analyst, "Wal-Mart is increasingly playing a role of kingmaker in the toy business."[16] As described by Nelson Lichtenstein in his chapter, toy companies line up to woo Walmart's buyers and to open offices near Walmart headquarters in Arkansas. Disney has been there since 1999; MGA, the creator of Bratz, is a more recent inhabitant; Spin Master moved in and doubled its sales to the chain in a year.[17]

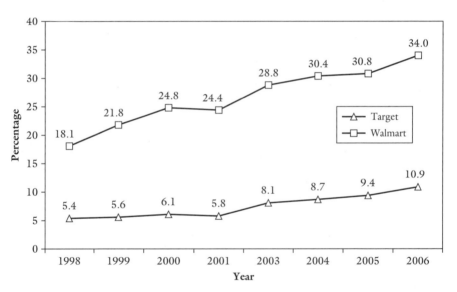

Figure 3.2. Dollar share of Walmart and Target in the U.S. toy market, 1998–2006. *Sources*: "Top 25 Retailers", *Playthings* 105, no. 11 (2007): 20–25; "Merchants of Mirth: The Top 25 Playthings Retailers," *Playthings* 104, no. 11 (2006): 22–6; "Playthings Top 25," *Playthings* 103, no. 11 (2005): 19–22; "Top 25 Toy Retailers," *Playthings* 102, no. 10 (2004): 9; "The Ranking: Top 15," *Playthings* 101, no. 1 (2003): 19; "The 'A' List," *Playthings* 99, no. 12 (2001): 38–44; "Playthings Top 50," *Playthings* 97, no. 9 (1999): 38–45; "Wired to Sell: Toy Makers Hope Gadgets Energize a Flat Industry," *Boston Globe*, December 5, 2004; "The Toy Industry Takes on Electronics," *TechNews*, October 5, 2006.

Walmart's overwhelming victory in the toy market has redefined the competition pattern of the whole industry, where more and more players are learning to safeguard their bottom lines by using Walmart's business formula, pursuing high-volume sales, lowering prices, and cutting production costs. Over the 1998–2005 period, Walmart increased the number of its stores in the United States from 2,433 to 3,189 (excluding the Sam's Club extension) and toy sales rose from US$4.95 billion to US$9.97 billion.[18] The sheer volume of Walmart's toy sales puts it in a position to drive a harder bargain with its suppliers, either with toy merchandisers using OEM suppliers or with Walmart's direct suppliers. For Walmart toy suppliers, it is a double-edged sword: they need Walmart for volume, but the profit margins can be small. As industry observer notes, "If you're a toy manufacturer, it's better to have Walmart [as a customer] than not have it. But even as you love them, you hate them. Walmart is always tough on suppliers."[19]

Walmart's toy business exemplifies the company's business model. Walmart uses toys as a "traffic booster" in its stores, so they are usually priced at rock bottom to pull in customers. Walmart sometimes even sells popular toys at cost to undercut its rivals. With global sales of more than US$250 billion and toy sales in the U.S. market of around US$10 billion, Walmart could give away toys free and hardly dent its bottom line. In 2003, Walmart triggered the most brutal price war in the history of the U.S. toy industry, dragging down average toy prices and pushing hundreds of toy retailers out of business because they could not match Walmart in slashing prices.[20]

Walmart's overwhelming clout in the marketplace has changed the competitive landscape of the toy industry, forcing companies on different layers of the supply chain to live with its low-price-driven business model. Pitting its suppliers one against another, Walmart is notorious for squeezing the lowest prices out of them. An officeholder of the Guangdong Toy Association complained, "U.S. buyers demand prices that are not reasonable, considering the growing labor costs. Walmart in particular puts a lot of pressure on prices, and as it orders so much from China, it has a large influence."[21]

THE RACE TO THE BOTTOM IN LABOR STANDARDS

The average toy price has been shrinking continuously. For instance, from 1991 to 2000, the average retail price of all toys in the U.S. market decreased 1 percent while there was an average 2.8 percent annual increase in all consumer goods prices over the same period.[22] Even the big retailers and merchandisers such as Toys "R" Us, Target, Mattel, and Hasbro, who dominate the toy industry, had to struggle to survive Walmart's low-price-driven business model.

According to C. K. Yeung, vice chairman of the Hong Kong Toys Council, "It's an open secret that the industry's profit margin is only razor-thin, and our business environment continues to get tougher."[23] An investigation in 2000 into the price of a Mattel Barbie doll, half of which was made in China, found that, of the ten-dollar retail price, eight dollars went to transport, marketing, retail margin, wholesale margin, and profit for Mattel. Of the remaining two dollars, one dollar was shared by the management function and transportation costs within Hong Kong, and sixty-five cents paid for raw materials from Taiwan, Japan, the United States, and Saudi Arabia. The remaining thirty-five cents was earned by the maker in China for providing the factory overheads, labor, and electricity.[24] Thus labor costs account for an infinitesimal slice of the retail toy price. Similarly, the results of a study by Hong Kong's Christian Industrial Committee into fifty toys produced for Mattel, Hasbro, McDonald's, and Disney show that, for one $16.99 doll, direct labor cost only 56 cents; for a $34.99 playset, 25 cents; for a $44.99 electric toy, 81 cents; for an $11.99 action figure, 66 cents. In none of the fifty cases was the cost of labor more than 6 percent; in one case workers earned as little as 0.4 percent.[25]

The combination of a low-price business model and top-down squeezing for lower production costs, coupled with brutal competition, has led to a race to the bottom in labor standards in the toy industry. Numerous reports by labor rights NGOs and news reporters during the 1990s revealed rampant sweatshop labor abuses in the global toy factories. Most of the accusations concern hazardous or unhealthy working conditions, forced overtime, long working hours, child labor, illegally low wages, and abusive labor discipline.

Occupational safety and heath issues are the most intensively criticized sweatshop abuses in toy factories. Many toy-making plants are so hazardous that workers die each year in fires, collapses, and other accidents, or from breathing in toxic fumes, and workers repeatedly report problems of headaches, dizziness, and skin rashes attributed to poor ventilation in factories. Incidents such as sweatshop abuses and major fires in factories have instigated confrontations with various civil society groups since the middle 1990s. Trade unions, shareholder organizations, and labor rights NGOs in the consuming countries and in Hong Kong have launched international campaigns against toy sweatshops and pressured toy merchandisers and re-tailers to regulate labor practices in their overseas supplier factories. Mean-while, labor practices in the toy industry have also caught the attention of the mainstream media, putting leading toy corporations under intensive public scrutiny.

CSR, THE MAKING OF A MONITORING INDUSTRY

Adverse publicity about sweatshop abuses and the consequent mount-ing of antisweatshop campaigns at one time had seriously damaged the high-profile brand images of several corporations. Leading toy corpora-tions have since been pressured to adopt codes of conduct requiring their overseas suppliers to comply with minimum labor standards. As the first company in the toy industry to take public action in response to antisweat-shop activism, Walmart created its code of conduct regarding labor stan-dards, "Standards for Suppliers," in 1992. This was followed by Hasbro, who adopted its "Global Business Ethics Principles" in 1993. In 1995 the International Council of Toy Industries (ICTI), the biggest industry asso-ciation of national toy trade bodies, adopted a "Code of Business Practices," and in 1996 it adopted a "Fire Prevention and Emergency Preparedness Guide" to encourage better labor conditions in toy factories around the world. In 1997, Mattel launched its "Global Manufacturing Principles," and in the same year, Toys "R" Us, then the largest U.S. toy retailer, developed its "Code of Conduct for Suppliers."

However, most of these codes have serious shortcomings regarding workers' rights or providing transparent and accountable compliance mechanisms. Most codes merely include "legal minimum" labor standards on forced labor, child labor, wages, work and overtime hours, safety and health, freedom of association and nondiscrimination. They do not ad-dress the fact that much national and local legislation does not provide sufficient protection of workers' rights. For example, in many developing countries where these codes are supposed to be implemented, local legal minimum wages are frequently fixed too low to cover workers' basic needs. Even where legal minimum wages are higher, ineffective state supervision of prolonged overtime work can make the legal minimum meaningless. The codes normally provide for freedom of association and collective bargain-ing, but usually fail to provide effective mechanisms that would allow work-ers to exercise these rights under authoritarian regimes where independent trade unions are banned or when workers face employers' union-busting activities.

More important, these codes are voluntary, and their application is not transparent, nor do they provide accountability. A number of internal, external, and independent monitoring mechanisms have been initiated to foster implementation of the codes. Walmart and Hasbro, two out of four top toy merchandisers or retailers—Hasbro, Mattel, Toys "R" Us, and Walmart—rely heavily on internal monitoring to oversee compliance with their codes, including first-party monitoring conducted by the corporations' own staff, and second-party monitoring by auditing firms or other for-profit organizations. However, as shown by Xue Hong in her chapter, suppliers' tricks have rendered the monitoring useless. Internal monitoring has been criticized for not being transparent because the monitoring reports are addressed to the factories investigated and not released to the public.

In response to the growing criticism, some toy companies have switched to external monitoring by auditors accredited by third-party organizations. For instance, Toys "R" Us uses the SA8000 factory certification program by which a factory is audited and assessed by organizations accredited by Social Accountability International (SAI).[26] Today, the most widely used external monitoring approach in the toy industry is the CARE (Caring, Awareness, Responsible, Ethical) process developed by the International Council of Toy Industries (ICTI) in 2004 and overseen by the ICTI CARE Foundation. In the CARE process, factories are audited by certified firms trained to audit toy factories against ICTI's "Code of Business Practices."[27] Major retailers like Walmart and Toys "R" Us are now working with ICTI using the CARE process. Hasbro and Mattel have declared that they are fully committed and are putting many of their factories through the CARE process.[28] By 2007, there were 1,022 toy factories worldwide registered under the ICTI CARE process, and 533 factories have been given the ICTI Seal of Compliance.[29]

Yet the credibility of external monitoring by for-profit auditing firms is just as questionable. The key concern is whether monitors selected, paid by, and accountable to the buyer companies have the necessary independence, motivation, and expertise to investigate factory conditions credibly. A major problem is the external monitors' concerns for profit, which could lead them to turn a blind eye to or cover up problems in factories.

Growing public awareness of the weakness of the internal and external monitoring systems and escalating pressure for reform have led to the development of "independent" monitoring. This includes monitoring by

NGOs, unions, or private monitoring firms not paid directly by the brands or factories.[30] A yet stricter type of independent monitoring is when NGOs use local experts in labor rights—labor lawyers, human rights activists, sociologists, and other academics—as monitors.[31]

Escalating antisweatshop activism has thus resulted in the growth of CSR practices in the global toy industry. All the biggest merchandisers and retailers have adopted codes and created various monitoring systems to inspect codes compliance. How effective have these monitoring activities been? The empirical study of two of Walmart's toy supplier factories in South China will provide us with an answer.

WALMART'S SELF-POLICING AND PUNISHMENT IMPLEMENTATION CSR MODEL

In 1992, Walmart adopted "Standards for Suppliers," which prohibit child, prison, and forced labor and require clean working conditions, reasonable hours, fair compensation, and compliance with national and local laws. However, Walmart takes a "legal-minimalist" stance, especially on issues of wages and workers' right to unionization. Although some NGOs have advocated a "living wage" because the legal minimum wage in many developing countries is set too low to meet workers' basic needs, Walmart officials argue that the company is not in a position to change the minimum wage standards of other countries or impose U.S. cultural standards overseas.[32] Also, Walmart's standards are silent on the right of workers to join unions, merely stating that suppliers must abide by local employment and labor laws. Such a weak position regarding the right of association means that in countries like China where independent trade unions are banned the promise on compliance is meaningless.

Walmart began to take the implementation of its codes more seriously in the mid-1990s when sweatshop abuses in its overseas supplier factories were intensively exposed to public scrutiny. Walmart published its first Factory Certification Program and authorized its exclusive agent for China, Pacific Resources Exports Ltd (PREL), to inspect labor practices in suppliers' plants. But as recounted in Nelson Lichtenstein's chapter, PREL was really an offshoot of Walmart. Besides, its monitoring system did not cover indirect suppliers producing goods for merchandisers who then sell to Walmart (for more details on this, see the chapter by Xue Hong). In the late 1990s, Walmart began to use PREL and auditing firms such as PriceWaterhouseCoopers (PWC) to inspect factories producing their private-label products. In 2002, when Walmart insourced the global procurement function from PREL, it began to manage the factory certification program directly with internal monitoring by Walmart staff, auditing firms, or other organizations hired by the company.[33]

"Self-policing," then, has become a key feature of Walmart's code supervision model. It gives Walmart unchecked control over how the monitoring methods are designed (e.g., whether factory inspections should be announced or unannounced), how audits are done, and whether or not the reports are published. Not surprisingly, Walmart's self-policing model has been criticized for its lack of credibility and transparency.[34] Civil society groups have tried to pressure Walmart, especially through investor activism,[35] to launch an independent system in which other stakeholders, especially local civil society groups and the workers themselves, can have a voice and a role in implementing the code. However, Walmart still insists on handling monitoring on its own terms. As Walmart spokesman Tom Williams states, "We [Walmart] have serious reservations about third-party involvement in the monitoring process.... Walmart is committed to eradicating abuse of labor. The point of contention centers on how that should be done."[36]

The entire Walmart code system is oriented toward punishment rather than problem solving. It can be said that Walmart has outsourced all responsibility for cleaning up sweatshop conditions to its suppliers. Those suppliers found to have serious noncompliance problems are excised permanently from Walmart's supply chain. According to Walmart's spokesman Tom Williams, "the threat of losing the huge chunk of business that comes from a colossus like Walmart usually moves factory owners to comply."[37] In 2004, Walmart reportedly dropped 108 of its 5,300 offshore factories for hiring underage workers or for other major violations.[38] Increasingly, progressive players in the global CSR community have moved on to discuss how to work with suppliers to improve labor practices through providing training, sharing costs, or reforming sourcing policies, but Walmart still sticks to a punishment-oriented model, simply severing relations with factories with bad labor practices.

WALMART'S CODE MONITORING AT TWO TOY FACTORIES

In order to assess the function of code monitoring, we have used two factories as our case studies: T_1 with monitored code and T_2 without code applied. Both factories are located in the city of Shenzhen Outer Zone. T_1 has a workforce of five thousand to six thousand workers, and T_2 only one thousand to two thousand workers.

T_1, established in 1992, is one of Walmart's major Hong Kong-owned toy suppliers in China. Every year it exports toys worth more than 40 million yuan (about US$5 million) to the United States and European countries for clients such as Walmart, JC Penny, Kay Bee, and K-Mart. Being so large, it is also very intensively monitored and has undergone many factory inspections by both Walmart staff and auditing firms during the past few years. According to the T_1 workers, monitors come three or four times a year, usually in peak seasons, and ask questions about wages, working hours, mandatory overtime, and so on. However, those who have witnessed many such Walmart inspections say that they have never had a chance to talk to the inspectors about the true situation.

The workers told us that all inspections are announced in advance, so the factory management usually coaches them on how to answer the auditors' questions. The factory management frequently told them that the factory would lose orders and workers would lose their jobs if the auditors weren't given the "right" answers to their questions. The management even promised fifty yuan (equal to six U.S. dollars, or nearly 10 percent of the monthly wage) to workers who answered auditors' questions according to the models prepared by the management.

The workers said that there were serious problems of cheating at T_1. For example, to ensure that T_1's workweek did not exceed the maximum of seventy-two hours set by Walmart's code, the management often required workers to punch out at 8:00 p.m. but made them continue to work several hours more, which were thus unrecorded and unpaid—this happened regularly during peak seasons.[39] One worker complained, "In early October [2005] when Walmart's auditor inspected the factory, we were required by management to work until 12:00 p.m. after we punched our timecards at 8:00 p.m." Although "working off the clock" is technically a code violation, Walmart inspectors checked mainly by reviewing time records and interviewing workers, who dared not mention anything of it. One worker recalled:

> One day, the line leader sent me to the office for a talk with the Walmart auditor. The auditor asked me how many overtime hours I took, how much I was paid, and if overtime work was voluntary. But I did not dare tell the truth, because right before I went to the office, the manager told me how to answer these questions "correctly," otherwise

the factory would lose the order and we workers would lose jobs. So I knew I should keep silent on the problems of working off the clock.

Logic would suggest that working conditions in this heavily monitored factory would be better than those at T_2, which is not monitored. But is this the case? In the next section, we shall examine the impact of these inspections on three important labor standards: working hours, wages, and living conditions.

The Impact of Walmart Factory Inspections on Working Hours

Toy retailing is a highly seasonal business with 45 percent of a year's sales squeezed into the six weeks before Christmas.[40] Such seasonality requires toy makers to employ a very flexible labor force, both in terms of the number of workers and their working schedules. At T_1 and T_2, the majority of production workers are Chinese migrant women employed on seasonal contracts, to allow the companies to adjust to fluctuations in seasonal orders.[41] In the peak production season, normally from April to November, the size of the workforce and working hours in both factories nearly doubled compared to the slow season from December to March.

These two factories have outbid many rivals to secure these large-volume orders placed either directly by Walmart or by its direct suppliers or agents. However, the problem caused by seasonality in orders remains fundamental. In terms of labor standards, our survey results indicated that they were just "Santa's sweatshops," like most toy factories in South China's Pearl River Delta region.

The research showed that Walmart's inspections of T_1 have had some positive effect on the problem of excessive overtime. The monthly overtime there of seventy-two hours was reportedly much shorter than T_2's, which ranged from seventy-two to ninety-six hours. Both factories did give workers one day off per week even in the peak season, which was much better than some other toy factories where workers are required to work seven days a week, or with just one day off per month. However, what is interesting was that, even though T_2 was not monitored by Walmart, it still allowed workers one day off every week. This means that monitoring may not be the only reason that factories treat workers better. Although Walmart's inspections were somewhat helpful in shortening the work schedule at T_1 compared to T_2, there were still gross violations of the legal working hours there. According to China's Labor Law, the legal working week is forty hours, with Saturday and Sunday off; and overtime must not exceed three hours a day, nine hours a week, or thirty-six hours a month, so the maximum number of hours per week is forty-nine. Although Walmart's code requires suppliers to "maintain employee work hours in compliance with local standards and applicable laws of the jurisdictions in which the suppliers are doing business," in practice Walmart lets suppliers meet instead its own laxer standard of a maximum of seventy-two hours a week instead of the sixty hours accepted by most companies.

The Impact of Walmart Factory Inspections on Wages

China's Ministry of Labor issued an Enterprise Minimum Wage Regulation in 1993, and in 2004 China's Ministry of Labor and Social Security revised the previous regulations and issued a new Minimum Wage Regulation. In 1995, the Chinese government reduced the national standard working week from forty-four hours to forty hours, so minimum wages in China mean minimum payment for a forty-hour week. China's Labor Law also stipulates 150 percent of the normal rate as overtime compensation during weekdays, 200 percent on Saturdays or Sundays, and 300 percent on statutory holidays. Walmart requires its suppliers to pay "workers wages and benefits that are in compliance with the local and national laws, or which are consistent with the prevailing local standards," whichever is higher.[42] Accordingly, Walmart requires its suppliers in China to pay at least the legal minimum wage for a regular forty-hour working week and overtime wages at the rates stipulated by the Labor Law.

As a result of Walmart's factory inspections, T_1's wage structure complied formally with the law. T_1 paid its workers a basic monthly wage that met the legal minimum wage (480 yuan in 2004; 580 yuan in 2005) and told the workers that they were getting the legal overtime premiums for workdays and Saturdays. They were also supposed to be getting bonuses and allowances, though with a deduction of 180 to 190 yuan for food and accommodation (contrary both to China's Labor Law and Walmart's code). However, workers' final take-home pay was just 600 to 700 yuan a month during the peak season. How could it be possible that, after working for so many hours of overtime during the peak season, workers' cash income was barely above the minimal wage? As a worker confirmed, "The company told us that we earned both the basic wage, which was 480 yuan in 2004, and then an overtime wage of 4.3 yuan per hour on week nights and 5.74 yuan per hour on Saturday. If workers' wages really were calculated this way, our monthly wages should have come to 1,000 yuan, but in fact we earn 600 to 700 yuan in the peak season and only 300 yuan in the slow seasons."

Our calculations suggest that, for workers at T_1 in 2004, their monthly wages in the peak season with the amount of overtime that they did should have given them a take-home wage of 991 yuan and for 2005, after adjusting to minimum wage increase, 1,197 yuan.[43] However, not only did T_1 in 2004 pay its workers only about two-thirds of what they should have received, but their take-home pay remained the same in 2005. Further, even workers who did not live in the factory dormitory also had $180 yuan deducted each month. Despite continual auditing, Walmart's monitors failed to note such serious violations both of the law and of the retailer's own code, largely because the factory was able to hide its practices behind its well-presented but heavily doctored records.

By contrast, workers at T_2 could earn about 1,100 to 1,200 yuan per month in the peak season, although they also made as little as 300 to 400 yuan in the slow season. There are some reasons for this huge wage difference. First, workers at T_2 worked longer hours than workers at T_1. T_2 workers were paid by piece rate, which is a bit more transparent to the workers than time rate, as it makes it more difficult for management to cheat the workers. Moreover, due to its long history and large size, T_1 may have more competitive advantages in the local labor market than T_2, in terms of offering stable jobs and guaranteed prompt payment for workers and in turn pressing them to accepting lower wages. Smaller factories like T_2 often have to pay higher wages or provide better working conditions in order to attract workers. Thus T_1 workers had food and board deducted from their wages, but this was not the case for the workers at T_2.

The Impact of Walmart Factory Inspections on Living Conditions

The quality of food and of living conditions are two important items inspected by Walmart monitors. At T_1, there was one new dormitory building, which was comparatively nice and was used as a showcase to convince the Walmart auditors that the factory's management had met its obligations. The reality, though, was that workers had to put up with food and living conditions that probably would not have met Walmart's requirements. One T_1 worker complained, "Meals tasted terrible and were not nutritious, so at weekends we often went to local friends' homes for better meals to keep ourselves healthy." As for dormitory conditions, "Rooms were crowded, shared by 12 people, but there was only one toilet and shower room on each floor, so normally we had to line up for 20 minutes to go to the toilet and 3 hours to have a shower."

Workers at T_2 enjoyed better meals and lodgings. According to the T_2 workers we interviewed, the dormitory was free and they only paid 5 yuan a month for water and electricity. Living conditions were considered acceptable, with a toilet and shower room in each room, which was normally shared by eight to ten people. There were two free meals a day, and workers working later than 10:00 p.m. could have an extra free night snack.

To sum up, both factories manufactured goods for Walmart, but the one being inspected consistently managed to underpay its workers substantially and provided them with substandard food and lodgings. However, the unmonitored factory paid more and provided better accommodations, although its working hours were longer—but at least the workers did get their overtime premium. It is clear that Walmart factory inspections are not an effective tool for improving labor standards if they could miss such obvious problems.

Going Beyond Walmart's CSR Approach

The global toy retailers, preeminently Walmart, have touted their CSR codes as effective means to establish minimum labor standards across national boundaries through private regulations. Our study shows, however, that such codes have done little to raise labor standards for workers. We argue that Walmart's codes clearly reflect the "legal-minimalist" approach dominant in current CSR initiatives. Such an approach limits the code's potential for upholding labor standards, especially on issues of wages and workers' right to freedom of association. Moreover, though Walmart opposes independent monitoring, its own internal and external monitoring systems are not sufficiently credible, accountable, or effective. First, this monitoring is "self-policing," giving Walmart unfettered control of the whole process of implementation and leaving civil society groups and workers without voice or power. Second, the model is punishment-oriented, focused primarily on excising from its supply chain sweatshops exposed to public criticisms, rather than on working seriously with its suppliers to improve labor standards.

Thus, after more than a decade of proliferating codes of conduct in the global toy industry, sweatshop labor abuses have clearly not been eliminated. Serious violations of workers' human and legal rights continue to hit the headlines of the mainstream media, and major toy brands and retailers such as Hasbro, Mattel, MGA, Disney, Walmart, and Toys "R" Us continue to be targeted by antisweatshop campaigns. This study and others have shown that multinational companies' codes do not provide a realistic alternative to state regulation, workers' empowerment, and prolabor organizations as effective regulatory mechanisms. However, in an age of neoliberal globalization, state protection of labor rights is being eroded in many countries, and unions are facing more challenges in organizing workers. Under such circumstances, totally dismissing the possibility that codes of conduct could improve labor standards will not help to protect workers' rights. To make codes more accountable and effective as tools for the protection of labor, alliances of international civil society groups advocating labor rights should continue to pressure companies like Walmart to accept more responsibility for the deterioration of global labor standards. They must be pressed to go beyond a legal minimalist standards and to use more credible and effective monitoring systems giving workers and local organizations more of a voice and more of a role. Above all, pressure should be placed on multinational firms to amend their business models and sourcing policy to make implementation of their codes financially feasible at the workplace level.

4 MADE IN CHINA

Work and Wages in Walmart Supplier Factories

Anita Chan and Kaxton Siu

To date there have been many case studies and reports about the work conditions of Chinese migrant workers in factories that produce for export to the developed world. These studies have raised international concerns. This chapter focuses on the labor conditions of such workers from a new perspective. It unveils the mechanisms of "sweated labor" in China's export industry by analyzing the relationship between wages and overtime work hours at nine Walmart supplier factories in the garment and toy industries.

"Sweatshops" and "Sweating"

"Sweatshop" is a popular word today that refers to the terrible conditions for workers in labor-intensive industries. The word conjures up an image of dilapidated factory buildings, dingy, dark, and damp, the kind of image that occasionally appears in movies set in the industrial revolution era of Dickens. Some of the sweatshops in China are right out of Dickens. But others are modern-looking, with state-of-the-art machinery and production lines and workers dressed in smart company uniforms. This is particularly true of the large factories that produce for brand-name products and that are the targets of "corporate social responsibility" (CSR) social auditing. Some of the factories in China that are Walmart suppliers are of this type.

Portions of this chapter and all of its tables and figures were previously published in Anita Chan and Kaxton Siu, "Analyzing Exploitation," *Critical Asian Studies* 42, no. 2 (2010). Reprinted with permission.

Are these really sweatshops, when the factory buildings are big, bright, and modern? Not from the outside. It is the "sweating process" that goes on inside these buildings which defines "sweating." "Sweating," unlike "sweatshop," is no longer a word in vogue. Like our image of the sweatshop, "sweating" conjures up a bleak nineteenth-century setting. The word emerged as early as 1848,[1] and the "sweating" problem prompted widespread social, economic, and political debates for many decades, resulting in a raft of regulatory legislation passed in the Western industrialized world in the hope of ameliorating the degradations of exploited labor.

The modern-day antisweatshop movement is reviving the issue of serious exploitation of workers. The antisweatshop activists are attacking corporations for underpaying workers, pointing to the same sorts of awful conditions that writers 150 years ago deplored. We have discovered that one common thread runs through and connects these two periods. As in yesteryear, today's reports on sweatshops involve minute numerical figures, down to a fraction of a penny per unit time or per unit piece. It is a reflection of the mean and stingy mentality of those who do the exploiting. In consequence, those of us who do research on the wages of these workers who are at the bottom of the global production chain have to deal with precision down to a fraction of a cent.[2]

A search for the derivation of "sweating" yields an imprecise concept that has changed through time.[3] At one time, it related to the abuse of a subcontracting system or applied only to home workers, not factory workers.[4] Even in 1892, when Sidney and Beatrice Webb wrote their essay "How to Do Away with the Sweating System," they could not provide a precise definition and chose to go by this: "Lord Derby and his colleagues finally decided that sweating was no particular method of remuneration, no peculiar form of industrial organization, but certain conditions of employment—viz. unusually low rates of wages, excessive hours of labour, and unsanitary work places."[5] In 1901, Nillie Mason Auten wrote in the *American Journal of Sociology*, "What is commonly known as the 'sweating system' is a general term used to designate a condition of labor by which a maximum amount of work possible per day is performed for a minimum wage, and in which the ordinary rules of health and comfort are disregarded."[6] Neither definition provided a specific standard by which to evaluate whether any given work constituted "sweated labor."

These two definitions, however, are in agreement that "sweating" shares three common characteristics: (1) it entails excessively long work hours, (2) remuneration is paltry, and (3) the workplace is unhealthy and toxic, causing occupational diseases and physical strains. In this chapter we shall restrict our discussion to wages and work hours and leave the occupational health and safety issues to experts on safe production.

Analyzing data on wages and work hours, based on a small survey that we conducted at nine Walmart supplier factories, can serve the following functions:

1. The quantitative data enables us to find out on average how much is paid for work performed. It thus enables us to evaluate the real impact of the official legal minimum wage on Chinese workers and to examine whether a wage that satisfies the minimum wage standard is no longer "sweated labor."

2. Comparing the quantitative data from two industries (garments and toys) helps us to unravel the hidden mechanisms of exploitation. The export garment industry in China normally pays by piece rates and the toy industry by time rates. A comparison of these two industries will highlight interesting differences not only in workers' objective conditions but also in their subjective consciousness.

3. We also believe that a survey of this nature can help to quantify the conditions needed to meet the minimum standard of work that is not sweated.

The Survey

Through very detailed questions on our survey questionnaire, we sought to find out as precisely as possible the wages and work hours of workers and attitudes toward these conditions.[7] The field survey was carried out in 2006 in two stages in various districts of Shenzhen City at factories that produce for Walmart—four garment factories in June and July and five toy factories in October 2006.[8] These two industries were chosen because such factories are numerous in this part of China, a region where production-line workers are all migrants from other provinces. The two industries provide an interesting contrast, given that the garment trade normally operates on piece rates, while toy production uses time rates. Since each of the factories had their own specific ways of rewarding labor, detailed questions had to be included to capture the complexity of the wage systems.

It did not prove easy to collect data on wages and labor conditions in these supplier factories. For instance, the ideal would have been to interview both factory managers and workers, but we were not able to gain access to factory management. Collecting information from workers could

only be done outside factory gates. Soliciting workers to answer questionnaires was not an easy task. The difficulty was compounded by the fact that
many of the factories that supply multinational corporations (MNCs) have
warned workers against talking to strangers about work conditions for fear
that they would leak information to the social auditors sent by corporate
clients. Moreover, the window of opportunity for surveyors to approach
workers each day was quite short, usually not more than an hour between
a worker clocking off for the day for dinner and clocking in again for the
night's overtime. The problem was further aggravated by workers often
having no days off a week. That means each surveyor's one- to two-hour
bus ride to a factory could yield at best two answered questionnaires, or
sometimes none. Thus it required great persistence, especially in the heat of
summer, for a few surveyors to fill in eighty-eight questionnaires from the
nine garment and toy factories. All of these factories supply multiple buyers, but a substantial percentage of their products are for Walmart.

The respondents could not state the exact number of workers or the
gender ratio at each factory. We overcame this problem as best we could
by using the mean distribution of the estimates for each factory.[9] Notably, too, due to the difficulty in obtaining respondents, the numbers of
questionnaires that were filled in at each factory are not proportional to
the size of the factories. To overcome this problem we have weighted the
sample when we compare data between the toy and garment industries.[10]
A summary of the number of respondents and the weighted means of respondents' estimates of the size of their factory's workforce is shown in
table 4.1.

Table 4.1
Sampled factories, number of respondents, and the weighted means for the
size of each factory's workforce

Factory (G = garment; T = toy)	Number of respondents	Weighted means of factory population estimates
G1	3	550
G2	10	169
G3	19	3,405
G4	8	900
T1	15	3,600
T2	14	2,733
T3	5	1,950
T4	6	321
T5	8	301

The Monthly Earnings Floor

Most of the factories in China's export sector are owned and managed by corporations from Hong Kong, Taiwan, and South Korea, which enter into contracts to manufacture for Western brand names. In the 1990s, as these supplier companies moved much of their production into China, they were soon plunged into an intense competition among themselves to acquire orders by offering lower prices, as described by Xue Hong in chapter 2. In this competition, a common way to reduce production costs was to squeeze the workers, who were largely poor migrants from the countryside. One Hong Kong buying agent put it graphically to us, "Suppliers still have places where they can cut fat, but the easiest fat to cut is workers' wages." One consequence is that the wages get squeezed down to what the manufacturers can legally get away with—the monthly legal minimum wage. Figure 4.1, drawn using official Chinese government statistics for Outer Shenzhen, shows the trends in the wages of both migrant and urban nonmigrant employees. Note the second line from the top, which traces the average wages of nonmigrants in the urban workforce after taking account of inflation. Much of the local urban populace fill jobs as foremen and white-collar staff or are on government payrolls. Real wages of the local populace tripled between 1993 and 2009. If we compare this to the monthly consumer price index (CPI)–adjusted legal minimum wage set for migrant workers for a forty-hour week, we see that the wage increase for migrants was much smaller. Such minimum wage levels in China are set annually by city-level governments, supposedly in accordance with the prevailing wage and the cost of living in the city. The legal minimum wage is then reported to the Ministry of Labor and Social Security in Beijing. However, local governments tend to be probusiness and eager to attract foreign investment. Setting the local legal minimum wage at the lowest possible level has been the policy for many years.

One of the authors has been to many dozens of factories in this region during the past two decades, and the monthly basic wage that the migrant workers have received for a forty-hour week *almost invariably has been the same* as the legal minimum wage. Most of these workers labor far longer than forty hours a week, and they are required by law to be paid a wage one and a half times higher per hour for all overtime and double for weekend work. In reality, however, most of them are paid at the same rate or just a bit more, and many workers actually make *less* per hour of overtime work than they do for their first forty hours. Because they are not paid enough

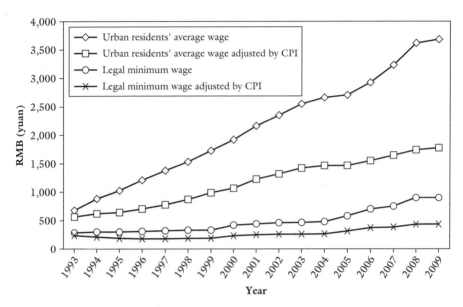

Figure 4.1. Wages of urban residents and the legal monthly minimum wage (migrant workers' base wage) for the Outer Shenzhen region, 1993–2009. *Source*: Shenzhen statistics yearbooks (1993–2009), http://www.sztj.com/main/index.shtml.

for their overtime labor, the overall pay of most of the migrant workers is far less than is stipulated by law.

Note, too, that the bottom line of figure 4.1 shows that real pay for the first forty hours declined slightly for a decade until 2004, when a labor shortage began to be felt. As a consequence of no real wage increase for so many years, by around 2003 many migrant workers no longer wanted to come to Guangdong Province, causing a shortage of labor that was widely reported in the international press. In 2004, the local government raised the legal minimum wage by an unprecented margin, 120 yuan (about US$15 per month) but as can be seen, it was still a modest increase when adjusted for inflation.[11]

One could argue that between 1993 and 2009, the legal minimum wage had gone up about 3.3 times, and after being adjusted for CPI the increase came to about 1.8 times. It seems from this that the migrant workers' livelihood in the city has improved considerably. However, this argument is only valid when migrant workers' monthly earnings are considered in absolute terms. When we compare migrant workers' earnings with the earnings of urban residents, we find that over the sixteen years urban residents' average wage has climbed 5.4 times, or 3.14 times when CPI is factored in. This widening gap between the urban population and the migrant workforce is well illustrated in figure 4.1.

Before a shortage of "prime" labor began appearing in 2003–4, factory managers were willing to recruit only young women between the ages of eighteen and twenty-three for most types of production work. The reasons provided by managers in interviews during the 1990s and early 2000s was that young female workers have nimble hands, are more obedient (*tinghua*) and easier to manage, and are faster and more meticulous. The factories were not interested in women older than twenty-three because it was said that by the age of twenty-four, rural women would return to their hometown to get married, and the factories did not want to deal with problems related to pregnancy. The factories also calculated that by the time a woman reached her late twenties she was too old to keep up with the rapid pace of work.[12]

A discriminatory hiring policy existed in these two industries. Men had great difficulty finding production-line jobs. They were hired normally only for heavier manual tasks such as loading and unloading, or tasks that required some technical skills, or in garment cutting, which requires taller and stronger workers due to the sheer bulk of the stack of material to be cut. Thus males usually accounted for 10 percent of manual workers in these two industries or even less before labor shortages were reported in 2004.

However, starting in 2003–4, with insufficient numbers of young women standing outside factory gates in search of a job, factories have had to hire older women as well as young men, and even men older than thirty. This can be observed in our survey. As can be seen in table 4.2, the mean age of the sampled workers at these Walmart suppliers is 23.8, which is older than the range of ages at which factories normally employed production-line workers in the 1990s.[13]

Starting in the mid-2000s factory-gate recruitment posters in the Shenzhen region often read: "Ordinary workers needed: 18 to 30 years old. Positions open for either men or women," whereas before a poster would read, "Women workers needed: 18 to 23 years old." This change in gender recruitment is evident in our survey sample, in which the males make up 26 percent of the workforce.[14] At one of the four garment factories it is as high as

Table 4.2
Worker ages and gender at the toy and garment factories

		Weighted mean		
Variable	Total sample (N=88)	Garment factories (N=40) 2005–2006	Toy factories (N=48) 2006–2007
Age	23.80	22.57	24.66
Male workforce (%)	26	31	19

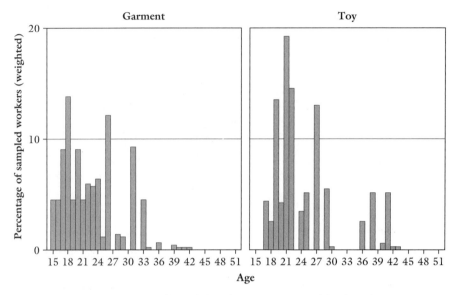

Figure 4.2. Age distribution of sampled workers in garment and toy factories (N = 88).

60 percent. This higher male gender ratio definitely goes against the widely held perception that China's garment industry is almost entirely staffed by young women.[15]

Figure 4.2 disaggregates the survey numbers. The widening age spread shown here appears to reflect a shift in factories' recruitment policy to alleviate the difficulty of recruiting what management considers prime labor—young unmarried healthy high-school-educated females. As seen here, as the pool of these prime workers shrinks, the factories cannot afford to be too particular but must take on both younger and older workers. Figure 4.2 shows that there were a few illegally under-aged workers (below sixteen years old) and a sizeable proportion of workers older than twenty-five, even up to forty-three years old. As nonprime workers, they feel vulnerable—and especially since the downturn in the global economy that began in 2008. Management made use of the nonprime workers' vulnerability to maintain cost competitiveness by continuing to force workers to do extensive overtime work at low hourly wages.

Wages and Work Hours

Managers invariably tell visitors that all of the migrant workers are eager to earn more money, and that they welcome as much overtime work as is available. There is some truth to these claims. In fact, one method managers use to penalize disobedient workers is to deny them any overtime work. But is it true that workers always want to work as much overtime as they can get? If so, why is it that when workers' complaints erupt into protest action, excessive overtime is almost invariably an issue? What do workers really consider is the optimal balance between wages and work hours?

Before proceeding further, we need to be more precise in our analysis by basing ourselves on concrete definitions and numbers. To do so, we will first need to define several terms:

Regular Work Hours: work hours as defined by the labor law as 40 hours per week. This amounts to 21.75 days per month or 176 hours per month.

Overtime: All work hours beyond the regular hours of 40 per week.

Overtime Wage (OT wage): wages received by workers for work beyond the legally stipulated norm of 40 hours. The legal rate for weekday OT is 1.5 times the regular wage per hour; 2 times for Saturdays and Sundays; and 3 times for public holidays.

Legal Maximum Work Hours per month: 176 hours + 36 overtime hours = 212 hours.

Received Wage: the total wage received by workers after various kinds of deductions were taken by the factories in the month prior to the survey.

Desired Wage: the wage that workers thought would be fair, when asked the question, "How high a wage do you wish to make each month?"

Legally Entitled Wage: total wage to which workers are entitled by law for the regular hours and overtime hours (legal and illegally long) that they have performed.

What does table 4.3 show us about the working conditions of the workers in the Walmart supplier factories in these two industries? When the extremely long hours are taken into account, the wage figures lie below the amount stipulated in China's labor law.[16] On average the workers in the sample worked 302 hours a month; of these, 126 were overtime hours (302 – 176 hours = 126 hours). This means that 90 hours (126 – 36 hours = 90 hours) of their overtime were illegally in excess of what China's labor law stipulates as the allowed maximum. The vast majority of the workers (88 percent) worked more than 11 hours per day, and 81 percent of them had fewer than 4 rest days a month. (A minimum of 4 rest days is legally required.)

When we compare the garment and toy industries, it can be seen that garment workers work longer and have a lower hourly pay than toy workers, despite the fact that garment factories require a more skilled workforce than toy factories.

Table 4.3
Work hours and wages per month, and the hourly wage for garment and toy factories (N = 88)

Variable	Weighted mean		
	Total sample (N = 88)	Garment factories (N = 40)	Toy factories (N = 48)
Work hours per month	301.92	308.00	297.63
Overtime hours per day	3.24	3.31	3.19
Days off per month	3.16	2.81	3.40
Monthly wage (yuan)	1,222.67	1,007.00	1,374.93
Hourly wage (yuan)	3.84	3.39	4.17

Ninety percent of the garment workers stated that on an average workday in the past month, they had worked more than ten hours, while only 78 percent of toy workers claimed this. Seventy percent of the garment workers regularly worked five or more hours of overtime on a workday. This means that for the majority of garment workers, a regular workday was thirteen hours or more, while for the majority of toy workers a regular workday was twelve hours or more. Sixty-one percent of the garment workers said that they had had fewer than two days off during the previous month, whereas only 15 percent of the toy workers claimed this. During peak seasons, 33 percent of the garment workers had no days off a month, up from 16 percent during off-seasons. The peak season for toy workers was less intense: 25 percent had no days off, up from 0 percent in the off-season. When asked how many hours was the longest continuous stretch they had worked, close to two-thirds of the garment workers (64 percent) stated they had worked between twelve and fourteen hours nonstop, and 16 percent claimed they had worked for twenty-four hours or more nonstop. In comparison, the longest continuous hours of work among any of the toy workers was twenty-two hours, and two-thirds of the toy workers (63 percent) said that the longest they had ever worked continuously was for twelve hours a day. Overall, garment workers work much longer than toy workers (see figure 4.3).

Since garment work is more skilled, and because they work longer hours, garment workers should logically be making more than toy workers, but this is not the case. They fall further behind their legally entitled wage (we surveyed garment factories several months earlier than toy factories, at a time of transition in the government-set minimum wage, so the legal wage entitlements for the two industries differ). If we compare their received wage as a percentage of their legally entitled wage, garment workers

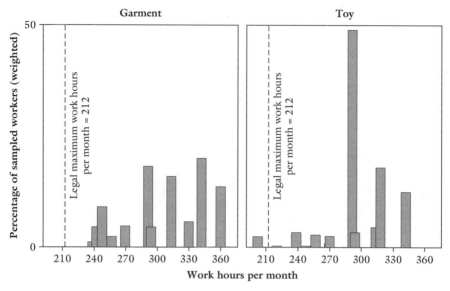

Figure 4.3. Monthly work hours distribution for garment and toy factories (N = 88).

received 75 percent of what they were legally entitled to (1007 yuan ÷ 1343 yuan × 100%), while toy workers received 89 percent (1374 yuan ÷ 1537 yuan × 100%) (see figure 4.4).

The invisible hand of market forces is supposed to adjust for the supply and demand for labor and set wages accordingly. Since garment workers are more skilled than toy workers, and since there is also said to be a labor shortage, according to economic logic garment workers should be paid more and have better conditions than toy workers. The results of the survey show, instead, what appears to be an irrational situation. For garment workers, the correlated coefficient between monthly work hours and received wage was 0.021; for toy workers, 0.13. In all cases, the correlations were positive but weaker in the garment factories. Twenty-two of forty garment workers (55 percent) labored more than three hundred hours a month, and eight out of the forty were paid less than three yuan per hour, which is less than half their legal entitlement. For toy workers, only sixteen out of forty-eight (33 percent) worked for more than three hundred hours per month and only two workers out of forty-eight received less than three yuan per hour. The weak correlations indicated irrationality in wage setting across the two industries, and as expected this was more pronounced in the garment industry. The maxim in China today of "more labor, more award" (*duolao duode*) does not apply.

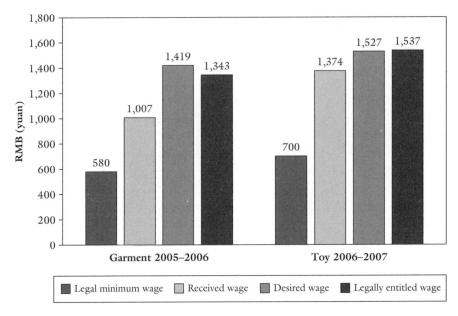

Figure 4.4. Legal minimum wage, received wage, desired wage, and legally entitled wage, per month (N = 88).

Workers' Desired Work Hours: Garments versus Toys

The quantitative data presented above tell us the objective situation. Workers at these Walmart supplier factories were forced to work those long hours and were paid illegally low remuneration. But what do the workers themselves want? What are their subjective conditions? How much do they aspire to earn each month and, for that amount, how many hours do they want/expect to work? While analyzing the data, we discovered that these attitudinal answers are most enlightening if studied comparatively between the two types of workers, as garment workers were on piece rates and toy workers were on time rates. This comparative perspective better brings out the complex relationship between work hours and wages, how the two types of pay systems affect this relationship, and which system is better or worse for workers.

Assuming that most workers want to make more money than they are presently getting, they were asked the question: "How much in wages do you wish to make each month?" We have labeled this the "desired wage." To see how this compares with the amount each worker was making, we constructed an index variable: a "desired wage index" (desired wage ÷ received wage). When the index is equal to 1, it means the worker accepts the present wage level as appropriate. Those who want more than they are receiving will score greater than 1 on the index; those who want less will score less than 1. Our hypothesis was that all workers would want to make more, and quite a lot more, as their wages are so low.

As wages are normally related to length of work hours, to find out how long workers want to work every day and every month they were asked two questions: "How many hours of work (including overtime) do you think is suitable for you?" and "How many days of rest a month do you think is suitable for you?" As shown in the survey figures that we have presented, many of these supplier factories give workers only two days off or even no days off each month, and our interviews reveal that workers become physically and mentally exhausted after a few weeks without rest. Their desired length of work hours and work days will give an indication of workers' tolerance level for exhaustion and for robotic, simplistic, monotonous, repetitive physical movements.

Regarding the first question, 75 percent of all the sampled workers wanted to work for 10 hours or less. If paid their current level of pay, 16 percent wanted to work for fewer than 10 hours, 59 percent wanted to work for 10 hours a day, and 25 percent wanted to work for 11 or 12 hours a day. On the second question, 50 percent wanted to have 4 days off each month, and another 13 percent wanted to have 5 to 8 days off a month. That means 63 percent wanted to have 4 or more rest days each month, and 37 percent wanted to have fewer than 4 days off. Combining the answers to both questions shows that a clear majority of all the sampled workers (60 percent) desired no longer than a 10-hour day and a 6-day week, which amounts to 260 hours a month (a 30-day month = four 60-hour weeks + 20 hours). While the workers in our sample were chalking up 302 hours a month (table 4.3), they wanted to work 42 hours less, which is still 48 hours a month more than the 212-hour legal maximum stipulated by the Labor Law. As interviews revealed, many workers felt that normal work days not exceeding 10 hours and having at least one day off a week were essential, to enable them to recuperate physically and mentally from 6 days of repetitive motions and numbing boredom on the production line. We can conclude that 260 hours a month can be regarded as the tolerance level above which most of the workers reach exhaustion.

Let us underline that desired work hours are not optimum work hours, but the maximum tolerance level for the workers. This coincides with a 60-hour week, which is the maximum set by many transnational corporations' codes of conduct. In that sense, the codes set the maximum work

Table 4.4
Garment and toy workers' desired working hours per day and desired days off per month
(N=86)

	Garment workers N=39	Toy workers N=47	All workers N=86
"How many hours of work (including overtime) do you think is suitable for you?" Desired working hours (including overtime) per day			
Less than 10 hours	11 (28%)	3 (6%)	14 (16%)
10 hours	16 (41%)	35 (75%)	51 (59%)
11 to 12 hours	12 (31%)	9 (19%)	21 (25%)
"How many days of rest a month do you think is suitable for you?" Desired days off per month			
5 to 8 days	2 (5%)	9 (19%)	11 (13%)
4 days	14 (36%)	29 (62%)	43 (50%)
3 days	8 (21%)	3 (6%)	11 (13%)
2 days or less	15 (38%)	6 (13%)	21 (24%)

hours at the level of the workers' physical tolerance. This also means that most of these Chinese workers are made to work many hours beyond their tolerance level.

Comparing toy and garment workers, we find that 69 percent (twenty-seven out of thirty-nine) of the garment workers wanted to work ten or fewer hours per day, compared to 81 percent (thirty-eight out of forty-seven) of the toy workers. On the second question, only 41 percent (sixteen out of thirty-nine) of the garment workers wanted to have four or more days off a month, compared to 81 percent (thirty-eight out of forty-seven) of the toy workers. Notably, 38 percent (fifteen out of thirty-nine) of the garment workers wanted only two or fewer days off per month. Clearly garment workers wanted to work more days, including all or most weekends, while the majority of toy workers wanted to rest at least every Saturday or Sunday. The factor, we think, that drove the garment workers to want to work such long hours was that their pay was too low for the work they put in, and the fact that they were on piece rates, which gave them the impression that if they worked longer and faster they could make more money.

Workers' Desired Wage: Garments versus Toys

Thus far we have looked at the distribution of the desired work hours of the sampled workers, but we still have to examine the variables that affected their desired wage. Why did some workers want to earn a lot more, and some just a bit more than they were making?

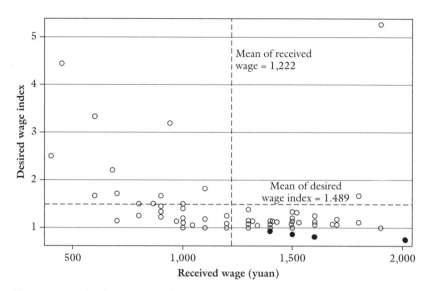

Figure 4.5. Received wage versus desired wage index (all workers; N=88).

To understand this, we ran correlation tests for a number of variables:

Received Wage and Desired Wage Index. It might be assumed that, since the received wage is low, the desired wage index will invariably be higher. When correlating the two variables, however, the situation is more complicated, as shown in figure 4.5.

There was a negative correlation between the two variables, with a correlated coefficient of –0.3643. Figure 4.5 shows that, as might be expected, all but four workers lie above 1 in the desired wage index (the four who lie below 1 are shown as black dots): that is, all but four workers wanted a desired wage higher than their current wage. Figure 4.6 shows that the mean of the desired wage index was 1.489, that is, about 49 percent more than the received wage, whereas only 19 percent of the workers thought that their present received wage was suitable, and 35 percent wanted only 10 percent to 20 percent more. Thus it can be said that 54 percent, just over half the workers, have no desire to earn more. Of those who have much higher desired wage indexes, 11 percent wanted 21 percent to 39 percent more; 13 percent wanted 40 percent to 80 percent more; and five workers wanted more than twice as much. We can conclude that overall the desire of workers to make substantially more money was not high.

What is most interesting, though, are the workers at both extremes in the graph—those who had unusually high desired wage indexes and those

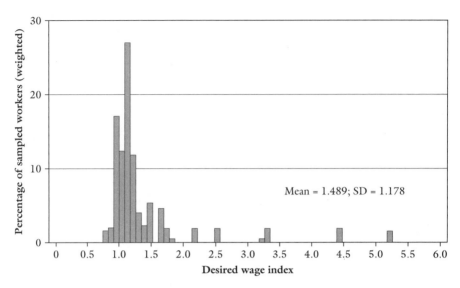

Figure 4.6. Distribution of desired wage index (all workers; N = 88).

whose desired wage was lower than their received wage. The five workers with the highest desired wage index (more than double their received wage) were all paid well below the legal minimum wage level while working extremely long hours. Two of them were working 340 hours a month, which is among the longest in the entire sample. These five workers all earned an *extremely* low hourly wage of 3.56 yuan, which was only about 60 percent of what they should legally have been getting. A possible explanation for this unrealistic dream of earning two, three, or even four times more than they were making is that it was a sign of desperation.

Even more interesting are the four workers who wanted to make less than they were already earning (shown as the black solid dots in figure 4.5). This finding is unexpected and disproves the all-too-common remark by managers that all workers want to do as much overtime as is available, to make more money. When we check these four workers' total monthly work hours, their numbers of days off, and their hours of work per day, we find that three of them worked for at least 318 hours a month, and two of them for more than 342 hours (12-hour days and only 1.5 days off a month), which are also among the highest workloads recorded for the sample. They worked many hours above the average tolerance level.

Furthermore, when we compare the hourly wage earned for the above two groups of workers (the group with highest and lowest desired wage index), the four workers who labored at least 318 hours per month only had an average hourly wage of 3.89 yuan (a mere 0.326 yuan more in their hourly wage than the first group of workers). This 0.326 yuan difference has both subjective and objective implications: on the one hand, the overworked workers felt subjectively that they were so exhausted that they would prefer to make less money, as a trade-off for a reduction in their excessive overtime; on the other hand, the objective 0.326 yuan difference signals that the government's policy that the overtime wage should, legally, be one and a half times that earned during regular work time is not followed in the sampled industries. Many factory bosses paid workers the same or just slightly higher for their overtime work.

Monthly Work Hours and the Desired Wage Index. The popular assumption is that, because wages are low, workers want to work longer hours to make up for the low wage. This should lead to a situation where those who work fewer hours have a higher desired wage index and vice versa. The correlations between the variables of monthly work hours and the desired wage index, however, were not significant for (1) all the workers combined, (2) garment workers, nor (3) toy workers. The correlation coefficients were also very weak (-0.1467, -0.2772, and -0.2636). This is evidence that length of work hours is not a determinant of workers' desire to make more money. This means that, compared to the received wage, the issue of working hours was less important as a factor affecting workers' desire to make more money.

The Monthly Wage versus Hourly Wage. Since a monthly wage package does not reflect rationally the relationship between hours worked and monetary award, to find out whether the worker is paid up to the legal minimum wage level it is essential that the wage rate is expressed as an hourly wage to determine accurately the extent to which labor is "sweated."

When expressed in terms of an hourly wage, it becomes clear that the most poorly paid workers at these Walmart supplier factories are those who do the most overtime work. We have divided the sampled workers into three groups: those with shorter work hours (less than 270 hours per month), medium work hours (270–300 hours per month), and longer work hours (more than 300 hours). We then examined the relationship between the length of monthly work hours and the hourly wage.

First, the mean values of the hourly wage for all sampled workers in their respective work hour groups are: short = 4.05 yuan (SD = 0.57), medium = 4.02 yuan (SD = 0.34), long = 3.56 yuan (SD = 0.49). Hence, for all cases we found that the longer the monthly work hours, the lower the hourly wage received. Second, when we split the whole sample into garment and toy workers, the trends were the same. The mean values of the hourly wage for toy workers in respective groups are: short=4.32 yuan (SD=0.56); medium=4.19 yuan (SD=0.16); long=4.06 yuan (SD=0.34); the mean values of the hourly wage for garment workers are: short=3.83 yuan (SD=0.48); medium=3.47 yuan (SD=0.14); long=3.20 yuan (SD=0.16).

The results clearly show that the more overtime the workers work, the lower the hourly wage. For garment workers, even though the minimum wage for the time when the survey was conducted was lower than for toys, the hourly wage was still extremely low. Thus garment workers who work longer hours than toy workers are in general much more exploited, even though their tasks demand higher skills.

The Hourly Wage and Desired Wage Index. As discussed above, the hourly wage is an indicator that takes into account both wage and work hours. For our sample, when a worker's hourly wage was correlated with the desired wage index, the outcome was highly significant for all groups: (1) all workers combined, (2) garment workers, and (3) toy workers. The correlated co-efficient for all workers combined was −0.1365; for garment workers it was 0.4037; for toy workers it was only −0.2661; in other words, the strength of correlation was far stronger for garments than for toys, though the relationships went in opposite directions.

A positive correlation between the desired wage index and hourly wage suggests that garment workers' desire to make more money increases in tandem with the increase in hourly wage. In fact, the opposite correlation patterns for two types of workers should not be surprising when we take payment systems into account. Garment workers on piece rates were under the illusion that they could make more money by either working longer hours or working faster. In either case, they believed that, if they tried hard enough, they might be able to augment their income through personal effort. As workers worked faster, the total number of pieces of garments increased, which contributed to a higher hourly wage. However, garment workers did not realize that the increase of their hourly wage stops at a certain point of work hours per month. In cases in which they work excessively long hours (say three hundred hours per month), their hourly wage begins to drop.

In contrast, a negative correlation between desired wage index and hourly wage suggests that the more the hourly wage toy workers earn, the lower their work incentive. This is the logic of work paid by time rates. Toy workers, who were on time rate, knew very well that at the end of the day no matter how hard and fast they worked, they would get the same amount of hourly wage.

A worker might have a higher than average monthly wage, but this could be a result of working very long work hours at a low hourly wage. The worker, in fact, could be terribly overworked and underpaid. Notably, too, the scatter plot of received wage against monthly work hours (see fig. 4.5) is more dispersed for garment workers because of an irrational wage structure and the individualistic nature of the workforce under a piece-rate system. The scatter plot for toy workers, however, is more concentrated, at close to 300 work hours per month, due to a greater uniformity in payments based on a time rate.

Speedups and Labor Intensity

Thus far we have used quantifiable figures to argue that the exploitation of sweated labor is serious. However, there is one factor that we are unable to quantify: labor intensity. Precise quantitative data on this can become available only through access to factory records on work hours and production. However, the evidence from the interview survey strongly suggests that, as the increase in the legal minimum wage outpaced the rate of inflation starting in 2004, an employer seeking to comply with the legal minimum wage law and to maintain or increase his profit margin turned to the stratagem of speeding up the production line. We asked respondents, "In comparison to 2006, did your factory request you to speed up your production in 2007?" We found that about 43 percent of garment workers and 56 percent of toy workers responded that they had to work faster. Fifteen percent of both types of workers said that the work speed was a lot faster. (See table 4.5.)

As management did not inform workers about the actual basis of their payments and their expected work speed, this was never made explicit in wage calculations, and workers were not paid more for working faster. In reality, greater labor intensity means increased exploitation and "sweating," as workers were already exhausted at the previous speed.

THE CODE OF CONDUCT AND WORKERS' ATTITUDES

The above statistical analyses provide evidence of prevalent, blatant labor violations in terms of illegally low payments and illegally long work

Table 4.5
Production speed, 2006 and 2007

Factory type	Speed	Number of workers	Percent	Cumulative percent
Garment	Faster by a lot	6	15	15
	Faster by a little bit	11	28	43
	The same	13	32	75
	Slower by a little bit	0	0	75
	Don't know	10	25	100
	Total	40	100	
Toy	Faster by a lot	7	15	15
	Faster by a little bit	20	41	56
	The same	14	29	85
	Slower by a little bit	0	0	85
	Don't know	7	15	100
	Total	48	100	

hours, especially in the garment industry. Walmart's code of conduct and its monitoring programs are supposed to rectify these widespread malpractices in supplier factories. On its website, Walmart boasts that it performed 13,600 audits in 2005, the largest number carried out by any corporation in the world, yet legal violations are apparent in our survey data. The purpose of these audits is thus unclear.

Some of the answers provided by the workers in the survey further explain why audits are not effective. The workers were aware of the auditing: in fact, 80 percent of the respondents knew that outsider auditors came to inspect their factory. Half of them stated that they were informed by management in advance. The majority, though, had little idea of what was being audited. Of the 80 percent who knew of the audits, only 3 percent said that the auditors were concerned about labor standards and work conditions; others thought the auditors were concerned mostly with product quality and occupational health and safety. The workers saw the inspections as having little to do with their personal well-being. Only twenty interviewees (23 percent) thought that the inspections could improve workers' work conditions or wages.

Relatively few workers knew that Walmart had set standards that were supposed to be audited. Only twenty respondents (23 percent) said that the Walmart code of conduct was put up on factory walls; 50 percent answered "no" and 24 percent "did not know." Of the twenty who had seen the poster, only eight answered that they had read what it said, and of these, only one person answered "yes" to the question, "Do you feel the factory has implemented the code?" These figures show that from the workers' perspective the corporate code is of no relevance: most did not know about it, and almost no one thought it was implemented. Given their low wages and illegally long work hours, they were obviously correct in this. The general failure of social auditing to detect violations of vital labor standards means that the CSR program of which Walmart boasts has had little impact on workers at the company's supplier factories.

COMING TO GRIPS WITH SWEATED LABOR

In both the Chinese and international press there has been much discussion (and lamentation among investors in China-based factories) that China's inexhaustible supply of cheap labor is drying up, driving investors away. The shortage, we argue, has been exaggerated. From the employers' vantage point, it has been a shortage of prime labor, which means young women under twenty-four, which has been alleviated by hiring older workers and male workers.[17] Use of under-aged labor (sixteen- to eighteen-year-olds) and even child labor has also increased to fill the gap.[18] The labor market is readjusting itself in Guangdong, but wages and work conditions have not been lifted beyond the "sweating" level.

To revisit our working definition of "sweating," it is clear that working hours are excessive, when the majority of the workers labor more than eleven hours a day with almost no days off, which is well beyond their tolerance level. Their wages are also "unusually low," as can be seen when we compare the earnings of migrant workers with the average earnings of the nonmigrant urban population. The hourly wages at these Walmart supplier factories can also be considered "subminimal" if we accept the legal minimum wage as the standard for "minimal."

Up to this point, our discussion of wages and work hours has been premised on the assumption that the legal minimum wage set by local governments is a fair minimum rate for a forty-hour working week—that because it is legal it must be fair. But is it? When workers labor more than eleven hours a day, and when many feel reluctant to work fewer hours because they desperately need the money, the wage structure is far from normal. A wage package that depends on a worker doing so much overtime before being able to secure a wage that amounts to less than US$190 a month is neither normal nor fair. To correct the problem of an abnormal wage structure, it must first be recognized that China's legal minimum wage level has been set too low.

The data show a disconcerting problem: workers' own notion of a fair wage is not high. Their expectation has been constrained by their assumption that a wage that is in compliance with the legal minimum wage is fair. We have yet to learn of workers privately or publicly demanding a higher legal minimum wage. The official minimum wage distinguishes legality from illegality and has gained an almost sacrosanct status.

The government and the trade union incessantly espouse the importance of "protecting rights" (*weiquan*), which is the current buzzword in China. This amounts to a right to be compensated up to the legal minimum wage. "To protect" is in itself a passive behavior; only if one's legal rights are being violated does one need to be protected. It does not suggest an active assertion of rights beyond the minimum. This explains why most of the workers in our survey, though aware of the legal minimum wage standard, were very modest in their aspirations. It is no coincidence, we believe, that the desired wage of the toy workers (1,527 yuan) was so close to the legally entitled wage (1,537 yuan), and the difference for garment workers was also slight—1,419 yuan and 1,343 yuan respectively (see figure 4.4). China's legal minimum wage distorts the perceptions of the workers, the authorities, and even the critics, including ourselves, the authors of this chapter. We, too, were caught up by this paradigm when we began our project. When we drew up the questionnaire, many of our questions revolved around the legal minimum wage framework as our benchmark. The discourse not just inside but also outside China has to move off this track.

We hope that our study can have some practical impact by raising the issue of the importance and necessity of expressing legal minimum wage figures as an hourly wage. Due to the lack of transparency and the deliberate complexity and arbitrariness in management's wage setting, workers have great difficulty understanding how they are being paid. In societies where trade unions are active, the unions take up this responsibility and negotiate with management on the intricate details of wage setting. In China, where collective bargaining is nonexistent in Asian supplier factories, it becomes particularly helpful to workers to express wage rates by the hour rather than by the month. Workers would then be able easily to calculate how much they should be paid. In fact, within the past few years the Chinese authorities themselves have begun expressing wages by hourly rates in order to clarify their own perceptions, but this usage needs to be popularized. It is unfortunate that developing countries today almost all use a monthly rather than an hourly wage, whereas in developed countries, expressing wages by the hour is the convention for low-paid workers.

If wages were generally expressed by the hour, workers would more easily become aware of underpayment. The piece-rates system in particular is confusing to them. Using that system, management has greater freedom to manipulate the wage package. The garment workers in the survey therefore not only made less per hour than toy workers paid on time rates, but worse still, their hourly rate actually decreased with longer working hours. They work at a rate of diminishing returns.

In a follow-up survey, when we asked a number of the garment workers in the survey whether their wages had gone up since the last legal minimum wage increase in mid-2006, they said that management had not informed them of an increase in the basic wage, and then followed up with, "since we are on piece rate it does not matter." Their answers show their lack of awareness that their pay was illegally low and that the more they worked the less they were paid per hour. Piece rates conceal from workers the reasons for their low wages. Instead, it encourages individualistic behavior on the shop floor. Labor NGO staff who work closely with garment workers remark that it takes more to convince garment workers to accept that they are paid less than the legal wage. Because of their individualistic outlook they tend to believe that the solution to their impoverishment is working faster and for longer hours.

In conclusion, we discovered that the exercise of figuring out hourly rates has some practical value in labor activists' advocacy work. Expressing wages in hourly terms will expose the hidden agendas of exploitation. It will help enhance workers' understanding of the award system and provide practitioners with a better tool for their advocacy work.

Our findings also show that Chinese workers in factories that supply Walmart are toiling far longer than the tolerance level—some 60 hours—at which most workers reach exhaustion. For the last two centuries workers in Europe and the United States struggled to reduce their work hours until the forty-hour week became the norm. Yet now, for the developing world, a sixty-hour week has been set as the norm in the CSR codes of multinational corporations like Walmart. This, too, ought to be rectified—and should become a goal of labor activists' advocacy work.

Workers in Southern nations toiling in the global supply chain are competing with workers in other poor nations for a share of the global labor market. Thus, even though Walmart sources most of its products from China, it is nevertheless in a position to require Chinese workers in the export industries to compete with Indian, Bangladeshi, Sri Lankan, Indonesian, and Vietnamese workers. The authorities who set the legal minimum wages in these countries are certainly aware of the highly competitive global market for cheap labor. Countries in the South need to begin to work toward a wage floor that stops a race to the bottom, and expressing wages as hourly rates is necessary for this.

The international competition was keenly felt in 2003 to 2006 when Outer Shenzhen's legal minimum wage had to rise to attract back to the region the migrant workers who had stopped coming due to wage stagnation. This in turn caused concern that the area would lose out to other low-wage countries. According to a newspaper report, a spokesman for Walmart's China regional office said that Walmart might start to shift its sourcing to Vietnam and India, due in part to China's rising exchange rate. In the coming year, according to the report, Walmart might reduce Chinese sourcing by 40 percent, from US$18 billion to $12 billion.[19] While the spokesman said that this figure could not be confirmed, the impact of such reports and the ongoing rises in China's exchange rate have placed pressure on Guangdong Province. In June 2007 it announced that there would be no increase in the legal minimum wage for 2007,[20] despite rising inflation during the first half of 2007.[21] This decision to preclude any increase was a noticeable break from the annual minimum-wage increases of previous decades, no matter how small and symbolic the wage rise. In 2009, due to the economic downturn, there was a second moratorium in the increase of the legal minimum wage despite continued inflation.

Workers whom we arranged to interview during July 2007 were concerned about the lack of an increase. They were aware of the legal minimum wage and had built up an expectation that it would be revised upward in the middle of every year, particularly in a year of rapid inflation. This expectation reflects a new level in workers' awareness. In July 2007, we became aware of three factories (not the ones in this survey) where workers had demanded higher wage rates for overtime work and limits on their daily production quota. In one factory, a group of workers demanded an unchanged pay level per hour even if there were not enough orders. These are big steps forward in workers' awareness and initiative. These new demands take into consideration what we have analyzed in this chapter—the relationship between legal minimum wage rates, overtime wage rates, piece rates, and speedups. Workers have begun to press on vital core issues that have been neglected by CSR codes such as Walmart's.

PART TWO

The Walmart Stores

5 CORPORATE CADRES

Management and Corporate Culture at Walmart China

David J. Davies

In 1996, when Walmart opened its first Chinese store in Shenzhen—the heart of the region where many of the goods it sells are manufactured—China became not just a sourcing location, but a destination for retail expansion. Having nearly saturated the American market with its gigantic stores, the Walmart corporation is investing a significant portion of the company's future on China's growing consumer class. After a slow start, in recent years it has been aggressively expanding to quickly establish a competitive economy of scale to push down purchasing and logistics costs—from only a few dozen stores early this decade they had nearly 200 stores by the end of 2010. Along the way, in late 2006, Walmart acquired Trust Mart (*Haoyouduo*), a Taiwanese retail competitor in the China market—adding 107 retail stores under Walmart's ownership. The success of this ambitious expansion, however, has depended on hiring and training thousands of new managers, and many tens of thousands of office staff, support staff, and store employees.

In this section on Walmart retail stores in China, it is appropriate to begin with a chapter that examines store management and corporate organizational culture. As the highest authorities at each retail store and those ultimately responsible for daily operation, staff performance, and profitability at the front line, managers are responsible for maintaining company standards, propagating the orthodoxy of Walmart's corporate rules, and

Portions of this chapter first appeared in David J. Davies, "Wal-Mao: The Discipline of Corporate Culture and Studying Success at Wal-Mart China," *China Journal* 58 (2007): 1–27. The author thanks Anita Chan and Xue Hong for their very helpful comments in editing this chapter.

interpreting corporate culture "on the ground" in the stores they manage. During this period of rapid growth, managers have been the teachers and role models of Walmart's distinctive corporate culture—its "corporate cadres"—introducing the corporation to the vast number of new employees and customers encountering it in China for the first time.

Taking "managers" as a group might lead to a tendency immediately to pit their interests against those of the "workers." As examples in this chapter suggest, however, there are many cases where such an oversimplification ignores the complex ways that the corporate structure subjects both groups to vulnerable positions of surveillance by one another and the Walmart customers they "serve."[1] Agreeing with Fiona Moore's observation that to understand the dynamics of transnational corporations, managers must be seen as more than "two-dimensional oppressors,"[2] Walmart managers should not simply be presumed to be exploiters of their subordinates' labor or banal rule-toting bureaucrats hoodwinked by corporate propaganda. In fact, thinking of them as "cadres" of Walmart culture is a useful metaphor because management is held to standards and expectations that discipline their behavior even as they must rely on these rules to discipline others as they manage day-to-day work at stores. Also, in the context of China, the term *cadres* (*ganbu*) may be used to refer to anyone in a position of authority and power.

Walmart is a highly structured, bureaucratic, rule-driven organization and while managers have power within an individual store's hierarchy, they are relatively powerless to influence the systems set in place by the global corporation to manage its empire of more than seventy-two hundred stores. The corporate system, for example, circumscribes store managers' power to adjust product lines, set pricing, allocate and rearrange shelf space, modify advertising, or adjust visible aspects of the corporate brand. These limits leave store supervisors with managing employee behavior and maintaining the physical space of the stores as their primary areas of control.

Working between regional and national corporate management and the retail sales floor, managers represent the corporation to employees and enforce its rules. At the same time they also represent their subordinates and the store itself to the larger corporation both regionally and nationally. In many ways they are more like the shop foremen of industry that Nelson Lichtenstein describes as "in the middle" between the dictates of corporate management and the needs of frontline employees.[3] Similar to foremen, store managers are responsible for labor discipline and "getting out production"—or in the case of a retail operation "getting out sales." From their position "in the middle," much of what Walmart managers "manage" is the implementation and enforcement of the company system. Edward, the store manager in the following chapter, "A Store Manager's Success Story," for example, describes some of these frustrations in detail as he explains how the limited power of his position affects his ability to generate profit for the company and deal with challenges such as the arrival of a labor union.

Walmart's rigid rules for store operation exist side by side, however, with a "corporate culture" that is more flexible because it allows employee thought and behavior to be more open to a variety of interpretations in local contexts. The company's distinctive and strongly promoted corporate culture is well known in the American business literature.[4] With roots in the words and sales ethos of Walmart's founder, Sam Walton, the culture consists of texts, quotes, images, and stories intended to communicate the organization's motivational and moral values. The messages of the culture are taught in employee training, sung in corporate cheers, practiced in public events, and prominently displayed in images and posters hung throughout the public and employee-only areas of all Walmart stores.

What began in the cultural context of rural southern America, however, has quite different associations in the context of twenty-first-century urban China. As this chapter describes, the messages of Walmart's corporate culture are formally expressed in language that resonates with and often mimics the family ethos and benign paternalism of a small face-to-face community of workers. References to egalitarianism, loyalty, service, shared sacrifice, and delayed gratification for a utopian future of corporate success—combined with images of a great leader—evoke uncanny associations to recent Maoist-era ideologies of an ideal workplace. In its Chinese context "Walmart culture" (*woerma wenhua*) has a localized Chinese flavor in dialogue with Chinese meanings of "culture" (*wenhua*) as an ideal form of human sociability. According to its logic, when expenses are as low as possible, the proper management of employees and the employee-customer relationship will naturally lead to profits. Unlike a Taylorist emphasis on assembly line workers' efficiency in production, the logic of this culture lies in the correct management of internal thoughts and attitudes. In such a community, compliance to the culture is not measured according to an abstract standard, but modeled for employees through social relationships—attempting to forge a sense of shared obligation and mutual responsibility for corporate success. With their decision-making authority circumscribed by the corporate system, managers rely on the more flexible messages of corporate culture to succeed at their jobs.

Store managers who provided data for this chapter often express deep ambivalence at being subject to the discipline of Walmart's corporate system—it is considered to be both a valuable formula for success and an impediment to doing their jobs effectively in a Chinese business environment. Often this ambivalence is resolved by considering employment at Walmart as a kind of business education. Walmart's expansion is occurring at a moment when Chinese corporations and individuals alike are competing amid the changing rules of the global economy. Successful individuals and successful corporations, both foreign and Chinese, are subjects of a popular cultural fixation with studying the "the art of success" (*chenggongxue*).[5] As this chapter describes, working at Walmart and subjecting oneself to the discipline of its strong corporate structure, the demanding Chinese customers, and the needs of subordinates are considered by managers to be more valuable than simply a paycheck—rather, it is important training in becoming "successful" (*chenggong*). Li Shan in chapter 7 expresses exactly this sentiment when, despite the difficulties of his day-to-day job, he writes of wanting to maximize his "potential" and being motivated to "systematically study Walmart's management style." Examining this corporate culture, and the ways that it is represented, taught, modeled, and practiced provides interesting insight into the operation of Walmart retail stores and how the global corporation is localizing in China.

RESEARCH METHODOLOGY

Due to the highly competitive nature of low-margin retailing, and the sensitivity of its global "brand" image, Walmart has strict rules for engaging outside inquiries for information that might become valuable to its competitors. This makes detailed long-term participant observation or survey research in a functioning store difficult if not impossible without direct support of the corporation. Visits to Walmart stores, interviews with management, formal tours and conversations with groups of employees are, however, much easier to arrange despite the fact that such requests must be routed through a bureaucracy of local, regional, and if necessary, ultimately national and international corporate affairs departments.

My first formal request to visit a Walmart store was in conjunction with an annual undergraduate seminar that I lead, which examines transnational production between China and the United States. The request began with a gracious e-mail exchange with Walmart's director of international corporate affairs at its global headquarters in Bentonville, Arkansas, inquiring about the possibility of a group of students touring a Walmart store in China. The conversation was then routed to national and regional Walmart offices in China where I was subsequently introduced to local managerial staff.

At the managerial level every Walmart employee I have met conveys a great deal of pride in the corporation's retail accomplishments and extols the virtues of the value they provide to customers. In China, managers see themselves as belonging to the "white collar professional stratum" (*bailing jieceng*) and take their job seriously and attempt to engage questions professionally and in detail. As a result, the managers I have met have been willing to talk at length about their day-to-day work and critically examine the functioning of their organization. This is particularly true of questions regarding the nature and functioning of Walmart's corporate culture. Although details about "numbers"—sales figures, customer purchases, and salary—could affect competition, and thus is a subject avoided in conversation, many managers are more than happy to talk about "culture" and introduce me to colleagues who could share their own experiences.

Through networking from my first contacts in 2004, colleagues to whom these contacts introduced me, and annual visits, the number of managers I have met and stores I have been able to visit has expanded. During the same period of time I have observed formal presentations of the use and function of Walmart's culture given during store tours tempered by descriptions of frustrations, editorial comments, and critical humor. In the absence of formal decision-making power within the Walmart system, the culture is an important system for managers to rely on to get their work done. They are also deeply aware—verging on cynically so—that the positive formal displays of the culture have a hidden coercive force. So while they often have "toed the line" in formal tours, it is precisely because they see themselves as white collar professionals that they seek to improve their organization through constructive critique. These critiques have emerged in our conversations and discussions in a variety of venues over a number of visits.

Initial data for this chapter were gathered from a single Walmart store during a visit in 2004, and longer periods in conjunction with annual seminars from 2005 to 2008. During an extended three-month research period in the spring of 2006 I collected data from an additional Walmart store and from some of Walmart's competitors. In 2007 and 2008 I visited two additional stores and spoke at length with managerial staff at different levels. The data on which this chapter is based includes both formal and semiformal presentations of Walmart's culture, formal and informal interviews with current and former Walmart employees, and participation at informal social events. Out of respect for their role as professionals I did not ask employees about "numbers" or other information that might be considered sensitive and put them in the awkward position of possibly breaking a company regulation. Such considerations were not necessary, however, in the case of former employees. All images used in this chapter were taken during official store tours with the permission and in the presence of local or regional store general managers. For reasons I will discuss below, all employees of Walmart China use English first names regardless of their English proficiency. Since the managers I describe in this chapter already use pseudonyms at work, in this chapter I have simply given them a different one so as to offer a measure of anonymity.

MANAGEMENT STRUCTURE

Chinese Walmart stores have a formal management hierarchy with job categories and supervisory roles generally consistent with American stores, although the number of employees in each position varies depending on a store's size. The position with the most authority at the store is the general manager (GM) who is ultimately responsible to regional and national corporate management for the correct functioning of each store. This includes, but is not limited to, implementation of the corporate system, store profitability, inventory, compliance, and worker morale. Typically two comanagers, each of whom is responsible for the two major categories of store merchandise—food items and nonfood items—assist the general manager.

Beneath the general manager and comanagers are four to five assistant deputy general managers (ADGMs) assigned to manage different categories of store operations. A typical breakdown often includes the following: a manager for front-end operations, including checkout and network technology; a manager for fresh foods, including produce, deli, fresh meats, and baked goods; a manager for dry grocery goods such as noodles, boxed goods, canned and bottled beverages; a manager for garments, and other various "softline" clothing items; and a manager for electronics, furniture, appliances and other "hardline" products.

The lowest formal level of management consists of the department managers and supervisors who manage individual departments within the store. At the bottom are hourly cashiers, sales associates, and other employees. In Chinese Walmart stores, "other employees" typically include representatives of vendors, supplier-provided stockpersons, and staff who do product demonstrations, which Eileen Otis examines in chapter 8. In addition, Chinese stores have a variety of spaces or counters leased out to small shops not affiliated with Walmart.

Positions within the management hierarchy are assigned according to a strict grading scale with corresponding pay rates.[6] At the top are "S" grade senior management employees subdivided into subgrades. S3 is reserved for the store general manager (12,000–25,000 yuan per month), S2 for the store comanagers (7,000–10,000 yuan per month) and S for assistant deputy general managers (4,000–5,000 yuan per month). Beneath are the "A" grade employees, consisting of department managers (3,000–4,000 yuan per month). At the bottom are the "C" grade nonsalaried "hourly" supervisors (1,500–3,000 yuan per month). Li Shan, the author of the diary in chapter 7 was a low-level supervisor of the "C" grade.

Outside of the management hierarchy there are four rankings. The highest of these are "B" level employees who work in the store office as translators or administrative assistants. Their pay is based on experience and skill and is generally in the range of 3,000 yuan per month. Skilled technicians, including butchers and cooks, are ranked at "D" or "E" grade (900–2000 yuan per month). At the bottom are the standard floor associates at the "F" rank (600–2,000 yuan per month).

Each employee's rank within the hierarchy is often posted in staff areas for co-workers to see and this visibility appears to be a technique of motivation for advancement. At two stores I noted a "staff development tree" (*yuangong fazhanshu*) posted near the employee changing room on which managers of grades "C" and higher were labeled by name and positioned according to their rank (figure 5.1). Each employee's name and basic information were printed on a long narrow slip of paper and pasted in hierarchical order on the outline of a green pine tree with a gold star at the top. Their Chinese name, English name, department and subdepartment, employment start date, and time at the current store were posted along with their current position and grade and next position and grade they will advance to up the hierarchy. For example, one slip read:

Deng Tuo, Fred; Fresh Food—Bakery—Baker, grade D; employed since 10/20/00; at current store since 2/5/04; will later move up to Fresh Food—Bakery Supervisor.[7]

In this way every employee at the higher grades could track their colleagues' advancement and the next step in each employees' promotion. On the highest "branches" each senior manager had his or her own slip at the

Figure 5.1. A "staff development tree" (*yuangong fazhan shu*) with the names and ranks of more than 150 management-level employees at a Chinese Walmart store. Note the letter ranks from C to S along the right side of the tree.

top of the hierarchy—but as colleagues all on the same tree their position was symbolically within reach of each employee below.

During my visits to Walmart stores in China over the past four years I have met five general managers at the S3 level, five comanagers at the S2 level, and more than a half-dozen managers at the S level or lower. In addition I have met a regional manager, two corporate affairs staff, and some staff in the purchasing division. With only one exception, everyone at the store management level or below is in their late twenties or early thirties and has worked their way up within the Walmart system over a period of six to eight years. Most came from regional or local Chinese colleges directly into Walmart as their first job. Two individuals were proud to say they had made it into a management position from a humble beginning as a basic associate with only a high school degree. As a group, managers come from all over China and are regularly transferred from store to store as they advance up the graded hierarchy. No doubt because Walmart first entered mainland China through Shenzhen and is headquartered there, many senior managers have spent time in southern China.

Walmart tends to fill management positions internally, dependably promoting managers from lower levels according to the strict hierarchy. Even employees recruited directly from college into its management-training program begin their careers at the lowest level of management, albeit often advancing upward very quickly, like Edward the successful manager whose story is told in the next chapter. Promotions, however, only occur if there is a vacancy in the current store, or if an employee transfers to another store. At the highest management grades advancement is slow and difficult without a ready willingness to move to a different store. Every single manager I have met has moved at least once in the past four years. All of the comanagers (S2) have moved up to become store general managers and two of the general managers (S3) have left Walmart to take positions with other retailers. Edward, for example, moved between four stores in his last four years at Walmart.

Moving from city to city to open new stores, to ascend management ranks and to gain new responsibilities is an exciting prospect for Walmart's young workforce. Moreover, every year Walmart sends select Chinese employees to the United States for management training—to "study abroad" in a U.S. Walmart store to learn about the larger corporation and the culture that founded it. They also gain the opportunity to improve their English, a valuable skill for communication and advancement within the company.

The geographic circulation of managers has the useful side effect of creating a primary affiliation with the corporation at the expense of relationships in the local community in which the store is located. All of the managers I have met at Walmart stores in China commented on the difficulty of constantly adjusting to new locations where they know very few or no local residents. One manager moved to three different stores in three different cities in the span of a year. With only one recent exception, all of the Walmart managers I have met live alone in rented apartments as close as possible to their stores—so they can get to work quickly or pick up and move if they were transferred to a new store. It is not uncommon for the families of married managers to live in different cities—permitting only infrequent visits. The distance from their families and their status as outsiders (*waidiren*) in the cities in which they work reinforces their identity as a Walmart employee. A manager who was lucky enough to stay in the same city for two years commented to me one evening that he didn't have a single friend outside of Walmart. Despite the sacrifices of their own time and effort, however, the individuals I have met with over the years are highly motivated, ambitious, and clearly anticipate that their hard work will pay off someday. In fact it is precisely this promise of future success that provides the rationale for enduring any immediate hardships or inconveniencies.

Among female managers, Walmart's strict and relatively transparent hierarchy provides a measure of protection from sexual harassment or discrimination. One female store manager in particular said that she felt women at Walmart were more protected than in the workplaces of Chinese competitors. I noted a number of female employees working at the highest levels of store management, in human resources, and other departments, and there does not appear to be the same kind of dramatic gender imbalance noted until recently in American stores. Of course, female employees face other challenges—male partners or family members might not be tolerant of the long work hours or other commitments of the Walmart "family."

Male colleagues commented to me that in its current period of expansion, Walmart demands a level of mobility and sacrifices in one's personal life—prerequisites for promotion at the highest levels of management—which put an incredible strain on marriages and families. Five of six female managers whom I met at Walmart were single, divorced, or separated from their spouses. The only manager who maintained a relationship did so by refusing to move to another city—and so remained stuck at the same management grade. Frustrated at waiting for an opportunity to advance, she later left Walmart to work in the same city for another foreign company.

Walmart Store Culture

Asserting a distinctive corporate culture is a claim of uniqueness in the realm of business activity. It is also the representation of an ideal model for interaction among employees and between employees and customers. While the ideal is not always reflected in actual practice, as Allen Batteau has observed, organizational cultures provide a repertoire of resources for imposing "cultures of rationality, inclusion, command and authority" while simultaneously eliciting "cultures of adaptation and resistance" among members.[8] As a "culture" with its many rules and regulations that specify normal store operation, Walmart store culture asserts a general set of values and expectations, which are constantly interpreted, negotiated, discussed, and contested by employees and managers alike as they go about their work. Often day-to-day practice of the culture may stray from the ideal, lending itself to interpretations that may contradict the rules.

Without a trace of irony, a company often seen by outsiders as coercive and exploitive represents itself as an ethically righteous, moral force for its employees. At Walmart in the United States, the corporate culture claims to uniquely emphasize the values, belief, and morality of the American rural heartland. Its corporate mythology is rife with examples of the simple lifestyle and "down-home" values of Walmart's founder, Sam Walton. His straight-talking, no-nonsense, no-frills rural persona is extolled as the epitome of American free-market capitalism. It is a persona that succeeds by thumbing its nose at convention—perhaps most famously illustrated by the commonly re-counted story of Sam Walton doing a hula dance down Wall Street in 1984.

In the United States Walmart positions itself in the use of populist language as the defender of the average American—its low prices offer-ing a higher standard of living that might otherwise be denied them by "the rich." Rick, a comanager at an American store framed this in language reminiscent of class struggle, telling me that his workers were "thick like thieves" working to offer low cost to people who could not otherwise af-ford things: "It is not fair for the rich to get richer and the poor to get poorer... average people kill themselves working on their jobs. That is just the way it is." He told me Walmart's newest American slogan, "Save money, live better," speaks directly to the core of Walmart's mission to provide for average Americans.[9]

Walmart's corporate culture codifies these values using language that speaks of higher morality and values such as individual initiative, hard-work, respect, honesty, and service. As Nelson Lichtenstein has observed, Prot-estant Christian values infuse the discourse on American Walmart stores. "Like the mega-churches, the TV evangelists and... motivational seminars," he writes, "Wal-Mart is immersed in a Christian ethos that links personal salvation to entrepreneurial success and social service to free enterprise."[10] More recently, Bethany Moreton offers a compelling historical examination of Walmart's ideas of free enterprise and the ethos of Christian service.[11] Historical authenticity at Walmart, however, still resides in Sam Walton's mythic persona and the story of the "genuine American folk hero cut from the homespun cloth of America' heartland" as expressed most grandly in Walton's biography, *Sam Walton: Made in America,* which is on the bookshelves of every Walmart store I have visited—in both America and China.[12]

In his history of Walmart, Robert Slater provides an introduction to its corporate culture created by Sam Walton and systematically written down in his memoirs in 1992.[13] In Slater's summary, the most elementary form of Walmart's culture consists of "three basic beliefs":

1. Respect for the individual
2. Service to the customers
3. Striving for excellence

To this are added "ten rules of business" written by Sam Walton himself:

1. Commit to your business
2. Share your profits with all your associates, and treat them as partners
3. Motivate your partners
4. Communicate everything you possibly can to your partners
5. Appreciate everything your associates do for the business
6. Celebrate your success
7. Listen to everyone in your company
8. Exceed your customer's expectations
9. Control your expenses better than your competition
10. Swim upstream

Walton added two more guidelines for daily employee conduct. The "ten-foot rule" mandates that "any time an employee comes within ten feet of a customer the employee is to look the customer in the eye and ask if he or she requires help of any kind." The "sundown rule" stipulates that employees are "expected to answer requests by sundown on the day the requests are received."[14]

Sam Walton intended that the store culture would create an exciting, motivational, and successful atmosphere among store employees. The atmosphere was predicated on the ideal of each employee learning and living out the corporate culture in dealings with other employees and customers. Walton believed that if the employees felt good, then it would be easy "to make customers feel good being at Walmart"—giving customers the impression of a warm, caring, and personal "hometown" relationship.[15]

In American Walmart stores, corporate culture is mentioned in employee training videos and training games but is most visibly deployed in a "culture kit" of posters and images distributed to stores when they are opened. While visiting an urban American store that opened during the same period of time I was collecting data from Chinese stores for this chapter, I noted parts of the kit displayed in various employee-only areas at the back of the store. On a break room wall, tacked to a bulletin board in very small print was a description of the three "basic beliefs" and Walmart's honesty policy, which will be described below. Affixed to the wall next to it was a small image of a middle-aged Sam Walton in a conservative blue suit with a starched white shirt and blue and burgundy striped tie. Nearby a few of Walton's famous business quotations were haphazardly tacked up. Unlike the many prominent displays of corporate culture in Chinese stores—often including homemade depictions by store employees in multiple locations throughout a single store—the display I noted in the U.S. store was modest, limited in scope, and appeared to be simply a compulsory posting. Communicating store culture clearly did not appear to be a priority for management or employees in the American store.

When I asked Rick, the American manager, about the value of Walmart's culture, he noted that the three beliefs were important and regularly mentioned in meetings, but that he had not heard of the ten rules of business for many years. One aspect of the corporate culture Rick told me that is still regularly practiced in U.S. Walmart stores is the Walmart cheer. Sam Walton introduced the cheer to Walmart as a morale booster in 1975 after seeing employees at a Korean factory do a morning cheer. Robert Slater summarizes the call and response of the cheer where a leader calls out each line and the assembled crowd of employees responds:

Give me a W!
Give me an A!
Give me an L!
Give me a squiggly!
Give me an M!
Give me an A!
Give me an R!
Give me a T!
What's that spell?
Walmart!
Who's number one?
The customer! Always![16]

The "squiggly" mentioned in the middle of the cheer refers to the dash that was originally between the Wal and the Mart in the company name. During the cheer the reference to the "squiggly" is accompanied by a twisting downward shake. Slater's version, however, does not include additional lines commonly found in current cheers. Following the letter-by-letter spelling of "Walmart" and before cheering about the primacy of the customer, two additional lines speak of the workers relationship to the company:

Whose Walmart is it?
It's my Walmart!

Later in this chapter I examine the implications of a culture that exhorts employees to identify with it as "My Walmart." For now, however, it is important to note that the cheer is not performed by a chorus of equals but directed by a cheerleader who manages each line of the call and response.

The basic cheer is the same at Walmart stores in China but it is common for additional lines and embellishments to be added at each store to make it unique. In the United States there are also regional variations in the expression of aspects of Walmart's corporate culture. For example, the human resource manager at Rick's store showed me a catalog of employee "incentive" pins worn on uniforms that display a wide variety of images, some of which clearly reflect the concerns of employees in different regions of the United States. As explained by Rick and his human resources manager, however, "the culture" appeared to be largely an incentive management practice quite different than the "spirit" displayed in Chinese Walmart stores. During our conversation I showed Rick images of the culture as expressed at various Chinese Walmart stores. While much of the content was familiar to him, he found its expression in posters and wall murals to be surprisingly elaborate, and he commented that there was "no way" he could motivate his American employees to engage the culture to the same extent.

WALMART, CHINA

During my first formal visit to a Chinese retail store, Frank, a regional manager, introduced Walmart in part by gesturing to a collection of posters and images hung on the wall of the office shared by the store's managers. The posters and images, Frank told me, would explain everything I needed to know. Outside in the hall near the staff changing rooms was a large and elaborately decorated "culture wall" (*wenhua qiang*) with further explanatory posters and images illustrating key aspects of store culture to employees. In the public section of the store near the entrance were even more posters presenting to customers Walmart's store values, a short corporate history, and the store's unique management structure emphasizing "servant leadership." In other words, the culture was something shown to workers and customers alike—shaping expectations of employee behavior and customer satisfaction.

While there are core aspects of Walmart's corporate culture that appear consistent across Chinese stores and no doubt constitute a standard package, there is also a degree of variety in representation. The many permutations of display and elaboration in different stores indicate a measure of local interpretation by managers and workers—culture is not simply translated from a standard American version. The formal displays of culture, as I describe in this section, provide a repertoire for managers and employees to interpret behaviors and underlying thoughts in the context of the store's corporate mission. Before discussing the culture in practice, it is important to examine the themes and general poetic impressions communicated through representations of the culture.

One aspect of store culture in China is the central role that images of Walmart's founder play in authorizing the various aspects of activity in the store. In public and staff-only areas throughout the store, the benevolent fatherly image of Sam Walton figures prominently—welcoming customers at the entrance, illustrating store history, and perhaps most often posted next to descriptions of store culture (figure 5.2). Interestingly, only one image of Walton appears to be in use at Walmart China and is repeated everywhere. It is an image of Sam dressed in a dark formal suit and conservative burgundy tie, his business attire blunted by a simple working-class Walmart baseball cap sitting slightly askew high on his head in rural American style. With an everyday red, white, and blue Walmart employee name tag pinned over his heart and his right hand raised in a partial wave of greeting, he looks out of the picture with a muted expression of pleasant indifference. The conventions of such a posture are strikingly familiar to the religious images of the bodhisattva, Guanyin, Jesus Christ, or images of Mao Zedong that circulated during the Cultural Revolution.[17]

In staff-only areas, images of the founder are frequently accompanied by displays of "corporate spirit" (qiye jingshen). Unlike the small "inspirational quotations" of the American "culture kit," at the Chinese store the quotations from Walton are much larger and more elaborately printed in plain white lettering on a solid blue background. As is common Chinese practice,

Figure 5.2. A huge image of Sam Walton welcomes customers at the public entrance to a Chinese Walmart store. Note the smiley face to the right.

a signature of someone with power and status authorizes the words—Walton's own handwritten name is reproduced at the bottom of the quote. Carefully affixed to foam backing and prominently displayed in backroom areas frequented by workers, in some cases the individual "Wal-quotes" are illustrated by hand-painted murals. In one store, staff ascending and descending the employee staircase from the city streets to the store pass nearly a dozen quotations and four images of the founder as they arrive and depart their work shifts each day. A selection of the quotations read:

Strive to make customers return to shop at our store...only through this can we reap profits.

Ensure the satisfaction of the customers, and they will continually patronize our store.

Do not allow yourself to land in an unchangeable predicament.

Listen to staff suggestions; they can come up with the best ideas.

Make us work together as one to do our very best to market our products.

Be grateful for every single thing our staff does for the company.

Outstanding product marketers are able to guarantee a supply of product on hand to sell at all times.

Only by concerted efforts to reduce costs, are we able to lower prices to the best of our ability.

We must achieve true honesty.

The difference between the competition and us lies in that we pay attention to cultivating staff consciousness about the products.

To be more frugal with our expenses than our competitors is to fight for competitive superiority.

It is notable that the quotations of Sam Walton communicate a moral tone that aspires to correct behavior in the workplace, and through their use of language evoke a sense of cooperative struggle for corporate success. These themes are reinforced by one of the most common postings of corporate culture—"The Ten Rules of Business" described in the previous section. In Chinese, however, the linguistic associations of the rules shift from the "marketing language" of the English original to a translation that accentuates a revolutionary, martial, or heroic tone.

The mundane "ten rules" become in Chinese the "ten laws" (*shige faze*). In some cases they are referred to as the "ten great laws for success with the cause" (*shiye chenggong de shi da faze*), where *shiye* ("the cause" or "undertaking") unites the success of the individual's career with the success of the company. Law number one, for example, which in English is "commit to your business," in Chinese directs employees to "be loyal to your cause" (*zhongyu nide shiye*). Law number three, which in the original speaks in the register of business to "motivate your partners," in the translation uses the word *jili,* to impel or inspire, a word used often in military examples of improving morale or struggling toward victory. In English, rule number five asks employees to "appreciate the work that fellow employees do for the business." The Chinese translation, however, replaces the congratulatory connotations of "appreciate" with *ganji,* a feeling of heartfelt gratitude and indebtedness. Rather than simply "controlling expenses" as rule number nine asserts, the Chinese entreats employees to *jieyue* "economize" or "be thrifty." Finally, in rule number ten where Walton challenges employees to "swim upstream," the Chinese presents a similar phrase, to "go against the current" (*niliu*), but adds an injunction in literary language to "forge new paths" (*pi xijing*) and to "not stick to conventions" (*moshou chenggui*).

Together, the "ten laws" formally represent the corporate culture in language and associations reminiscent of revolutionary struggle in a form resonating with the many lists of rules for proper conduct common to the language of Chinese Communist Party propaganda. The "ten laws," for example, are similar both in form and content to rules such as the Red Army Code of Discipline's Three Main Rules of Discipline and Eight Points for Attention (*sandajilu, baxiangzhuyi*), which stipulate obeying orders, frugality, interacting with others fairly, and being honest in interactions with others. Anecdotally, in the summer of 2007, I learned that managers at one Walmart store were busily discussing a popular new management book promising a uniquely Chinese way to successfully manage a Chinese workforce consisting of a large mass of workers—by looking at the "management style" of the People's Liberation Army (PLA). The book suggests how the revolutionary tactics of the PLA can be useful in struggling for success in the contemporary global market.[18]

Honesty and obligation to colleagues in the workplace is, furthermore, evoked by the "ten laws" through the formal use of *tongren* as a translation for "associates"—a common term in Taiwan and Hong Kong to address a public audience, but not by Chinese mainlanders who use the expression *tongshi* (colleague). While both Chinese terms may be translated into English as "colleagues," the latter term *tongshi* emphasizes sharing a common cause, while the former *tongren* connotes shared humanity or morality between people. An assistant Walmart store manager explained that, unlike *tongshi*, which is just a "co-worker," *tongren* means "hearts united" (*xinlianxian*) for a common cause or vision. Historically *ren*, or "benevolence," foregrounds the ethical qualities of personal relationships and implies that they are properly constituted by subduing oneself to the proper social rituals of human interaction. The formal moral tone established in the language of the "ten laws" is reinforced in the language of the "gift policy" posted in employee areas. Also posted on the break-room walls of American stores, the gift policy seeks to restrict interactions between Walmart and its suppliers to "simply business"—through a moral injunction to employees not to be corrupted by personal relationships. Given China's gift-giving culture and the prominent role of relationships in doing business, the "work principles for gifts and gift giving" (*lipin he kuizeng gongzuo yuanze*) are guidelines especially emphasized in the China operations. They are also the most thoroughly explained:

No matter if one is a staff member whose duty is large or small, no one may, for his or her own personal benefit, accept any gift, tip, compensation, sample or anything that appears to be a gift. This is a basic principle of this company.

These gifts may include: tickets for entertainment activities, commission paid in cash or products, a discount given to any staff member, sample products, travel paid for by a supplier, holiday gifts or other such gifts. Any staff member who receives gifts such as those outlined above is requested to please return it at the expense of the other party.

Treating a guest to dinner is also a type of gift. If there is a need to have dinner with a supplier, staff from this company and the supplier should each pay their own costs.

The principles outlined above are to be followed by all staff members of Walmart and Sam's Club. If an individual makes any request for personal remuneration from a supplier for personal benefit, please directly inform a high-level company leader.

That Walmart's corporate culture is more than simply a list of rules that employees should follow at work, but something with a moral quality that is intended to affect one's thoughts as well as behaviors, is overtly stated in a standard poster of the "three basic beliefs." Authorized by the image of the president and CEO of Walmart China, Ed Chan, the beliefs are translated into Chinese as "basic principles" (*san xiang jiben yuanze*), suggesting moral standards or rules for living. The transformative value of these principles is clearly stated:

These [principles] are not simply rules for a style of work, but are "a kind of way of life": we must take these convictions and dissolve them into every hour and every minute of our lives, furthermore embody them as colleagues work together in the process of serving our customers.

There is probably no better example of this all-encompassing culture than the ubiquitous smiling face in Walmart. Yellow "smileys" are everywhere in Chinese Walmart stores, constantly reminding staff and customers alike of the expectation of a pleasant experience at Walmart (figure 5.2). A smiling face and the impression of care for the customer is implicit in the "ten-foot rule," modified in China to the "three-meter principle" (*sanmi yuanze*). Employees at one store are reminded of this expectation every day by a huge five-foot diameter yellow smiley face painted on a wall, which greets them everyday as they punch in for work. At a different store, a full-length mirror near the employee lockers is topped with a yellow smiley face and the question "Are you smiling today?" written above, so that employees can "check their smiles" before heading out onto the sales floor.

This culture is also embodied in the "the sundown principle" (*riluo yuanze*), which urges workers to complete each day's work before the end of the day. Like the "ten-foot rule," it scripts a behavior that a customer, colleague, or client can interpret as care—appearing both engaged with and friendly to customers, regardless of true underlying feelings. In this way it redefines the normal mundane work of day-to-day business interactions with others as opportunities for demonstrating morality. Like the smiley face, the sunset rule is featured in official posters and as motif in murals and images in store backrooms.

Ed Chan's call to adopt the basic principles as a "way of life" that serves others finds its roots in the rural origins of American Walmart's culture—echoing Protestant Christianity's emphasis on realizing belief through "living a Christian life." However, in a Chinese context, the corporate values are cast using distinctly Chinese motifs. The culture—as *wenhua*—scripts a harmonious exchange among colleagues and between employees and customers and the company by requiring employees to submit to a ritual of social interaction. One does not need to believe in the principles and rules as a necessary precondition for them to be efficacious—the morality of the employee is demonstrated through social practice.

While the examples I have described to this point are shared generally among different stores forming a set of core representations there are also instances of local interpretations. These are interesting because they show cultural diversity but also maintain a consistency with the emphasis on morality, collegiality, and community. In one case I noted a hand-painted slogan describing the "Eight Operational Honors and Disgraces" (*yingyun barong bachi*) for store workers modeled along the lines of the "socialist concept of honor or disgrace" (*shehui zhuyi rongru guan*):

Eight Operational Honors and Disgraces

Take love of company culture as honorable, words that don't match deeds as disgraceful.

Take work on the floor as honorable, lingering in the back of the store as disgraceful.

Take sincere care for staff as honorable, being cold and indifferent as disgraceful.

Take honest, direct communication as honorable, complaining to extremes as disgraceful.

Take being a marketing specialist as honorable, slow-witted inflexibility as disgraceful.

Take skillful management of data to be honorable, managing blindly as disgraceful.

Take fast, nimble implementation as honorable, being messy and sloppy as disgraceful.

Take seeking substantial results as honorable, lying low and giving excuses as disgraceful.

That certain behaviors are honorable (*rong*) or disgraceful (*chi*) elevate them from the realm of formal operational rules to that of "spiritual civilization" (*jingshen wenming*), and as moral behaviors they are subject to social scrutiny. The implications of this injunction even extend to a warning against shoplifting posted in a men's restroom—reminding customers to cherish their own reputations:

Shoplifting is criminal activity that will be investigated for criminal or civil liability. Please cherish your future and reputation, avoid breaking the law so as not to regret it later.

MANAGEMENT DISCIPLINE, DISCIPLINING MANAGEMENT

It might be easy to dismiss the formal expression of the Walmart culture described above as corporate propaganda designed to create the appearance of a morality where none exists—nothing more than a ploy to cover up a "deeper" corporate management strategy. Without denying the possibility that it was constructed to hoodwink employees, in practice the culture has concrete effects. Taken together, the cultural representations frame normative behaviors that delineate membership in the organization and impose specific claims on each worker.

While Walmart's corporate system strives to reduce relationships between its employees and other companies to "just business," in practice its culture does the opposite, defining colleagues through a moral code of correct behavior that makes Walmart more than merely a place to work. While, for example, official policy might stipulate maximum hours that an employee can work each day, the culture rewards those who "demonstrate loyalty to the cause," "feel indebted to their colleagues," and "control expenses" by working around the formal rules. The culture as a moral system can be coercive. Precisely because it is public, other employees will use this normative standard to evaluate others' commitment to the organization.

Of course, the messages of Walmart culture could be very powerful if used by a manager to squeeze more work from employees. However when I suggested this scenario to the store general manager in the next chapter, he responded that it would be very difficult to use the culture to coerce workers overtly, because many would ignore it or don't believe in it. He did explain, however, that managers reward individual employees who demonstrate corporate values in their work—particularly exceeding expectations or volunteering for projects. If the messages of the culture are coercive, it is because employees who voluntarily go above and beyond minimal expectations will be promoted faster. In other words, the culture is less about penalizing those who don't measure up, as much as providing an ideal performance goal for those who seek to advance. In his diary, Li Shan in chapter 7 describes at a number of moments the coercive nature of Walmart culture and the employees who "volunteer" to work overtime. At the same time, he often observes how the "mysterious knowledge" of the culture works so effectively to create a positively motivated workforce.

In fact, this "positive" coercive effect is actively reinforced among managers and store staff through "Great Job" cards. Managers give simple blue cards, about the size of a name tag, to other managers, superiors, or subordinates when they have done outstanding work. On one side in English are the words "Great Job" and a quote from Sam Walton, which reads:

> Share profits with all colleagues treating them as partners. In return, they will also take you as a partner and together you will eventually create unbelievable performance.

On the reverse is a space for the manager to briefly describe the exemplary behavior and sign and date it. Staff who collect a specific number of the cards—at one store it was five cards—will get a monetary reward of one hundred yuan.

Working in a system where they have little control over the vast majority of store functions, and having themselves benefited from moving up through the ranks of corporate management, it is in the best interests of managers at all levels to reinforce the messages of the culture. They get more work out of employees who contribute "willingly," and the ones who follow the cultural aspirations most closely become ipso facto the most desirable employees to promote. These outstanding employees then reinforce the system as they too are promoted higher up the management hierarchy.

It is important to note that managers are not working outside of this system but are also subject to it. The manager interviewed in the next chapter, for example, describes his own swift advancement in the Walmart system by getting noticed by superiors. At the same time, he notes instances where, even as a store general manager, he was compelled to work around official operational policies or even break them outright, due to a sense of obligation to superiors, former trainers, or other colleagues. Even when breaking the rules brought no financial gains, the cultural expectations of being a Walmart employee called for certain actions. As he sums it up, "The culture makes you work more than you otherwise would."

Rather than simply a job where employees are compensated for the work they do according to fixed rules and expectations for job performance, at Walmart the culture is used as a flexible measure by which managers evaluate relative performance and the expression of internal sentiments. On a formal tour, for example, Frank, the regional manager who first introduced me to Walmart, proudly showed off a huge airplane suspended from the ceiling above a product display, put together from cardboard advertisements by a team of employees. They had borrowed two floor fans to place under the wings as "jets" and had used a small ceiling fan as a propeller in the plane's nose (figure 5.3). The team's work was not professionally done, but it was significant to Frank because it symbolized the care and commitment the workers had for the welfare of the customer and the store "family" (*jia*).

Through the interpretive lens of the culture, the self-initiated creation of a team of employees cobbled together from throwaway junk, represented "economizing" on costs or "thriftiness" in the face of the business competition. By not hiring a professional designer, the employees saved money for the company—and by extension their self-reliance helped to lower costs for the customer. In Chinese Walmart stores it often happens that staff members team up to design and set up product displays or serve as advertising models for company promotions, and they may also suggest new customer service techniques and ways to improve product sales. All of these activities are taken as symbolic of their sense of ownership and participation in their store "family."

The ideal of employees working together in a spirit of honest collaboration for the welfare of all in the Walmart family is one of Walmart's explanations why it doesn't need organized labor unions. If employees speak

Figure 5.3. A symbol of worker ingenuity and cooperative spirit, a product advertisement made by Walmart employees

honestly with one another and fulfill the obligations of their different positions in the spirit of the culture there is no need to pit one group against another or involve outside organizations to intervene in internal problems. In fact, the arrival of unions at Walmart stores in China was explained by Edward, the manager in the next chapter, as the embarrassing failure of managers to educate workers fully about the corporate culture. If the staff had really understood the force of Walmart's "open door policy" (*menhu kaifang zhengce*), so the explanation goes, they would have realized that they didn't need unions; they could speak to any other employee or member of management honestly and frankly at any time.

Steve, a charismatic and capable young manager originally from South China, repeated this to me the summer before unions were established, remarking that at Walmart each employee can speak frankly to any other employee—including a superior. He was proud that as a manager he was not immune to criticism. He explained:

Before, at my old job, I had to listen to my boss and follow his instructions, but here [at Walmart] any worker can talk to me. Working at Walmart we practice egalitarianism...for example, nobody calls me Manager Wu; only Steve. This is practicing the aspect of American culture of freedom and equality and respecting the individual...the female staff are particularly not used to this. This really is completely an American lifestyle.

Emphasizing the egalitarian nature of work at Walmart, every manager that I met has at some point or another commented on the fact that store general managers do not even have their own offices, but share an office with the entire management team. When they were not working on managerial tasks in the office they were expected to be out on the floor among the employees and customers—engaged in the face-to-face work expected of a Walmart employee.

A key technique for improvement of which Walmart management is proud of is the wide variety of opportunities that all employees have for input, feedback, and criticism. After all, if Walmart is a family, the opinion of each member of the organization is valuable, and they have an obligation to share it to make the company a better place. While there are anonymous means of feedback, some of which I will discuss below, the most common means involve face-to-face techniques for soliciting worker input and for correcting improper behavior. In fact, as more than one manager corrected me, employees at Walmart are not "punished" (*chengfa*) for inappropriate behavior, but are guided by their "coaches" (*jiaolian*) about their errors and how they may correct them.

Perhaps the most regular opportunity for this face-to-face feedback among managers is the morning meeting held on the sales floor prior to the workday. Unlike the typical arrangement of similar meetings in Chinese companies, where superiors stand facing subordinates to do morning exercises and communicate important information, the Walmart floor meetings are convened with management standing in a circle for discussion. When a manager speaks, he or she moves to the comparatively more vulnerable center of the circle to address his colleagues. At floor meetings managers of specific departments are praised for high sales, criticized for poor performance, and encouraged to suggest improvements. More generally, photographs are posted regularly on management boards, sale products chosen by a specific employee for extra promotion to customers, performance charts posted near break rooms, and on worker name badges. Responsibility for specific jobs and their resulting successes and failures is always tied to a specific face.

Figure 5.4. A diagram at the entrance to a Walmart Store illustrating the concept of "servant leadership" (*gongpu lingdao*). The store general manager is at the bottom of the inverted pyramid with his comanagers and assistant deputy general managers immediately above, and department managers at the top.

In the most explicit form of feedback, the faces of managers and their roles they play in managing the store are portrayed through the image of a "servant leadership" (*gongpu lingdao*) posted at the entrance to every store (figure 5.4). This features an inverted pyramid placing the store manager at the bottom, with assistant managers and other managers stacked above them. At the top are the "lowest" levels of managers. The formation illustrates the manager's role of "balancing" the pyramid from the crucial tipping point at the very bottom. From this lowest position, the manager must, as the accompanying illustration says, "provide workers with the opportunity for success."

The inverted pyramid—putting the masses at the top—and the appeals to "serving" both customers and workers is strikingly evocative of the revolutionary class hierarchy of Maoist socialism and the role of the postrevolutionary party leadership as "serving the people" (*wei renmin fuwu*). In this case, however, the culture as displayed inverts the true store hierarchy represented behind the scenes in staff areas by displays such as the "staff development tree" (figure 5.1). While managerial positions are at the top of the corporate system's hierarchy of authority and responsibility, the cultural concept of "servant leadership" provides workers with a measure of power to make claims on managerial performance through moral obligation. If managers, as standard bearers for the corporate culture, do not sufficiently perform the role of "servant leader" or follow the "laws" stipulated by corporate culture, employees are empowered by moral authority to criticize them and seek redress.

Employee dissatisfaction can be expressed internally through the use of anonymous "suggestion boxes" mounted in employee areas, but the external conduits that go around store management, such as the ethical violations hotline, appear to be the most effective means. In one store, the notice "Worksite Code for Moral Behavior" (*gongzuo changsuo xingwei daode guifan*) was posted immediately next to Walton's "ten laws" and provided a telephone hotline and e-mail address to report ethical violations either to Walmart's ethics office in China or directly to corporate headquarters in Bentonville, Arkansas. The hotline is clearly intended to catch serious violations of ethical behavior such as embezzlement, corruption, or gift giving. It does, however, also open the door for allegations of behaviors broadly defined as "harassment" (*saorao*) or "discrimination" (*qishi*). Because the hotline is anonymous, employees may use it to complain about any managerial behavior, no matter how trivial.

While individuals may or may not make use of the opportunity to complain, serious or frequent accusations by employees are investigated, and some managers admit that it undermines their effectiveness, especially in comparison to managers working for competitors who do not have to deal with such systems. In fact, more than one manager commented that Walmart is so forgiving of employee behavior that it is like giving them an "iron rice bowl" (*tiefanwan*). Managers mention to me even in official store tours how difficult it is for them to fire someone at Walmart. One manager offered an example, explaining that he could not demand workers take shorter smoke breaks for fear that they would complain; instead, he had to "convince them" that it was not in their, or the store's, best interests for them to take more time off than allotted.

Of course, the culture does not subject employees and managers only to mutual surveillance. If it did, then the inverted pyramid of servant leadership would only need to be displayed in staff areas, not publicly posted at each store's entrance. As Eileen Otis describes in her chapter, customer satisfaction is an effective and economical way to police the behavior of floor staff at stores. However, this policing does not stop with floor staff. Publicly displaying the faces of the "servant leaders" subjects management to the scrutiny of customers. Above the managers' portraits at the pointed base of the inverted pyramid are, presumably, the staff and—most importantly—above them, the mass of customers at the very "top." The pyramid instructs customers about the hierarchy of management and employees there who are serving them. In fact, the most prominently displayed "face" in Walmart stores is that of the store general manager, along with his or her phone number and the following message, at the end of every one of the dozens of checkout aisles:

> Thank you for shopping. We are committed to providing you with fast, friendly and efficient check-out service. If we don't do this, please call me.

Contrary to what one might expect, however, it does not seem that all managers resent how the culture compels them to work more, or pressures them to demand more work from their employees. In fact, managers often gleefully share examples of innovations that save money and encourage the ideal behavior. When I was visiting in 2006, Frank showed me the creative idea that a group of employees at one store had devised as an incentive for good customer service. Walmart promises each customer the best customer service possible, and the employees came up with a method that would make this service not only visible, but also subject to immediate penalty in the event that the customers' expectations were not met. Eventually they decided that a one-yuan bill should be clipped underneath each service employee's name tag. If a customer was dissatisfied with the service received from an individual employee, he or she could take the one-yuan bill as compensation (see figure 5.5).

Figure 5.5. During a formal tour, a manager describes with pride how employees created a new way of ensuring customer satisfaction. The text on the button reads: "If I have forgotten to ask how you are, or have not offered Walmart's outstanding customer service, this money is yours."

In his explanation Frank did not clearly indicate how the decision was made, but the store management did agree to provide the bills to support the idea. In line with the expectations of the culture, however, the innovation was described as the creation of a group of committed associates.

The interesting thing about the button and the bill is that it makes the customers the enforcers of the rules and makes their dissatisfaction public—not only to other customers, but to other employees as well. Having one's yuan taken—or rather, allowing a customer to take one of their yuan back—is not only a loss of profit, but a loss of face for failing cultural expectations. Managers were not immune: in fact, expectations of them were higher—they had to wear a five-yuan bill.

"WALMART PEOPLE"

"My Walmart" is a popular corporate slogan and part of the corporate cheer common to Walmart stores in the United States and China alike. Who the "my" refers to is left open, permitting employees to assert a claim to employee ownership and customers to expect a level of personal service from "their" Walmart. In both cases, that Walmart is "mine" as opposed to "someone else's" sets an expectation for loyalty and commitment to the company—uniting each employee's performance with the success of the company even as it claims to satisfy consumers' desires at the lowest possible cost. Stories of satisfied customers and committed employees who speak of how "my Walmart" took care of them in tough times or taught them new skills is part of the Walmart corporate ideology.

That Walmart is "theirs" establishes the ideological foundation for the company to make claims on employees' time and "commitment to the cause" beyond a paycheck. Like other aspects of the culture, it makes external work performance a reflection of internal personal morality. After all, if Walmart is "mine," I should treat it with all of the love, care, and concern I show to any of "my" things or "my" relationships. Such claims work around the formal rules of the company, reminiscent of the paternalistic ethos of a family business.

From the point of view of a salaried store general manager who must basically live for Walmart, describing the store as "My Walmart" is not unreasonable given the sacrifices they make in their personal lives to be successful. Even moving down the salaried hierarchy, it is not uncommon to hear managers comment on the extent to which they have devoted themselves to Walmart by referring to themselves and others as "Walmart people" (*wo-erma ren*) or as "Walmart's" (*woermade*). Depending on the context, this can be a positive comment used to refer to individuals who exemplify the ideals of the culture and seriously "believe" in them, but can also be used critically to express the way that the culture subjects employees to its expectations.

One evening over dinner, for example, King, a sourcing manager, discussed the problems of Paul, the general manager of a Walmart store in a nearby town. Paul had successfully moved up through the company to be a store manager but had remained a poor leader. He was loyal to Walmart, but the culture had made him too dependent, concerned with protocol and worried about offending subordinates. As a result, he had become a good part of the corporate machine but could not be an effective leader. "That's *my* Walmart," King said sarcastically, referring to the Walmart slogan. Walmart was no longer Paul's, but that Paul had become Walmart's. The company discipline had made Paul a good follower but had robbed him of the ability to make independent decisions that would make the store competitive.

A key area where this independence is limited is in store purchasing. While most of Walmart's major competitors have a great deal of local control over purchasing, more than half of the goods at Walmart are purchased centrally for distribution countrywide. According to a former employee, Carrefour, one of Walmart's main competitors, permits local stores to purchase up to 90 percent of goods locally, reflecting local markets and local tastes. If more than half of the goods at a Walmart store are purchased centrally the brands and styles might be from areas unfamiliar to local customers and thus not sell well. At Walmart, store management and product purchasing are separated, reducing the store manager's ability to influence what is for sale in a given store and how it is displayed. While this reduces the potential for corruption—by receiving kickbacks for providing preferential shelf space—it locks out an entire area where managers could make decisions that would dramatically influence a store's profitability. As things currently are, managers are evaluated by profit they generate selling goods purchased by someone in central purchasing. King commented:

Walmart just pays attention to the system, and not the people. But seriously, we should ask, does the system manage people, or should the people manage the system. [Walmart] is like an ostrich with its ass in the air and its head in the ground...the culture is too closed...Walmart can be too insular, seeing the world like a frog from the bottom of a well. And this has a huge impact on the ability to be competitive.

Mark, a store general manager, described the feeling of being held responsible for performance despite a corporate culture that shackled their decision-making as caught between "rules and reality" (*jiufeng qiusheng*). He gave an example of Walmart's strict corporate rules that do not permit employees to accept gifts or have dinner with their vendors. He could not even have dinner with government officials, and "you know what China is like, everything is done over dinner! If a supplier asks me out for dinner, I tell them 'I am sorry, but I cannot. Our company does not permit it.'" This can make Walmart appear very strange in the eyes of other companies.

King felt that the problem lay with the fact that the company teaches employees that they are already the best and don't need to learn outside of the company. The culture was far too *quanmian*—all-encompassing in its control of employees—to the point that it inhibited managerial ability to actually make the decisions about products, placement, hiring, and purchasing that would make much larger profits. He argued this was not the way that one can be a successful retailer in China.

> [Walmart] wants to change China, but this is still China. They have not done a good job localizing control. Managers have some freedom, but are very restricted by the system.... It is like a prison yard, where prisoners are free to move around within the walls. There are guards along the walls and in the towers restricting [manager's] movements, and they all have guns. Their culture is their gun.

Conclusion: Cadres of Corporate Culture

King's description comparing Walmart's cultural system of monitoring and control to a prison yard is a powerful image familiar to many social researchers who have engaged Michel Foucault's examination of disciplinary regimes of the prison.[19] In King's version, prison discipline is enforced by the coercive force of the culture in the hands of superiors who are above store management—and also potentially foreign. Yet, while King describes the "guards policing along the wall" as an external force that keeps managerial decision-making in check, the idea of being a "Walmart person" or "being Walmart's" illustrates the extent to which corporate performance depends on *internalizing* the messages of the culture and its expectations for behavior. In other words, it is not necessary for Walmart staff to actually believe in the corporate culture—although some certainly do and ascribe their success to following its dictates. It is interesting to note here that even after sharing the difficulties of his work as a low-level supervisor and ultimately deciding to leave, Li Shan, the author of the diary translated in chapter 7, proudly identifies himself as a "Walmart person." In fact, the narrative of his diary is rife with examples in which he expresses disdain for the culture that he begrudgingly admits often works very well—he complains about employment issues while also being sure to work on his Walmart cheer. Employees need neither like the culture nor believe in it, but they are expected to master the performance of its normative expectations.

Of course, the idea of performance implies being visible to an audience of informed viewers—the gaze of a judging viewer who knows and understands the culture. As this chapter has described, in multiple locations and in a variety of ways the culture is publicly displayed to staff and managers at various levels, and to customers in ways that shape expectations for behavior. That the culture makes all employees, including management, visible to others ensures that someone is always potentially watching and evaluating even as they are subject to the same gaze.

Interestingly, while culture displays are intended to educate various groups about appropriate behavior, even if the target group does not get the message, the employee has an incentive to perform their roles correctly. For example, it is not even necessary that customers take the time to read the "servant leadership" display publicly posted in the store that communicates what customers can expect from Walmart staff. It is enough that employees know it is there and that a customer might potentially expect the behavior. Similarly, the display of cultural messages in the backrooms among employees—managers and their subordinates alike—make all employees as "colleagues" visible to one another and potentially subject to critique and promotion.

Yet, as described earlier in this chapter, the store culture is not a static creation that is exclusively introduced and enforced from above. Within stores there is an ongoing metadiscussion among employees, especially management, about refining and perfecting the messages and practice of the culture—increasing visibility among staff and between staff and customers as a means of policing staff behavior. Couched in terms of competition, improving efficiency, or rewarding initiative, employees are recognized for innovations—such as the customer satisfaction rewards or through "good job" cards that actually increase the level of cultural policing. The messages, in other words, are always being edited, changed, refined, and reworked in a process of improving their efficacy.

Even at the top, however, as King describes, store general managers are not immune to, but "imprisoned" by, a culture that subjects them to both the expectations of subordinates and regional heads. Because of its discursive emphasis on egalitarianism among colleagues, the culture places managers in a visible position as models at the top. It creates for them a position as "cadres" of the corporate culture who must exemplify its messages. Failures to do so make them vulnerable to criticism by subordinates or customers. In this way the culture acts as a policing mechanism for the structural power they have as the managers in the formal store hierarchy that squeezes as much value as possible out of them as they "get out sales."

Of course, certainly many frontline employees lower down the chain outside the management structure would no doubt agree with King that the culture is a disciplinary structure. Indeed, as other chapters in this volume show, workers privately are less positive, satisfied, or motivated than they outwardly appear. No doubt many would agree with King's prison metaphor, the only difference being that the "guards along the wall" would have the familiar faces of managers at their store.

Management cannot throw out the culture, however, because as this chapter described near the beginning, the Walmart structure places limits on the local decision-making power of the managers at the store level. As a result, managers themselves have a vested interest in modeling and perpetuating the messages of the culture, because they depend on its persuasive morality as a primary tool to manage the behavior of employees and the space of the stores. Managers need the social power of the culture to manage, even as they perpetuate their own subordination to it by extolling its virtues and refining its messages. For many managers that have I met, however, their own subordination to the culture—agreeing to the surveillance of the guards along the wall—is considered a short-term sacrifice to gain training and experience that prepares them for future success.

6 A STORE MANAGER'S SUCCESS STORY

David J. Davies and Taylor Seeman

There is a tendency, given Walmart's controversial history as a global mass-market retailer, to assume that store managers are primarily responsible for the exploitation of lower-level frontline workers. As the previous chapter has described, however, at Walmart China this assumption misses the more complex forces within the company's structures, rules and systems that strategically limit the power of managers, often reducing them to banal functionaries within the larger corporation. As the previous chapter argued, the corporate culture provides limited flexible resources that management must often rely on to deal with employees in the day-to-day retail work.

To gain a more nuanced understanding of the way Walmart works, it is important to also consider the larger contexts of the personal motivations of workers to join the company and the way that work at the company relates to the individual dreams and desires to be successful in the market economy. The next two chapters address this issue of context by offering personal narratives of two store managers of different ranks and experiences. While one might question to what extent their stories represent the many hundreds of managers currently working at Walmart stores in China, they are important because they offer a detailed portrait of how working at Walmart becomes part of a larger life—revealing the way that being a "Walmart person" is an often contradictory process of being acculturated into a new work regime.

In both cases, these stories already publicly represent work at Walmart. Edward, the manager whose story is recounted in this chapter, was described in an article in the Chinese business press and in Walmart's own training materials as a model Walmart "success story." Li Shan, the subject of the next chapter, chose to publicly share the narrative of his experiences at Walmart through an online blog. Taken together, their personal stories of life at Walmart provide faces and experiences that flesh out many of the issues taken up in other chapters of this volume.

The first-person narrative presented in this chapter was edited from the transcriptions of a number of recorded open-ended conversations that both authors had with Edward during the summer of 2008.[1] After spending his entire career at Walmart, Edward had left the company six months earlier and had just begun work for another American retailer. Thus it was a very transitional period for him, and the topics of conversation ranged widely from very personal reflections on his time at Walmart to more descriptive accounts of what it was like to be a manager at Walmart. Because he was no longer an employee, Edward felt free to speak candidly and in some detail about many things, offering a nuanced description of his life path, some challenging aspects of his work at Walmart, and ultimately his reasons for leaving. As he describes, his ultimate departure from the company was a difficult decision—one that reveals aspects of Walmart's powerful corporate culture and the relationships and dependencies it creates.

The arc of Edward's career at Walmart was one of continual advancement and promotion through the management ranks—certainly the image of opportunity and "success" that Walmart wants to portray to its employees as it seeks to grow. Throughout the narrative, we see moments where the contradictions of work at Walmart emerge and catch glimpses of the source of its persuasive power—its emotional connection to its employees. At times, Edward's descriptions closely reflect the sentiments of Li Shan in the next chapter. In both accounts, and others in this volume, Walmart in China emerges as a company that employees seem to both love and hate. They love it because it provides upwardly mobile urbanites with the promise of success, and a larger purpose to mundane retail work. The opportunity, the camaraderie, and the meaningful performance of belonging to one of the world's most powerful corporations cannot be underestimated. Edward like Li Shan is in awe of Walmart's global dominance, and both of them dream of learning the secrets of Walmart's success.

As Edward's narrative progresses, however, he describes how he comes to understand how he is so clearly exploited by the company and its policies. He does not mind the hard work. He is proud of his advancement and enjoys the challenges of retail work. Slowly, however, he comes to realize how submitting himself to a Walmart managerial culture removes from him exactly the thing he wants to develop—his own personal management style and ability. Often the glue that keeps him at Walmart is only the feelings of obligation to personal relationships with colleagues and teachers that trained him into the Walmart system.

Edward speaks very highly of Walmart and its model while also lamenting the hold it has on him—clearly expressing the contradictions of working there. Like Li Shan in the next chapter, he doubts it even as he wants to believe in it. Walmart is very successful at giving its employees that sense of mission, but as Edward observes near the end of the narrative, he has also observed the way that his initial excitement about the possibility for personal growth and advancement of the early years has succumbed to the comparatively stultified day-to-day monotony of life as a manager who only needs to implement a corporate system.

Edward's story begins with the negotiation of a dream and a disappointment. As a recent graduate from a midlevel regional university, he explains that another international corporation had already offered him a job when he decided to take the job with Walmart. He chose Walmart, however, because it was a top Fortune 500 company and a global success that would have much to teach him—even though the decision immediately meant he would be separated from his future wife as they were transferred to different stores.

Edward's personal disappointment is offset, however, by the valuable training and opportunity that he gets as he quickly advances up through the management ranks. His descriptions of first impressions of Walmart vividly evoke a mass of colleagues all working together toward a common goal—driven by the promise of opportunity and the optimism for a bright future of almost limitless growth for Walmart in a market of more than a billion potential customers. Commitment to the company and the realization of his own desire for success are expressed through uncompensated overtime work, short breaks, and even working out of uniform off the clock. Yet, as Edward explains it, the sacrifices were made for the promise of promotion or on behalf of colleagues with whom he had developed a sense of obligation. As a member of Walmart's management training program he and others were favored for accelerated advancement. Those who did not advance as quickly, such as Li Shan in the next chapter, were disappointed.

The second section of Edward's story continues with a discussion of the differences between Walmart in China and the United States. Edward spent a year abroad as a management trainee in the United States, so his comments directly compare experiences in both locations. In the United States, Walmart has been successful because of the highly centralized nature of its procurement, shipping and distribution logistics, and the standardized experience of each store. As a manager in China, however, Edward complains that centralized distribution and non-Walmart vendors compromise the consistency of the store experience. Perhaps most important, the highly idiosyncratic, inconsistent, and corrupt interpersonal practices of government in each city present an ever-present challenge to managers who must negotiate the legal obligation of the stores to not engage in gift-giving with the everyday expectation of favors for doing business.

The combined effect of these differences, as Edward outlines them, is that Chinese managers are effectively impotent in the face of the macrolevel forces that affect the lives of employees at each store. Managers have little to no control over merchandising, composition of store employees, and local officials that can make everyday work at the company challenging. In each case addressing any of these issues necessitated an appeal up the management hierarchy to a higher authority.

Having spent a year at a Walmart store in the United States, Edward observed that managers in the United States have much more authority than those in China. Managers in China, as he explains in the third major section of his narrative, respond to the things they cannot control by more carefully managing labor numbers and maintaining smooth operations. This smooth operation—"operation standard"—depends on individual managerial efficacy managing the culture of the workplace. This is primarily accomplished, as Edward explains it, by social recognition, employee-employee "coaching," customer relations, and carefully deploying sales figures to motivate employees.

It is here that Edward reveals his understanding of how Walmart's management culture most directly exploits workers. It is a culture that is confident in its efficacy—so confident that he admits that he never doubted that it would be successful. Furthermore, it naturalizes personal sacrifices and overtime work by making them necessary aspects of individual development. In everyday practice, however, Edward explains how linking new employees together through obligations to one another—particularly through "coaching"—creates this context. Coaches model behavior, mentor employees on a career path, and teach new concepts. As Edward explains, the desire not to disappoint the coach that has taught so much is motivation to follow the rules—and, of course, this also is a standard for promotion.

Of course, the interpersonal obligations between an employee and his or her coach suggests in Edward's case that a primary affiliation at the organization may be first with the coach and only second with the company. While this has the advantage to the company of potentially getting more work out of the employee, the downside is that the desire to impress leads to various forms of corruption. As Edward describes, however, various forms of corruption—negotiating with vendors for special placement on store shelves, working around inventory rules and regulations, and creatively avoiding Walmart's own corporate policing—are part of everyday work as a manager. He admits that his motivation for doing these things was to impress his former coaches and superiors to cement their trust in him and, of course, with an eye toward further promotion.

Edward was a manager at one of the first stores in China that were unionized in late 2006. The issue of unions is an important aspect of examining Walmart, China, because the company has been virulently anti-union in the other countries within which it works. It is perhaps for this reason alone that Edward's comments about unions, in the fourth section of his narrative, are important. They are interesting, however, because the description he offers is not of the adversarial relationship between workers and managers—as much as what might be called a company union. In the narrative, he frames the drive to form a union as a competition between locals in various parts of the country to be the first to unionize Walmart. In the stores, the local unions sought to bargain directly with the highest authority—the store manager. Edward, however, describes how within the Walmart system he had no authority to bargain with the unions on behalf of the company. In fact, he clearly expresses frustration with being stuck in the middle unable to do any more than placate local union members and wait for further instructions while the corporation negotiated at the highest levels with the national union in Beijing.

It is, however, Edward's reflection on why the push for unionization at Walmart began in the first place, that reveals much about the assumptions managers have about store culture. Unions emerged, he explains, because he and other managers failed to properly acculturate workers. Had the workers really internalized the family ethic of Walmart and had trust in the system, he explains, they would not have felt it necessary to go "outside." In this way, the unionization drive was perceived as a failure of correct management according to Walmart's culture.

In the final section of Edward's personal story, he explains why he ultimately chose to leave Walmart after working there for nearly a decade. Slowly the combination of personal sacrifices and frustrations at work began to build. On one hand, the lower salary, distance from his family, and long work hours demanded much of him. On the other, he became increasingly frustrated with being rendered powerless by a corporate system that did not allow him to make the important decisions at the local level that he felt necessary to do his job. The fascinating narrative of his decision to leave it indicates the way the corporate culture affects individual subjectivity. Feeling "brainwashed" by the promise of a bright future, Edward describes how thinking of leaving made him feel "guilty." The guilt emerged from a sense of obligation to individual teachers and trainers that had done so much for him. Ultimately it was the departure of some of these managers that convinced him to leave.

Edward concludes his story with some reflections on change within Walmart in China. In an interesting comparison to the history of the People's Republic of China, he frames the change as one that moves from the early years of heady optimism and struggle for growth to one of an instrumental rule-bound organization that demands subordination to a standardized system. While the former enticed him with dreams of a bright future, the latter drove him away with its insistence on simply following rules. In the end, he concludes that there was no "secret" to business success at Walmart that he could learn and take away with him. Walmart's success as a global retailer and Edward's own success as a "model employee" derived only from being a faithful and willing cog—"able to follow the policies and complete the routines"—within the corporate system.

※

Edward's Story

THE ENERGY TO ADVANCE: A WALMART MANAGEMENT TRAINEE

I began working at Walmart in 1999. I first learned about the company when they held a recruiting event at my university, the South China Provincial Foreign Language and Trade University. Xiao Wei, my girlfriend, who is now my wife, and I both applied for positions there and were hired directly into Walmart's management training program. This appealed to us because Walmart was ranked at the top of the Fortune 500 companies. So, we thought it would be a great company to work for.

Actually at first I hesitated to accept Walmart's offer, because UPS had already offered me a position and a higher salary, and would have let me stay in Guangzhou with Xiao Wei. In the end we decided to go with Walmart because we assumed that if we were both hired they would place us in the same city—perhaps Walmart's Chinese headquarters in Shenzhen. This, however, did not happen. Two weeks after we started with Walmart, we were notified that our training would be over sixty kilometers away at the store in Menggang. We never expected to move to Menggang, but by then there was no choice.

The management training program was designed to give us six months of training first as associates and then as lower-level managers with the expectation that we would later be quickly promoted. The training was conducted mostly by the store's department general managers, each taking charge of eight trainees. Each day they worked with us—coaching us and offering advice. As management trainees, we learned a lot about Walmart culture, its management style, and how to work with people.[2] I was most interested in how they taught us to become good businessmen. We learned how to recognize potential products, how to get higher sales by choosing the right products, and how to coach others to do the same. After I left Walmart last year, this management training has been very useful for my new job with another American retailer that was just getting started in China.

Of the eight members of my trainee group, four of us remained at the Menggang store after the six-month training program finished while the other four, including Xiao Wei, were transferred to other stores. I remained in Menggang for three years.

Shortly after the training I was promoted to the level of supervisor. I remember the speech I was asked to give at the first associate meeting after completing my training. Assembled before me at the meeting were more than one hundred associates in the red Walmart uniform sitting on the sales floor. I was very excited, but also nervous. I remember very clearly my first words, "This is the first time I've stood up here and have seen so many of you wearing red shirts—I feel like I'm looking at a great red ocean (*hongse de haiyang*). Already I can feel your energy, and the energy of Walmart," and I remember them applauding.

Even now I remember that energy. Walmart employees are very diligent and hard-working. They don't care how much overtime they have to give to the company. They just don't care. Store policy says you have to clock out after an eight-hour shift. But they clock out and go back to work without being asked. Everyone does. Of course, not *everyone*—but many do, and it's not just managers or higher-ranking employees, the associates do, too. When I started working with Walmart, I wondered why everyone was so motivated to work so hard. My colleagues' only reply was they love their job and want to advance.[3]

The Menggang store was one of the first few stores in China, and the management there always explained to us that Walmart associates would have a bright future. After all, there were three thousand stores in the United States for only about 200 million people. In China there were only a few stores, and over a billion people! You can imagine how people aspired to the opportunities that lay ahead. Even on their days off, many associates would come to the store without wearing their red Walmart uniform—stocking shelves, ordering products, checking inventory, or talking to vendors and merchants.

The energy of that work environment affected me deeply. It was contagious. Soon I started feeling the same way and found myself taking ten minutes for lunch or ten minutes for dinner and getting right back to work. At that time, our careers were undoubtedly the priority for both Xiao Wei and me. Three years after we began working at Walmart, we got married. We couldn't live together, however, because she was working sixty kilometers away at the store in Bao'an.

At the time, however, I felt fortunate to know Paul, the general manager of the Menggang store.[4] Paul was an American-born Chinese whose family was originally from Fujian Province. He was a very good coach, and I learned a lot from him. Not only from him—but from the whole management team. Part of my enthusiasm for Walmart was due to their influence. Paul created a learning environment that offered opportunities to everyone. When he coached me I took lots of notes and followed them. I did what he said and it worked. Our store's sales volume kept going up. You would be promoted depending on how well you listened to your coach, and of course the profit you made, your sales, associate morale, things like that were also important.

Management trainees were the only college graduates hired by the company picked for the management-training program with the intention that we would be potential leaders for Walmart. Our superiors saw to it that we learned fast and did well, so they gave us the greatest opportunities. This situation, however, also led to dissatisfaction and caused some associates to complain—some of them had worked for the company longer than we had.

"DIFFICULT THINGS": PRODUCTS, PEOPLE, AND POLITICS

After working for Walmart for only three years, I was promoted to store deputy department manager. I remember the day and the moment very clearly. I was very busy selling chicken necks on the sales floor of the Menggang store, when I was paged to the store manager's office. I wondered what was going on and was concerned that maybe I had not been selling enough. When I got to the office, however, my store manager told me about my promotion and congratulated me! After my promotion, I was transferred to go and open a new store. The next morning I left with Samuel, who would be my new store general manager. I was excited to be instrumental in opening a new store.

Since then, in the Shenzhen area, and then later in other parts of China I helped open new stores. I learned that the two most difficult things in opening new stores are the localization of products and local government relationships. Finding workers is not a problem. It's not hard to find people who want to work at Walmart. Merchandising, on the other hand, involves getting to know the local people. In China, people are very different in different regions. You have to know what they like—what brands they like. China has some national brands, but local brands are usually more popular.

Merchandising—this is quite a big concept, and a very important one in Walmart in China. It is something that the company needs to continuously work on. They have localized the people and store operations, but still have not localized merchandising. It is still too centralized. Stores in different regions cannot get the kind of local merchandise they need, and when customers can't find the things they want at Walmart, they go to the competitors. After a few years, however, they finally began to put some localized merchandise like fresh food in stores. This was a big change for Walmart—in U.S. stores, there is no city merchandising team.

In Chinese stores, there are many vendors whose employees work side by side with Walmart employees. They are staff who don't work for Walmart directly, but work for and are paid by the company whose products they are selling. The Walmart store management team manages them. If they do not perform to Walmart's standards, managers will talk to their vendors and they will be fired. Customers don't always distinguish between Walmart employees and vendor-employees, so we have to watch them closely to make sure they are not hurting Walmart's image. Depending on the size of the store there may be two hundred to three hundred vendor-employees. At one store I managed there were four hundred vendor-employees, nearly as many as regular Walmart associates.[5]

The second thing I learned while opening new stores was how to handle relationships with local government. At the corporate level, Walmart has a good relationship with the central government in Beijing, but that doesn't mean there is necessarily a good relationship with local governments in each region and city. At the local level, officials just know Walmart is a huge global company, which means it brings jobs and pays a lot of taxes. The members of local government are pleased about these things, but they don't understand that Walmart's culture has very strong rules about relationships between store employees and officials or product vendors outside the company. The company's honesty policies state that no staff members can give or receive gifts of any kind.[6] The government employees expect store managers to take them out to dinner, like local Chinese companies do. This is the way business is typically run in China, but that is against Walmart's policy. It's forbidden in America, and Walmart is an American company. Local government officials are uncomfortable with this rule and concerned that if they let a company like Walmart into the area, it might set a precedent for other companies to act in a similar way. As a store manager it is hard to handle a situation like this. Usually I tell them we want to be a good member of the community, but we can't engage in the types of business practices they are used to because it's against Walmart's company policy.

It is important to have a good relationship with local government officials, because once they permit the store to open, they will come with all kinds of requests. For example, maybe they'll plan a community event and they'd like us to sponsor a specific activity. However, this usually means we have to pay the government to take part in it, so we can't participate. After refusing this kind of request a number of times it is easy to get a bad reputation over time.

The local government also uses their regulatory power to check on store operations. There are all kinds of inspections, such as fire and sanitation. One specific inspection that I remember involved parking. In China, Walmart China offers free shuttle service to its customers. Sometimes even if we park the shuttles in a place that is legal, a representative from the city transportation department will come to me and say, "You can't park here." After pressing them for an explanation, they asked me, "Did you give my boss a Walmart giftcard?" I know it sounds odd, but in China, that is common business behavior. But American companies cannot engage in this kind of behavior. It's a tough dilemma for Walmart managers. Sometimes the corporate Home Office helps out—they have what's called a corporate affairs manager. If the situation is really bad they send someone out to invite the government officials to dinner, acting as a liaison between the company and the government.

It's not only in this instance where store managers have limited power. There are many things about which we are not allowed to make decisions. But it hasn't always been that way. It's different from Walmart USA because it's newer. When I started in Menggang, the store manager was American, and his decision power was very big—it operated just like a U.S. store. The store manager could do competition price matching, lower prices if he wanted, even sell below cost if he thought it would somehow help business. Later, after management became more localized, and more Chinese were promoted to store manager positions, issues of managers doing their own thing began to surface. Chinese are really clever. Too clever. To get results, they would try all kinds of things, methods that American managers would never imagine.

So, policies had to change. More and more rules and stricter procedures were put in place about what store managers could and could not do. The power of store managers was limited. For example, six or seven years ago, a store manager could change the setup on the shelves if he wanted to, but now he can't. Actually, right now they are changing the policies to give back some control to managers.

One thing managers do have control over is how many people we have in the store. We have a budget, and under these constraints, store managers can move people around from department to department, and promote people all the way up to comanager, though with the permission of the district manager. If you want to hire more people going beyond the number of staff set for the allotted budget, you have to prove that if you do, the return on investment will be worth it—for 1 percent over the budget, you have to have a 5 percent increase in sales. On the other hand, you can't just fire people if the store is not making its sales goal.

Besides hiring and firing, the biggest responsibility of the store manager is on the operations side. It is the responsibility of the store manager to make sure the store is run according to company policy, and that everything is maintained and runs smoothly from the time the store opens to when it closes. This is what we call "operation standard." I'd venture to say that a store manager takes 80 percent of his time keeping "operation standard." When I was a store manager, I spent a lot of time thinking about the best way to do things, the ways to be a good manager. How to be a good manager is a big question—entire books have been written about it. But for me being a good manager means listening and dealing with changes.

The basic requirements of success are not that complicated: recognize people—associates, managers, everyone. Ask them, "Are you taking care of your customers today? Do you have the merchandise your customers want today? How many customers are you greeting today? How are your employees working today?" Everyday, as a store general manager, you have certain responsibilities. This is, of course, a manager's primary concern. For me, every morning I would get to work early and make sure the store was ready for opening. We would have a morning meeting with everyone in the store where we shared information, recognized valuable contributions to the store, engaged in coaching, and got information out to different department managers or supervisors to make sure they knew the day's work. After the meeting, I would typically look at the sales reports from past days and see which departments had the most opportunities for improvement—departments where sales had dropped compared to the day before or week before or the same time last year. I would go to the department to understand the situation—then we would work on the problem together and try to fix it. In the afternoons, I would usually go out on the sales floor to greet customers, clear shelves, help out other employees, make sure they were working efficiently, checking stock levels, or just make sure everything was in good shape. Sometimes I also would take customer complaints and other things like that.

It wasn't until I'd been a manager for a while, however, that I realized how Walmart takes advantage of their workers. I already mentioned how the culture somehow gets people to work more and expend more energy without getting more pay. In a way, it is like being "brainwashed" [*xinao*]. The eight of us who were in the management trainee program had never had any other work experience. We came to Walmart right from college and so we didn't have an opportunity to develop our own management or business styles. Like blank sheets of paper we eagerly took on Walmart's way of doing things. We accepted the Walmart culture, and thought, "Yes, this is the way to be successful. All we have to do was follow it and do everything we can to achieve the goals they lay out for us." We think we were very, very useful to the company, and we also learned a lot from them. I never doubted the possibility of success at the time. But as I rose in the company and interacted more with other companies and different people—my former classmates, relatives, and friends—I discovered that diligent, hard-working people like those of us at Walmart could make more money elsewhere. Walmart's culture and the coaching lead you to assume that it is natural to work extra. Your coach is both a person you work with and the person you get recognition from. He represents Walmart culture to you.

All of my colleagues in the management-training program wanted to develop as individuals. Walmart's culture sends the message that you will have many opportunities to develop, so you agree to work extra. They are very smart about this—touching on what a person really needs. You know that pyramid, Maslow's pyramid—the one with the levels of needs? It starts from the bottom with survival needs, then security, and then social recognition. Well, the top level is self-satisfaction, right? Walmart is very good at providing that by making employees satisfied and excited with what they are doing. Of course, if you don't buy into this Walmart culture, the extra hours and need for development, it's not like you get fired. You just won't get promoted. In my new job as manager at another American retailer, I don't have this same feeling of opportunity yet. Maybe it is because I just started working here, but I feel that the culture is different—a very different energy.

Because pleasing your coach, being considered for advancement, and creating new opportunities are so important to many employees, it can lead to some integrity issues. It is a written store policy that no associates or managers can talk to vendors in the store at anytime, except for the merchandising team. This is because some managers and employees were receiving kickbacks from vendors for special placement of products. For example, they might tell Procter & Gamble, "Give me a little extra cash and I'll put your product in this hotspot where a lot of customers will see it." An integrity issue like this one is something you can get fired for immediately at Walmart. Other, smaller infractions warrant verbal and written coaching. If the situation degenerates or the person can't be coached they are fired. Several store managers got fired for making deals with vendors.

It's natural for a store manager when doing the inventory to want to make themselves look better by making it seem that they have sold more. For example, if I were to give that hotspot to Procter & Gamble, in return I ask for two extra pallets of soap. When I receive it, I do not include it in the inventory system. It's totally free. But when we do the inventory we count it. This makes the store sales appear higher, or it can make up for missing, damaged, or stolen product. This makes you look like a better store manager.

Besides minimizing missing and damaged goods, managers also are under a lot of pressure to record high sales. If you don't make the budget, you get a lot of pressure from above, all the way from headquarters in Shenzhen. Managers are no longer allowed to lower prices without permission from headquarters, so we can't use that option to increase sales. The sticker price of items on the store floor have to remain the same, but if someone comes to the manager to buy in bulk there is another way to offer a lower price. For example, say the bulk customer wants 10 pallets of soap from Procter & Gamble marked at 2 yuan apiece and the customer will buy 10 additional pallets if we can sell them at a price of 1.9 yuan. Technically this is impossible because our purchase price is 1.95 yuan. Since I obtained two free pallets from the guy from Proctor & Gamble in exchange for preferential placement on the shelves, I can use the free product to offset the price reduction. That's how managers can offer a kind of "discount," though it's completely against company policy.

I'm sure Walmart's corporate office knows this kind of thing goes on, but they can't prove it. They try to find out from associate reporting, sending teams to check, calling customers and asking what price they paid. They also have store cameras. If someone is found out, they will be fired. So why do managers do it? Some employees wonder that themselves. Some think it's worth it to take that risk. I think they choose to do it because they're so brainwashed by Walmart culture. They're so devoted to the company, and they just want to achieve the goals the company gives them. Usually they don't even get any personal gain out of this type of activity. They just think that they're paying back their coaches for treating them well and giving them opportunities to develop.

I understand that feeling of wanting to give something back to the manager who coached you. I wanted to do anything I could to pay back what my manager, Frank, gave me. He promoted me multiple times, and promoted my wife, too. I felt like I owed him. This feeling of obligation is a common sentiment among successful employees. We are proud for our bosses to get recognized by the company. If they get recognition, if their region is seen as the best in the company, then we ourselves also get more chances and opportunities.

UNIONIZATION

Walmart in the United States doesn't have any unions, but in August 2006 the stores here in China were unionized.[7] The first union was actually formed at a store in the small town of Jinjiang in Quanzhou City, Fujian

Province. I heard later that some employees there decided to first form a union because they wanted to get a good reputation by being the first to form a union at a Walmart store. I was the store manager at one of the first Walmart stores to unionize right after Jinjiang. The unions were very strong and had a long history in the city where I was a manager. So, when the Jinjiang store announced the news that they had set up a union first it really pissed off the union in my city. Right away the union in my city blacklisted me. I'm not exactly sure why, but I think they assumed I wasn't going to cooperate with them. It wasn't true, though, I didn't even know they intended to form a union!

After workers in Jinjiang unionized, people at several levels sought me out to talk—workers at my own store, union representatives, other managers at my store, and then my superiors, the regional manager and representatives from the corporate office in Shenzhen. At the beginning Walmart didn't have a clear strategy for working with unions. So in my city I just did things and said things that seemed sensible to me in order to cooperate with them. I didn't want to piss them off more. At that time, the only direction we were getting from corporate headquarters in Shenzhen was to hold off cooperation with them and not promise anything to the union on behalf of the company. That's all the guidance I got from Walmart's corporate offices. A few weeks later the office in Shenzhen set up a team, led by Walmart China's vice president of human resources, to negotiate directly with the chairman of the All-China Federation of Trade Unions in Beijing. After the negotiations, the team then gave us guidance through a memo announcing a new strategy for store managers. The memo discussed how to cooperate with the union and said that having unions in Walmart stores could happen if things were done right. It listed associates who corporate headquarters agreed could be head of the local store union, and then explained what levels of employees were eligible to join it. All store employees with the exception of the senior management—store managers, comanagers, and assistant deputy general managers—were eligible to join the union.[8]

After a few months, though, this policy didn't hold up. Associates didn't care. Whoever wanted to join just joined. Everyone wanted the benefits. Members get a gift at various holidays, such as a towel, two bars of soap, and a bottle of shampoo, or something like that. That's what state-owned companies do for festivals. Also, union members get free tickets to things, and a bonus at the end of the year, maybe 150 yuan. Things like that. The memo also said that a union committee should be set up, specifying who could head the committee, and what percentage of people from different departments could be involved. The union and Walmart had an agreement. This is where unions in China differ from the United States—here it was set up by the corporate office.

When all of this was discussed at a company meeting it sounded simple—we just had to follow the directions in the memo. But when I went back to the store, I found that it wasn't as easy as I anticipated, because from the beginning the union had assumed I wouldn't cooperate with them. As I said, I was, in effect, blacklisted. So I talked to some of the heads of the union in my city and paid several visits to their headquarters. We had some good conversations. The local union in my city was clearly upset that Jinjiang had been the first city to establish a union and didn't want to lose face to them. So while I thought we were discussing and working together, the union people were actually secretly organizing. One day an associate in my store informed me, "We have a union." I said, "What?" And they showed me an article in the newspaper. Until that moment, I was in the dark. They set up a union in my store without telling me. It was out of my control. They explained that they couldn't wait to complete our discussions but had to push ahead because they didn't want to lose face.

There was a troublesome associate at my store, Richard, who contacted the local union himself, and they gave him directions. He and about forty people held a meeting, had elections, and elected committee members and a chairman. I couldn't believe who they elected as chairman. It was a college guy named Michael who had only been with the company for a week! The only explanation was that he was a Communist Party member. I heard that Michael didn't really know what he was getting into. The union called him to a meeting where they said they were going to discuss issues pertaining to the Chinese Communist Party, and when he arrived he was just told he was elected. I think Michael felt a bit guilty because at that point the company was not encouraging people to join the union. Later, he wrote a letter to me explaining it wasn't his intention to be the union committee chairman; he was just put on the spot. I told Michael that it was all right and later he cooperated with the store.

Richard, the difficult associate who called the local union to set up a union branch in the first place, however, caused a lot of trouble. He controlled the committee's finances and the large amount of money they were given by the parent union. Since Michael, the committee chairman, had just graduated and had no business experience, he didn't really make decisions—leaving Richard to exert control. Richard was the type of guy who was lazy and always late. Finally a representative of the city union told the human resources manager at the store that they had been in such a hurry to form a union that they had made a mistake selecting Richard. He was the wrong guy to be put on the committee. So we started working together to have another election of committee member to try to replace him, but it didn't work out. The rules for holding another election were too complicated. It would have required holding a meeting attended by two-thirds of the members, and they would first have had to vote on whether or not to have a reelection, and then hold the election itself. It was just very complicated. I left Walmart not long after that, so I'm not sure how things ended up.

I think it is different now. Now, they want a very good worker working on the store's union committee. They want an associate with very good relationships—someone with influence in the store—so he can do union work. Walmart management provides the name of that worker, and if the union agrees, he or she will become the union chairman. We are very careful in choosing these people. For example, at my store I chose one HR manager who was also a party member who used to be a management trainee. His title itself gave the impression that management was helping him to advance. We gave him a lot of opportunities to get promoted, so the union was happy about that, and we had a shared understanding. They didn't want to mess around any more with people like the problematic associate, Richard.

At any rate, Richard didn't affect things too much, and after a few months, the committee gave the store money to do all kinds of activities for the associates, like outings, camping, things like that. They didn't make any other requests, they didn't ask to improve working conditions or change hours or have more time off. This is another difference between unions in the United States and in China. The Chinese union's requests were mostly about entertainment and social activities. I'm not sure if they eventually plan to go further than that, but I suspect they will.

One thing they did want, however, was to have a contract on their terms. Walmart has contracts with each employee, but these were Walmart's contracts on Walmart's terms. I was asked about it, so I asked Walmart headquarters, and they said they would work on it with the Beijing Union. A store manager does not have the authority to negotiate these things, but the local union still talked to me about it and wanted me to do something. They didn't understand Walmart's ways. Big decisions like employee collective contracts are made at the company level. I sort of felt trapped in the middle. I had no control over the decision; I had no bargaining chip with the union.

All Walmart told us was to say we were cooperating and that we would have answers later. We were told to "keep in touch" and "just talk to them." If the union branch had any specific requests we were to write them down and report them to headquarters. Actually I didn't care what any of these requests were, because the answer to anything was really just "no." My corporate offices told me to say no, and I know there was a risk to agreeing to anything or signing anything. It was like a finger in the hole of a dike. If you make one concession, everyone at all Walmart stores would want the same thing. So we couldn't do anything at all. I did everything I could, serving as the middleman—writing down complaints and passing them upward. The only response I got, however, was that they were working on it with Beijing. That's how they do it—that's the Walmart way. Relations are not negotiated horizontally or locally at store level, but downward from the center at the very top to the stores. Negotiations like those with the union are done at the highest level, Walmart's top level with other organizations' top level. The local union wanted to be successful in the negotiations to earn points with Beijing and get an award. Each local union was in competition to be the first to get a contract signed with Walmart.

I think that the reason unions began at Walmart in the first place is because the management team at Walmart didn't do their job well. They didn't create a strong Walmart culture, so there were associates who felt weak and thought the union would be their channel to air their grievances and to negotiate with the company. If the employees felt like they were a part of the culture, why would they go to the outside for help? In the end, that they unionized is proof of an internal failure. They didn't get what they needed from the store management and didn't understand why. Remember Richard, the troubled associate I mentioned earlier, he had asked his supervisor and the department manager to move his wife to a new department. When they said they wouldn't he was not satisfied so he went to the union. He then told everyone that he was not treated fairly. Most of the cases are like this. They say they "weren't treated fairly," and I suppose sometimes it's true, but not the whole truth. If you are a store manager and cannot do what an employee asks, there are always other ways to meet their needs. In my case, I feel like I failed to uncover and identify problems before they exploded into larger issues. It was also a failure of my management team that they did not identify serious matters that really meant a lot to someone like Richard.

Since the establishment of the unions at the stores, there is a new channel for grievances, but most associates don't think the union is of much help because they know what most Chinese unions do—they do nothing.

They don't come to talk to you so that the feedback can go upward. The union in my city didn't really care about the employees at the Walmart, they just want to set up one more union to look better. Later, when store employees discovered this, they lowered their expectations for the unions. As new stores open up, there will always be employees who don't understand Walmart's feedback channels to voice their concerns. There are things like the store manager's suggestion box, or one could call the headquarters directly. There are a lot of channels within Walmart to complain or offer suggestions. As long as we open new stores in new places, that problem will be there—the new associates often only see one side and have the illusion that they need more help.

All in all, I think Walmart will have a good relationship with the trade unions. The unions don't cause too much trouble, they help us hold social activities, and even finance associate recognition programs. It's a pretty good deal for Walmart. I don't think it will weaken the Walmart culture among the workers. The company has established a very good system with the culture built into the store. Of course, unions are subtly different in different locations. In Shanghai, for example, all Walmart stores are actually incorporated as one company—but each store has its own union. It's all really too complicated to explain.

It has been four or five months since I left Walmart, and I have to admit that life outside Walmart has not been as exciting as I imagined it would be. I haven't been too sad that I left Walmart, however. Actually, when I was in Menggang, my first store, I had considered leaving—especially because of the low salary and constantly being apart from Xiao Wei. There are hundreds of better-paying jobs, I thought. But even at that early stage I was already brainwashed. I was told over and over again that I would be very successful at Walmart and I would have a very bright future. I believed it, and I really wanted to prove that it could be true. The reason I stayed was simple—I liked my coach, my store manager, and I got a lot of encouragement from my girlfriend when I had bad times. That's why I stayed. I just focused on the good aspects of work at Walmart. Every year I was promoted until I became a store manager, and it was then I finally started to think about my future. Occasionally I would ask myself if it was a waste of my time and talent to stay with Walmart, but as soon as such a thought entered my mind, I immediately shut it off. I was very loyal to Walmart then, and thinking those kinds of thoughts made me feel guilty. I hadn't yet paid back my coach for all that he taught me, and the opportunities he gave me.

In fact, I think perhaps I was less loyal to Walmart as a company than to my coach. But in the end, I figured out that I wouldn't be happy if I continued working at Walmart. I don't think Walmart is the kind of business where I can learn what I want to learn, get what I want, what I need. Also, the salary was a big temptation. I also wanted a more profitable position.

Perhaps working at a big company like Walmart is not the best for an individual's development. The company's regulations are too detailed and comprehensive. There's no room for creativity. But I like to be creative. I would always propose new ideas and nothing would happen, so I decided I wasn't happy there anymore. I was frustrated. I worked from 7:00 a.m. to 7:00 p.m. sometimes, and I just didn't want to continue contributing that much time. It didn't matter.

They sent me to training in the United States, and I think it was there I realized that I would not spend the rest of my life working at Walmart. While training in the United States, I could see the future of Walmart China, and it's not something I'm sure I want to be a part of. Its corporate culture is the culture of thirty years ago when Sam Walton was still alive. And even after he died, that culture was maintained for several years in the United States and even longer in China. It was that culture that encouraged people to see Walmart as more than a job, as a cause to which they could devote themselves and their lives.

If you want a good career with Walmart you shouldn't think too much about salary. You work there because you just want to work with those people and be part of that culture. But now, I think that culture is disappearing. Shareholders are demanding higher profits and results. It's not a very exciting place to work anymore. Eventually it'll be just like the U.S. stores. Anyone can ultimately become a store manager just like in the United States. You don't need creativity, you don't need to have ideas, you just need to be able to follow the policies, complete the routines. And if you do it long enough, you may become a district manager. It wasn't fun for me.

When I was in the United States, I didn't see much Walmart culture over there. It's ironic. Walmart sent me to the United States for a whole year to learn the culture, but I didn't really learn much about the culture, I just learned the system. I think Walmart China is on its way to being like that: a system where you don't need good leadership abilities, just the ability to follow the rules, follow the policies and the guidelines. Maybe chain stores like Walmart have to be this way. Maybe it's not the company's fault. It's just the kind of business it is. If you want to be big, you don't want to hire too many creative people who might rock the boat. People who may take risks and become a liability to the company. My wife left Walmart for the same reasons.

Funny, it is sort of like the end of a revolution—"seek truth from facts" (*shishi qiushi*) rather than "struggling for a future revolution" (*wei weilai de geming fendou*). But that culture worked well years ago, when Walmart was smaller. Now it's huge in the United States, and it's expanding quickly in China. We have a saying in China, "A big tree attracts the winds" [*shuda zhaofeng*]. That's one of the reasons I chose the company I am currently working for. It's still small.

Actually would you believe I had been considered a successful model employee created by Walmart China? A few years ago I was interviewed by the news media, and they put my photo and my story in Walmart's recruiting and training materials. I suppose I was considered "a success" because I started out as an associate and in five and a half years I became a store manager of some of Walmart's largest stores. To them, I was a model of success. Even now that I have left, I imagine they are still using those materials.

7 PRACTICING CHEER

The Diary of a Low-Level Supervisor at
a Walmart China Store

Scott E. Myers and Anita Chan
Translation by Scott E. Myers

From mid-2005 to early 2007, a Walmart employee in China kept an online diary documenting his experiences working at the retail giant. Writing under the pseudonym Li Shan, the blogger spent eighteen months exploring and reflecting on life on the job at a foreign transnational corporation. Selections from his 200,000 Chinese-character blog have been translated for this chapter to show the working life of an ordinary Walmart employee in China.[1] Since it was not possible to include such a long document in full, we had to use some discretion on what to translate. We concentrated on entries that show the everyday life of a low-level supervisor at Walmart China and offer a glimpse of the blogger's views on some of the issues discussed in other chapters of this volume. Of particular interest to us was how the Walmart culture described and discussed in earlier chapters molds or fails to mold the individual into what Li Shan calls a "Walmart person." Thus we include his detached and self-conscious observations at a company meeting; his remarks—one moment critical, the next venerating—on Walmart's management system; excerpts showing his attitude toward his superiors (as well as toward those working under him); and comments reflecting false perceptions he held of Walmart operations in the United States. We also included diary entries showing aspects of his life outside working hours to give readers less familiar with China a sense of how one Walmart employee in that country lives.

It is not clear why Li Shan chose to document his professional life and share it online with an anonymous community of readers. We do know he was proud—initially, at least—of being employed by the world's largest corporation. Perhaps the exhilaration of entering a new stage in life made him eager to communicate his experiences to anyone who would listen. Perhaps the blog became a space for him to describe and reflect on the challenges and contradictions of his new identity as a Walmart person. After all, given his background, adjustment to life at Walmart would likely have been a complex, perhaps disorienting affair. Having graduated from a top-tier Chinese university with a degree in marketing, Li Shan was an unlikely candidate to take a position as a shop-floor supervisor at a retail outlet.[2] Relocation to a new city, Taiyuan, forced him to take on the identity of a migrant worker, a marginalized social status he was unlikely to have embraced. Moreover, there are clues in the diary suggesting he felt the position was below his abilities and qualifications. Entering Walmart as a "C" level employee—the lowest rung on the supervisory hierarchy—Li Shan held a much lower rank than Edward, the employee whose success story was told in the previous chapter. Whereas Edward had little difficulty accepting Walmart culture, in part because he was quickly promoted and in part because of his more conformist personality, Li Shan is haunted by a deep ambivalence. His relationship with the company is marked by constant inner struggle, a relentless skepticism that always positions him on the edge of rebellion against the company even as he strives to adapt to it. In the end, however, Li Shan does not rebel against what he comes to regard as the deadening tedium of life at Walmart (not, at least, in any way that could have had a far-reaching impact), but instead abandons it for new career opportunities.

Li Shan's diary tells the story of a young person in twenty-first-century China entering the workforce at a time when human labor had again become a market commodity following Deng Xiaoping's economic reforms a quarter century earlier. Along with more than fifty thousand other "red collar" Chinese nationals employed in more than one hundred retail units across China,[3] Li Shan became one of more than 2 million Walmart employees worldwide enmeshed in a vast organizational scheme. Such subordination of the individual to the politico-social machine is not, of course, new in China (or elsewhere). It was exemplified by Lei Feng, the paragon worker posthumously celebrated as a model do-gooder and seamless cog in the wheel to be emulated by all Chinese youth under the Maoist socialist system.[4] Whether in a socialist or capitalist society, hyperconformists like Lei Feng are necessary to ensure that structures of social, economic, and political power remain intact. But while Li Shan is far too critical of authority to accept it unquestioningly, his rebelliousness has a limit. As his blog shows, he is adept at analyzing power relations on the shop floor but stops short of directly challenging the authority management exercises over him and his co-workers.

Although the diary reveals little about Li Shan's family background, there are indications that he might have grown up in poverty—for example, the apparent obsession with meat reflected in the fervor with which he devours the roasted chicken served in the company's fast-food eatery, a reward for cleaning a filthy kitchen. The diary also reveals his resentment against foreign capital in general and Walmart in particular, though he is initially elated to land a job at a foreign company of such immense global stature. Approaching the world with irreverence, Li Shan has a love of wordplay exemplified by tongue-in-cheek use of oxymoronic platitudes such as "the body is the capital of the revolution." At other times, he quotes Mao with heartfelt sincerity, using the chairman's thought as a critical tool with which to understand the world around him. Socialized in a contradictory social and political environment, Li Shan revels and takes pride in his shrewd ability to approach the world with cynicism. From his first day as a trainee at Walmart, he regards the company with detachment, portraying himself as an outsider looking in at all times except when the fleeting feeling of real or imagined empowerment causes him to jump enthusiastically into the job. He writes well and his remarks are observant, self-confident, sarcastic, and sometimes arrogant.

Li Shan's first six months at Walmart were spent in on-the-job training at a store in Taiyuan, capital of Shanxi Province and a major industrial city about four hundred kilometers southwest of Beijing. There, he lived with other new recruits while training in various departments of the store in accordance with company policy. His diary shows him particularly—and rightly—distressed during his first week on the job, when he discovers that despite working for the world's largest corporation, he can barely afford to eat. But neither his innate cynicism nor the real financial difficulties he encountered prevented him from seeking success in his new career. Throughout the diary he expresses his determination to climb the company ladder and transform himself into a good manager, an ambitiousness perhaps in line with the oft-repeated mythology of Walmart's rise to global dominance after starting from humble origins in the American South. When his stint in Taiyuan was over, he had some say in deciding his permanent location and was transferred to a branch in Beijing, where he continued working for another year before leaving in January 2007, just five months after the All-China Federation of Trade Unions (ACFTU) captured the world's attention by successfully unionizing Walmart stores throughout the country.

Li Shan's position as a "C" level supervisor placed him just a notch above the regular floor workers. Sandwiched between the rank-and-file and upper management, his world was a shifting and contradictory one. The dilemmas he faced would have been familiar to supervisors around the globe: he identifies at times with the daily struggles of his co-workers, at times with the authoritarian impulses of management. On the one hand, he has strong aspirations to attain the status of high management and writes cordially, if paternalistically, about the employees working—not far—below him. But he also has deep resentments of upper management, whom he characterizes as arrogant, ignorant, self-serving, and capricious in the exercise of power. He speaks highly of the antibureaucratic tendencies supposedly enshrined in Walmart's business ethics but also offers a frank critique of the exploitation of labor on which the very corporate philosophies he admires are built. He recognizes the exploitative nature of the "voluntary" unpaid overtime required by management of its employees but complies because he knows this is the only way to get a promotion. When an employee in his department is fired by a superior, Li Shan finds the act heartless but says nothing. On another occasion, however, he speaks up on behalf of his co-workers, telling a manager, for example, that his crew required a meal break. Thus, while it would be easy to dismiss Li Shan as conflicted, his diary shows it was the milieu in which he worked that was itself full of contradiction: democratic yet authoritarian, egalitarian yet hierarchical, voluntaristic yet coercive, creative yet stifling. This was the world of clashing values Li Shan had to accept and adapt to if he was going to get ahead.

Throughout the diary, Li Shan upholds Walmart as the consummate example—in word, if not always in deed—of what an honest, principled company should look like. His perception reflects the powerful image Walmart has projected to consumers in the United States and around the globe, in which the central imperative of the bottom line is seemingly secondary and business practices appear to be governed by a folksy, community-based ethos. A related image, equally available to the Chinese public, is that Walmart stores in the United States are meccas not only for consumers but for workers as well. Such representations lend themselves easily to the Chinese imagination. Walmart preaches honesty, discipline, frugality, collective spirit, egalitarianism, and a host of other values, all consistent with the virtues upheld by Confucianism and by Maoism.[5] Like most Walmart employees in China, however, Li Shan was unaware that the largest foreign company in China is notorious in its own country of origin as a key symbol of exploitative global capitalism and that it has become a chief target of union organizing campaigns from Buenos Aires to Jonquière, Quebec.

Many Chinese workers tend to be deeply impressed by the seemingly egalitarian and casual culture of foreign, especially U.S., companies. Gestures such as addressing co-workers, senior management, and even CEOs by their given names are virtually unheard of at Chinese workplaces.[6] Within half a year, however, symbolic perks such as these were not enough to hold the attention of Li Shan, who increasingly found the monotony of the job unchallenging to his intellect and stultifying to his creative impulses. Rules and regulations emanated directly from Bentonville U.S.A., imposing a strict corporate hegemony standardizing each aspect of employee behavior on the shop floor. Feeling trapped in this kind of environment, minor infractions of procedure became the only way for him to alleviate his boredom and express his individuality. Far from sabotaging corporate interests, however, Li Shan's rebellion is always oriented toward the fulfillment of company objectives. In one diary entry, he intentionally moves items to the wrong section of the store because, he believed, this would make them more visible, thus promoting sales. Li Shan is not anticorporate; he just wants to see things done differently. To occupy his time during off-duty hours, he immersed himself in the world of diary-writing, chatting with friends in cyberspace, and diligent improvement of his culinary skills, this last pursuit resulting in a few diary entries containing lengthy recipes. Still, while he was willing to share certain aspects of his private life, there was a limit. We know he made some friends at work and that some of these, unable to stand their jobs any longer, left Walmart in less than a year. But there is little information about his personal relationships outside of working hours. There is no discussion of his family (he fleetingly mentions his mother once, his father twice), and while he mentions he has a girlfriend, he says little about her. Perhaps he felt personal relationships were outside the scope of what he wanted to accomplish with his blog. Perhaps it was a conscious decision he made to protect his identity.

For our purposes, the gap in knowledge that is most frustrating is our inability to know what happened to Li Shan and his co-workers' attempt to set up a trade union in their store branch. This was a real, if not remarkably aggressive, effort made by store employees a full year before the spectacle of rapid unionization of Walmart stores in China attracted international attention. On August 18, 2006, two days after Walmart and the ACFTU signed the five-point memorandum and thirteen months after the blogger's first day of work,[7] Li Shan wrote:

> Walmart is unionizing!!! This is serious stuff. A year ago, whenever we asked about the union, [manager] Lao Tang kept finding a million ways to brush us off and avoid the subject. But this afternoon when I was in the employee hallway I found a handbook with information about the Beijing union. The union! It looks like Walmart is getting closer and closer to it every day. My heart skips a beat just thinking about it.

Three days later, on August 21, Li Shan wrote of a management meeting held at his store. There, not only was the issue of establishing a union discussed, but Li Shan also walked away from the meeting feeling confident, if somewhat bewildered, that the union had the full support of management. "All of a sudden Walmart has this enthusiastic attitude about the union and I can't figure out why. I need to get online immediately and figure out what's going on."

These are the last words in Li Shan's diary on the trade union issue. Odd indeed! He and his co-workers had tried to speak with management about setting up a union—an unusually courageous move—and he is plainly excited when unions begin appearing in other stores. And yet, instead of digging into the subject to share his findings with blog readers as promised, he lapses into total silence about it, leaving the reader somewhat disappointed by the lack of development of this issue.

This makes us wonder whether there was more going on than the diary reveals. The store where Li Shan worked was one of the three Beijing stores described in chapter 10. As far as we know, representatives from the neighborhood-level trade union went to Li Shan's store to discuss setting up a union with management.[8] Soon after, and with management approval, union staffers returned to the store to provide workers with information about trade union laws, medical insurance, social security contributions, and procedures for establishing a union. To ensure that employees were properly informed of the upcoming union election, two lunchtime meetings were held. There, workers were invited to join the union; seventy-three did so. These events were followed by a union election and a founding ceremony, all held in the store. Li Shan could not have been unaware of these activities—and yet, they were not recorded in his diary. Five months later, he handed in his resignation.

In a personal correspondence in 2008, Li Shan was somewhat vague about this, telling us only that he lost interest in the union because online research led him to regard the ACFTU as a weak and ineffective organization.[9] The implication was that establishing a union would have been a waste of time, so why bother? Still, we wonder whether fear of retaliation deterred him from openly supporting the union. Li Shan's diary reveals a sharp and critical mind, but he is also ambitious and career driven. Perhaps in the course of his research he learned about Walmart's staunch antiunionism. Perhaps he came to feel that it had been naïve of him to agitate for a union and decided to back off when he realized what it might mean for his career. If this was the case, it might explain why he failed to dive into union activism at the very moment when conditions were most ripe for him to do so. It was, after all, dissatisfaction with Walmart that prompted his interest in a union to begin with. When the news reached him that union branches were appearing in other store locations, he would have been an obvious candidate to seize the opportunity to become an active preparatory union committee member. If he had run for a union committee seat, it is likely that he would have been elected by his co-workers. But something happened. Perhaps awareness of events taking place at other Walmart branches made him realize that management would not permit him and his co-workers to function as a proper union. Perhaps open support for the union prompted his superiors to warn him to retreat. Perhaps a management meeting he attended alerted him to the possibility that being an active trade unionist would somehow jeopardize his career. But whatever the reason, it cannot explain why he made no further reference to the union in his diary. Perhaps he was silent on the subject because of embarrassment and guilt. Perhaps the distractions and pressures of daily life simply caused him to lose interest.

Despite these and other unknowns, Li Shan's diary is a valuable document in that it offers a daily record of one supervisor's socialization into Chinese operations at the world's largest corporation. It is, of course, only one person's story, but it is surprisingly frank and rich, with detailed observations that resonate with other chapters in this volume. Li Shan's story shows that while many people in China are repelled by the culture of Walmart, in other cases it captivates hearts and minds. Although Li Shan, like Edward, leaves the company when new opportunities for career advancement arise, he nonetheless remains grateful to his first employer for giving him the opportunity to gain job experience and learn how a corporation works. In the end, he tells us, he has indeed been forever transformed into a "Walmart person."

Selections of Li Shan's Diary, translated by Scott E. Myers

July 15, 2005: Friday

The weekend is here. Finally, a day when I don't have to go to training. For the first time since starting this job, I can actually sleep in.

For the past two days, it's been eight hours a day of full-time study, something I haven't done in ages. Even my last year of college wasn't this stressful, probably because I had a solid grasp of my thesis topic. When I think about it now, I realize what a great year it was. But these last few days have been just the opposite: training all morning without a break, a forty-minute lunch, then more classes until 6:00 or 7:00 p.m. when we finally get back to the hotel they put us in.

We didn't get back until 7:00 tonight, despite the fact that Human Resources made us clock out at 5:20. Walmart doesn't like us working overtime, so you're supposed to get everything done within normal working hours. If you're really not done with your work and there's no way around it, you can do official overtime, but only if you get the General Manager's signed approval! Obviously, the whole thing makes no sense. So what we end up doing is "clocking out" on time, but then just keep working. Fucking bullshit.

Walmart is always pushing this idea that honesty is everything. I guess that's why everyone gets along so well and relationships between employees feel so natural and uncomplicated. Obviously, that's a good thing, since it improves efficiency and also ensures that employees maintain a positive attitude. But I also feel like it's a bad thing. We're like seeds in a greenhouse, unable to grow anywhere but here. What will happen when we leave Walmart? Where will we have learned everything we need to know about the world to survive? I don't know. Maybe things aren't so bad in the real world, but I'm still worried. It just makes me feel like this place is some kind of camp for idiots. At the end of the day, all they're doing is spitting out a bunch of people who won't be able to face the cruel test of society.

July 16, 2005: Saturday

Today, our only real job was to go downtown and discover the true meaning of "prosperous Taiyuan."

In the morning, we carried forward the fine college tradition of sleeping in late. The reason for this, of course, was to skip breakfast so we wouldn't have to worry about where it was going to come from. Then we headed to Yingze Street, the city's main shopping district. The cab ride was cheap, only ten *kuai*,[10] but there wasn't a single place to eat on the way. By the time we got there we were all starving, so we went straight to the pedestrian street. Finding a restaurant was easy enough, but there were only a few things on the menu. We ended up ordering one of their specialties. I don't know if the people in Taiyuan are just friendly or what, but it was almost entirely beef, hardly any noodles at all. What could we do? In the end, we were still hungry.[11]

When all this was over, we went and sat for a while in the usual suspect: KFC. Then we took a cab back, thus completing the day's journey. I took a shower and immediately started worrying about food again. None of us knows what to eat or where to go for food. Anytime we spend money, we have to worry about whether the company is going to reimburse us. Walmart, the stingiest company on the planet, has the following rule: they'll reimburse you, but only for what you've already spent, and only within the per diem specified. It's a major pain in the ass, and it also raises a practical problem: How do you get a receipt from a street vendor for a breakfast that costs two *kuai*? We can't afford to eat at real restaurants. So now other than worrying about food, we don't think about anything else. The cruelty of fate!

July 18, 2005: Monday

Walmart doesn't help us with the food situation, so there's no choice: we have to figure it out on our own. Yesterday we skipped breakfast as usual, then went to the noodle shop outside the hotel to get a bite to eat. But when we got to the front door—*bam!*—closed. There was nothing we could do but go to work and try to find something there. When we got there, we walked around for a while but couldn't find anything that looked even remotely edible, so I decided to just get some fried rice. But after I ordered it, I found out they wanted six *kuai* for it! WTF?? At school it would have been at most two *kuai*. Who decided Shanxi Province shouldn't grow rice?! Anyway, later in the day I walked around the store for two hours before finally buying some sliced bread and strawberry jam. That was going to be my dinner. I looked in my pocket: 1.7 *kuai*.

I swear, other than food, there's nothing else we think about. At this point, eating is by far our greatest source of anxiety. This isn't what life is supposed to be about. Here we are at the biggest corporation in the world and we don't have money to eat? Don't tell me this is what I came for!

In the evening, I mobilized everyone to go for a jog in the neighborhood. I ran for half an hour straight. I don't know if half an hour is actually a long time or if it just feels like it because I'm getting old, but either way I'm determined to keep it up. As they say, the body is capital for the revolution!

It was more employee training today. The training itself is easy enough, but my work clothes don't fit at all. The shoes are uncomfortable and I don't have a belt. It's not the end of the world, though, since you don't have to walk around a lot. I had two meals at work—breakfast and dinner. I guess I'm finally learning how things work around here because I actually managed to eat pretty well. My stomach was full, at any rate. Later tonight we might have to go back to the store to practice our cheer.[12] Anyway, I'm off. I have homework for my employee training class and there's a test tomorrow.

July 22, 2005: Friday
Capitalist exploitation has truly reached a new low. On the surface of things, they solemnly declare they don't permit overtime and cite numerous examples of people getting fired for violating this policy. But this rule has a huge, glaring loophole. They say the company doesn't "recommend" or "advocate" overtime and that if an employee must work overtime, they have to get the deputy general manager's signature. But since the company doesn't want us working overtime, the manager is by definition never willing to sign. So, what if you really have a ton of work and there's absolutely nothing you can do about it? There are two ways of dealing with it. First, you can just not finish it. Leave on time and do it the next day. But Walmart has this "Sundown Rule,"[13] which means you have to finish everything before going home, so leaving when you're supposed to isn't really an option. In most cases, people who leave on time eventually end up leaving the company. The second option is to clock out when you're supposed to, but then just keep on working. Tonight I bumped into a co-worker who was supposed to get off at 3:00 p.m., but there he was, still working when we left at 8:40.

Maybe all foreign companies are like this. If you can grin and bear it, you might have a shot at getting promoted. But if you can't take it—*see ya!* According to what this one co-worker was saying, 90 percent of the people he came in with are gone now. The only ones left are the ones who can put up with it.

What this all adds up to is a whole lot of employee resentment. Everyone's pissed off at the company, but nobody has the guts to say anything.

July 26, 2005: Tuesday
Today I want to talk about Walmart's management system.

There are ninety-two departments. Departments with around three thousand different product types have one supervisor and around four employees. You have to admit, it's a pretty efficient team. As one would expect, the company relies heavily on its computer system. I've heard Walmart can perform an entire global inventory within three hours. Any other company and this would be "mission impossible"! Still, regardless of how great the technology is, I think all the behind-the-scenes work is also a major factor. Just think of the way the U.S. Army is organized. An army brigade doesn't just have ground troops. First and foremost, it has to have a strong rear detachment. Nor can you do without aircraft and missile operators, military engineers, medical personnel, logistics staff, and on and on and on. Add it all up and you've got around 300,000 people. Walmart is just like that.

There's one general manager, two executive deputy general managers, four department managers, two assistant managers, six human resource officers, two administrators, and three universal product code people. The remaining 450 people you could call regular employees. It's an extremely tight ship and, of course, there's hardly a trace of bureaucracy! But then, of course there's no bureaucracy. How else could they have such an efficient management system?

Employees often "volunteer" to work overtime but don't ask to be paid for it. There's no distrust between people here. They're like a big group of school kids: naïve, but working together toward a common goal. That, I tell you, would be unimaginable at any other company. How does this place pull it off?

August 11, 2005: Thursday
If it hadn't been for the last ten minutes of work, this would have been the day from hell. But, fortunately, the gods granted me those last few wonderful minutes, thus bestowing a fleeting moment of happiness on my life.

A few of us had gone to the cafeteria to eat. I'd heard the food was pretty good there so I was looking forward to it, but the minute we showed up the supervisor told us to clean the kitchen! My god! This was the first time I'd ever cleaned a kitchen. Only now do I realize how filthy they are! Especially the drains. Full of rotten garlic, tea leaves, swollen green onions. Every disgusting thing you can possibly imagine—and I had to dig it all out with my bare hands. To make matters worse, there was this huge, heavy grate covering the floor drain. The sides were sealed over with some kind of shit-colored substance that got all over my hands when I lifted it up! Ugh! It was so disgusting! If you still have an appetite after that, be my guest. When we were done cleaning the kitchen, the supervisor immediately had us turn around and start selling chicken legs. After four hours of greasy, roasted chicken, I was so saturated with the smell that I practically lost my appetite.

Now, those last ten minutes. We couldn't take it anymore, so I told the supervisor we were hungry and wanted to have some of the roasted chicken. He said okay, then pulled out a big vat from the kitchen and told us to have as much as we wanted. When I asked him if I could have just drumsticks, nothing else, he said yes. I went crazy over them. Here I am, a grown man, and never in my life have I eaten chicken with such unbridled pleasure. Hello, meat!!!

February 13, 2006: Monday

There was a management meeting all afternoon today. It took five fucking hours. It's never taken that long before. Next time I swear I'm going to download a video game to my cell phone and play to the final round. Marshall talked even more than usual, on and on nonstop like a train.[14] Everything he said you could have clearly stated in about a minute, but he has this fussy, long-winded way of saying everything. I truly can't stand that guy. Then they brought in a little food, and I had to go over some stuff with the toy manager. It was 9:00 p.m. before we got out of there and I didn't even have any dinner. When we were finally done, I had no choice but to pay six *kuai* for one of those boxed meals from the cafeteria.

Meng Liang says he's handing in his resignation tomorrow. He says the day he made up his mind to quit was the best day of his life. I completely understand how he feels because I've imagined myself in his place a thousand times. One thing's for sure: the allure of Walmart is definitely fading fast. All I want is to maximize my own potential without wasting precious time on this kind of trivial shit. When I first got here, I was feeling all ambitious and ready to systematically study the Walmart style of management. But it didn't take long for me to figure out that when I'm at work I don't have time to think about that kind of stuff.

Some people might say I'm restless. I've thought about that too. But I've come to realize that that's not the issue. All I want is to be able to figure out the most efficient way to use my time. I realize this job is going to create opportunities for the future, but I still can't stand this miserable environment. This kind of mechanical work should be given to machines to do. The greatness of human beings is our ability to engage in creative work. That's what I'm striving for. Is it really too much to ask?

February 17, 2006: Friday
Only last night did I finally start getting used to the night shift. I got a good amount of work done, felt a sense of accomplishment, and wasn't even particularly tired when I finished. No longer am I a mere functionary.

There were two big projects going on. My job was to coordinate everything, put it all together, and tell everyone what to do and how to do it right. I also ended up doing some really menial, mindless physical work that didn't require any brain activity. I just wanted to give them a hand. I'm beginning to realize that my multitasking skills are way beyond doing just two things at once. I'm sure I could juggle a number of projects at the same time, and further down the road I'm sure I'll kick even more ass!

There's this one employee in my department whose performance is pretty strong. His administrative skills are excellent, probably better than any I've ever seen. I admire the guy. He's always throwing ideas out, though I have to admit I don't know if it's because he really gets flashes of inspiration or if it's just because he's been here so long. Still, there are a lot of areas he would have to improve in if they were going to train him to become a supervisor. I mean, otherwise he would just become a manager overnight! In any case, if I end up having the misfortune of staying at Walmart for a while, this place could turn out to be the perfect stepping stone. This job may be the only way for me to get the qualifications I need to move up in the career ladder!

February 21, 2006: Tuesday
Today I got up early to go to the big staff meeting. I'd been wanting to see what the monthly meetings at the Xuanwu store in Beijing are like. Originally, I heard that Marshall acts like a total megalomaniac, that he's trying to create his own cult of personality and everything. I heard he makes the entire staff scream his name for five minutes, then clap for two more minutes before he even gets on stage, and that the rest of the time he's basically not there. In fact, it wasn't quite like that, at least not this time. The main point of the meeting was to thank everyone for their hard work during Chinese New Year. Everyone was laid-back and in a good mood, and you could feel the Walmart cheer reverberating from one department to the next. The content of the meeting was great too, though I was having a bit of a hard time hearing.

Just as everyone was starting to loosen up and have a good time, the boss jumped up on stage and yelled: "Do you guys like your jobs?" Only a few people—the ones who'd come up from Shenzhen—answered "Yes!" and everyone else was completely silent. I guess the boss was thrown off by this, because after fumbling through a few more lines, he suddenly yelled out: "Do you guys like your team?!" Everyone went crazy, screaming "Yeah!" I couldn't tell if they really meant it, or if they were just trying to compensate for having messed up the first time.

In any case, Walmart really is good at team building. There's essentially no suspicion or hostility between anybody. It's like all these people from different countries coming together to build a beautiful home without the slightest bit of self-interest. I can't figure it out. It's like some kind of mysterious knowledge, something you'd never be able to understand without taking some time to dig into it and figure it out.

Anyway, back to the meeting. Everyone seemed to forget that it was, in fact, supposed to be a formal event. The only thing employees care about is hanging out and having fun. I guess that's why management tries to get all crazy, yelling things out and egging people on to engage in these ridiculous stripteases (although, so far, the action has always stopped short at screaming; I haven't seen the striptease go any further, ha ha). If it was any company other than Walmart, I wouldn't use that word: striptease.

There's this guy in my department who just got the employee-of-the-month award. He's a truly capable guy, a rare kind of employee. I really hope he has the chance to turn into a good manager, a manager with a little professionalism.

February 23, 2006: Thursday
Got up at three-thirty on the dot this morning. I never used to be particularly wild about soccer, but ever since starting this job I've had so few chances for that kind of thing that I've actually begun treasuring moments like these. There wasn't a cloud in the sky and I was feeling great. I was certain it was going to be a good day.

All of this changed in the afternoon when River came to talk to me again. It appears that one of the deputy general managers thinks I'm not suitable for the toy department and wants a more appropriate person to take over. In other words, they're giving me the boot so they can put their own person in! River tried explaining it a million different ways, saying they'd already found me a C level position at the front of the store and all this kind of crap. I never would have thought something like this could happen at a place like Walmart. Actually, you know what? I did know getting sidelined like this could happen here. Just look at the way the appliances manager treats people.

If this is really how things work around here I guess there's not a lot I can do about it. I can't change a place as big as this overnight. All I can do is find another place that suits me better. But what I don't understand is what I could have done so wrong in just two short weeks. Call me lazy, but I really don't think I have to be overly enthusiastic about this job. There's an incredibly structured system in place here that makes everything run smoothly. I don't know. Maybe other people's thinking about this is completely different from my own. I just don't want to force myself to adapt to some environment I don't identify with. But for the time being, I have nowhere else to go, so I may as well suck it up. When River told me I had to go up to the front, I told her pretty firmly I wanted to stay in toys because I have confidence in my ability to do well in this department. But then I thought: you know what? Just forget it. It's not worth fighting for.

Next month when I get an Internet connection, the first thing I'm going to do is dive into a new job search. At the very least, I know this branch isn't the right one for me. I'm definitely getting out of here. So many good employees—all wasted.

I don't want to talk about it anymore. I'll just do the new job and try to learn a lesson from the experience. All I have to say is this: don't believe what Walmart teaches you in its trainings. This place really is a microcosm of society. Whatever's going on out there—in the outside world—in here it's exactly the same. At least when I get out of here I'll know how to play the game.

February 25, 2006: Saturday

Today was my first day in my new department, section 82. So far, it's better than I expected. There's actually not a whole lot going on there. All the employees pretty much know what they're doing and get things done without you having to tell them.

In the morning, though, something really moving happened. An employee who found out that I had left the toy department came up to me to ask why I'd disappeared without saying a word. Then he asked if he could come with me to my new department. When I asked him if he was serious, he said all I had to do was fill out the transfer application form and he'd be there in a minute. That was nice. Moments like these make me feel I haven't been sticking around here for nothing.

Section 82 is the impulse buy section and they expect you to have a pretty good sense of how things are selling. It's interesting enough, but the section is small and isn't considered particularly important, so if I ever wanted to bail I won't get a lot of points for having worked there. But it's a decent area to work in, and at least now I'll be able to use my time to think about other stuff. With everything comes pros and cons.

March 10, 2006: Friday
I can't believe we stayed up last night talking till past 3:00 a.m. All we talked about was Walmart. The good and the bad.

With many companies the idea of corporate culture is just empty talk. Even global top 500 companies like B&Q are a mess when it comes to corporate culture.[15] Walmart, on the other hand, is the only company out there that truly has its own unique culture. Take training, for example. Walmart and B&Q both stress customer service, but at B&Q it's taught in this incredibly didactic way, as if customer service were nothing more than some kind of technical skill. It's different at Walmart. Here they teach with real-life examples so that you, the employee, can really develop a customer service mentality. They don't just pull out a set of guidelines and hand it to you. They make sure that learning happens from the inside out, that the employee is led, step by step, toward conscious, self-chosen adoption of the customer service mindset. Eventually, that mindset becomes a habit, and the habit in turn becomes a culture.

We also talked about one troubling aspect of Walmart management. Walmart needs administrators, not innovators. Walmart needs people who can follow 100 percent of the orders, not be 120 percent excellent. That's why some people say Walmart is a stable company but not a particularly fast-growing one. Since it only requires people who can carry out orders, the absence of any one person doesn't affect the organization as a whole. Even if the manager died tomorrow, it wouldn't make a difference. The store would just keep on functioning like clockwork. Everything moves forward in such an orderly and predictable way, before long they'd just churn out another Walmart-style manager. And while individual store managers may have different kinds of management styles, their ability to shape the overall culture is limited to the particular store they work in, and even then their power is extremely limited. Real management power is concentrated at headquarters. They are the program writer, the central processing unit. We're just the semiconductor.

March 18, 2006: Saturday
I have this employee. A smart, hardworking guy who notified me—by text message, oddly enough—about another employee who, he said, isn't doing

his job, doesn't respect the work, and deserves to get canned. My initial reaction was: *Yes, this is indeed a problem. But not only because there's an employee who's not doing his job. The bigger issue is that there's a conflict between two employees.* The truth is, I didn't even care whether what he said about the other person was true. Obviously, I would have to see it with my own eyes to believe it. But then I started thinking: what if it was someone I really knew and trusted who had told me? Would that make me take it more seriously, or even just automatically believe it? I need to be suspicious of everything, to approach everything with a question mark. Believing things too easily makes you a child.

It's pretty interesting stuff, trying to get inside other people's heads. This interplay between me and my employees—it's like a game of chess. Play too cautiously and they get bored. But if you play too aggressively they get frustrated. The key is finding the right balance.

March 21, 2006: Tuesday
Today is my favorite day of the year: the first day of spring. From now on, the sun hangs in the sky longer. People work harder. Maybe it's the Leo in me, but I love the sun. From this day forward, I think everything's going to be okay.

This morning I suddenly got a call. They told me one of my employees showed up two hours late, then sat in the back of the warehouse reading a newspaper. A supervisor saw him and told the manager, who asked him to hand in his resignation. Obviously, I couldn't say anything about it. After all, I have no idea what really happened. But then it suddenly occurred to me: the people working under me—I mean, to just throw them out like that! It's just like the depictions of class struggle you've seen a million times in the movies.

April 1, 2006: Saturday
Happy April Fools' Day!
Today when I got online to look at my blog I discovered I've been gently reprimanded by one of my readers, a member of the older generation, you might say. You know, I really do hear what you're saying and I often try to remind myself of the same point. But you have to understand there are real, objective forces diluting the culture of Walmart. Yes, I realize the store in Shenzhen is top-notch. Yes, I realize the stores in the United States are even better than that. But here at my store, I'm powerless. I can't make myself assimilate into this environment. I just don't know how. Don't get me wrong.

I don't have a problem with Walmart. I admire it, I worship it. It's just that I can't deal with this tedious, petty little world. Maybe if I can swing it, a change of store locations will help. Maybe.

April 11, 2006: Tuesday
This morning when I went to look at the attendance rates I learned that yet another employee has resigned from the toy department—and this one was voluntary. This is getting too close for comfort. I mean, it's all around me—before you know it, people are just gone. Is there really nothing here to make people want to stay? Gone, just like that—and no turning back! You know, some of the employees working under me have expressed their desire to leave. Actually, I really support them and even adjust their schedules so they can go to interviews. If you think a job isn't right for you, if you don't like it or whatever, then you need to go out and find a new one. At a minimum, one has to be happy!

April 17, 2006: Monday
There was a policy exam today.[16] Everyone in management was nervous, even the deputy general managers. They were the ones who had to take it first. At first I was secretly happy about it because I knew the exam would give those smug, arrogant bastards a run for their money. But then I got a report from a management insider who told me that the moment the exam was over, the two of them (let's call them "Manager A" and "Manager B") went straight to the Human Resources office to get their exams back so they could change the answers. That in itself is bad enough, but even that's not the worst thing going on in this store. A much more serious issue is the fact that every Thursday when we send missing stock reports to the China general manager in Shenzhen, those same members of the leadership just randomly enter barcodes on the missing stock report form. They don't even go out to the floor to scan the shelves. All they care about is submitting reports that look good!

This is exactly how bureaucracies are created. Everything that's real is overlooked and attention is paid only to form, to surface issues. For these people, the important thing isn't finding real solutions to real problems but covering things up and not getting caught. It's work for the sake of appearances, for no reason but to kiss the asses of the higher-ups. It's meaningless, repetitive labor. It's the campaign style of doing things.[17] This is exactly what people mean when they talk about "formalism." What's the point?

Fuck. The more I think about it, the more pissed off I get. Are these people really this apathetic about their jobs, or are they just incompetent? From what I can tell, the answer to both questions is *YES*. But at least now I know what the problem is and I can do my best to make sure I don't turn out like that.

I have to keep reminding myself that the process is just as important as the outcome, and in some cases it's even more important. Only through process can you make real advances and begin to understand what the actual issues are. Process is movement through time; outcomes are mere points in time. I can't tell you whether the outcome of something will be good or bad, but I do know that understanding the process will help us move forward. Chairman Mao said: "Mistakes and setbacks teach us and make us stronger." This is exactly what I'm talking about: valuing the process.

Anytime you do something, you need to ask yourself if it has any meaning. You have to ask yourself where it will get you. Meaningless work? No thanks! I hereby promise that anytime I or the people under me do something, it will always be for a meaningful reward—not just to reproduce mindless work!

April 19, 2006: Wednesday
This afternoon I went back for another boring day of work. I don't even know what I'm doing anymore. All day it was just "discovering" new promotional products for the impulse buy section. There was nothing good though—just a bunch of crap! That day when I was doing research at Carrefour, I noticed they only put a few items on each display rack. I don't know if the employees were just trying to get away with doing as little as possible or if that was their way of promoting specific items, but it gave me an idea. Instead of just throwing a bunch of random things up on the shelves, I think it would be better to specifically promote a few key products. Give the customer a visual impact!

I also did something against policy today. I took the electric baby bottle warmers out of the household appliances section, brought them to the infant section, made a space on the shelf and stuck them in. I think it makes more sense that way. I also arranged them in a way that violates the company's four-inch display policy. Apparently I've set myself a very low standard: do one meaningful thing each day.

August 12, 2006: Saturday
The results of yesterday's inventory came out around four o'clock today. We're at – 0.26 percent, not bad at all. We had a champagne celebration. Lao

Ma, the manager, said a few sentimental words to mark the occasion and I suddenly had the feeling that maybe this store is finally getting on its feet and entering its finest hour. I didn't feel the slightest bit of personal happiness about the success of the inventory, but I was excited about possibilities for the future. During the meeting, the bigwigs got up on stage to fire us up with their speeches, then everybody went home. Now we can finally take a break after twenty-four hours of nonstop work. There's no denying it: Walmart people truly are hard working.

Today is the ten-year anniversary of Walmart in China. Some of the employees have been here ten years too. That's persistence.

August 18, 2006: Friday
Potato Beef:
- Take beef slices, potatoes, carrots, and onions. Stir fry in oil. Add a little salt.
- After it's fried, put it in a big pot. Add MSG and a little wine. Boil until the potatoes and carrots are soft enough to poke with a chopstick.
- Turn down the heat. Add curry and soy sauce and continue to boil, the longer the better. Make sure the sauce doesn't stick to the bottom of the pot.
- Put white rice on a plate. Put the curry mix on top and enjoy!
Walmart is unionizing!!!

This is serious stuff. A year ago, whenever we asked about the union, Lao Tang kept finding a million ways to brush us off and avoid the subject. But this afternoon when I was in the employee hallway I found a handbook with information about the Beijing union. The union! It looks like Walmart is getting closer and closer to it every day. My heart skips a beat just thinking about it.

August 21, 2006: Monday
Today at the management meeting they formally brought up the subject of the union. This whole thing has happened way too fast. Ever since the day Jinjiang went union,[18] there have been seventeen stores in all that have established union locals. What I just don't understand, though, is how this whole thing developed. All of a sudden Walmart has this enthusiastic attitude about the union and I can't figure out why. I need to get online immediately and figure out what's going on.

September 18, 2006: Monday
Today I was so bored at work that I called one of our suppliers just to talk. I ended up feeling like an ass, though, because he was in the middle of a

project and didn't have time to chat. Then Lu Jun came by and we had a long conversation. He's from Guangdong Province. Those southerners aren't so bad.

Tomorrow we have this bullshit "Cultural Competition." We're actually supposed to answer such questions as: "What was the name of Sam Walton's first dog? When did he get married? When was his first son born?" It reminds me of the way the Cultural Revolution is portrayed by some of those avant-garde filmmakers.

November 20, 2006: Monday
The inventory victory party was spirited and fun and everyone seemed to be having a great time. I was the only one sitting on the sidelines, just observing. From my perspective, the event had nothing to do with me; I was completely unable to integrate myself into my surroundings. It was only when Ah Hao got up to sing "Glorious Years" that was I able to muster up even the slightest trace of the enthusiasm I once felt,[19] but even that had nothing to do with Walmart. It seemed like everyone got an award, but then, maybe only a few people did. I was probably the only person in the whole room who didn't think it was unfair that there were some people who didn't get an award. I didn't care because it had nothing to do with me. It was just like what Lao She says: "Happiness is their happiness. It has nothing to do with me."[20]

December 26, 2006: Tuesday
First thing this morning, I went to GfK, the third largest consulting firm in the world and a pretty impressive outfit.[21] An entire half-floor of the Ren Shou building is theirs, and that's only what they have so far, and only in Beijing. I spent a full hour before the interview filling out paperwork and taking a written exam, but the interview itself was short, around twenty minutes. I feel pretty good about how it went. My only worry is that I might have overstressed the fact that I see the position primarily as an opportunity for professional growth, a stepping stone for future undertakings. This could have made me lose a few points. My lack of technical skills might also be an issue, since I'm not very familiar with statistical analysis software. All in all, though, I think it went pretty well. Maybe it will turn out to be the right place for me.

January 16, 2007: Tuesday
Without even planning it, today suddenly became my last day at Walmart. When I got to work, I went to Human Resources to find out whether they

were going to be giving us our bonuses at the end of the month. They said they weren't. In a moment of frustration and feeling somewhat liberated, I handed in my resignation. And that was it. The paperwork went smoothly; management gave me their signatures without batting an eye. I filled out the necessary paperwork and, at the end of the day, swiped my timecard for the very last time, exactly on time. I didn't stay a second beyond my shift. If you're gonna go, you may as well do it in style.

Today is the 16th. Exactly a year and a half has gone by since I came to Walmart. The days have truly flown by. In these eighteen months, I've written more than 200,000 characters documenting my experience. Perhaps this record contains a lot of inconsequential garbage, but at least it documents my own growth process. One day in the future, I'll look back at this thing. There's a lot of personal growth and transformation here.

I'm not saddened or hurt by this. Everyone has their own way of moving forward. It's just that, for me, I didn't expect this day to come quite so soon. I'll treasure these eighteen months at Walmart. This was my first job, my first real step into the world. I think it's been a great success and I'm grateful to Walmart for the experience. From this day forward, I'll proudly state to anyone I meet: "I am a Walmart person!"

8 WORKING IN WALMART, KUNMING

Technology, Outsourcing, and Retail Globalization

Eileen M. Otis

In 2001 Walmart Corporation established one of its first China retail branches in the relatively remote capital of Yunnan Province, Kunming,
the "City of Eternal Spring." At that time foreign investment barely trickled
into Kunming's service sector. By 2007 there were three branches of the
global retail giant in Kunming. With the retail behemoth poised to expand
rapidly in China several questions arise about its retail labor practices: Will
it import its draconian employment practices and "charismatic" management ideologies to China? Or will it make adjustments to adapt to the local
environment? If so, how will the company adapt to local labor conditions?
To address these questions, I organized an in-depth study of Kunming's
first Walmart branch.

Despite the name, logo, slogans, and pictures of Sam Walton bedecking
the interior, this Walmart looks unrelated to its American cousins. Instead
of being sited in a distant suburb, this branch is centrally located in one of
Kunming's commercial districts. The Kunming Walmart is not surrounded
by an oceanic parking lot. On one side of the store there is a modest plaza
where locals gather each morning to practice tai chi. Entering the store
requires negotiating a warren of small, independently owned stands selling
watches, electronics, clothing, nail care products, and shoes. Inside the retail space, crowds pry their way through the aisles as hawkers chant slogans
about their wares, plying customers with free samples of chocolate, coffee,
jelly, dumplings, peanut paste candy, dried fish, shampoo, toothpastes, and
creams. A saleswoman pounds on a drum as she cries out the day's discount
on instant noodles. Other salespeople shout about their wares through
megaphones. Shelves are piled high with local goods: Customers can find

"Tibetan Stubby Barley Wine," Yunnan coffee, tobacco bongs filled with local rice wine, full-belly clay pots brimming with condiments like eggplant paste, soy bean paste, ginger paste, dried green bean paste, and ten different types of dumplings (*jiaozi*), ready to eat.[1] This is utterly unlike the spacious and ordered Walmart outlets in the united States. Despite the difference in outward appearances, Walmart, Kunming, adapts familiar technologies and outsourcing labor strategies to this new retail labor environment. Indeed, I found that underlying the festivallike atmosphere of the store were two sets of labor practices designed to control workers. One is indirect and commission-based, and uses surveillance technology indirectly; I call this labor regime "entrepreneurial-hegemonic." The other is highly centralized and technology-driven; I call it "techno-despotic."

Walmart is well known for extensive use of innovative technologies to organize and control their suppliers (see Lichtenstein in chapter 1 of this book). Less well known is how Walmart also uses technologies to control and optimize the labor of its retail workers in China who provide services for customers. The existing scholarly literature on service work reveals little about the role of technology in interactive labor, especially retail labor.[2] This work instead tends to focus on fundamental differences between service work and manufacturing, with manufacturing taken as technology-intensive and physical while service work is conceived as primarily social and affective.[3] In manufacturing, labor is controlled by management, and there tends to be a fairly linear hierarchy of power and decision-making descending from managers to workers. Employers organize technology not only to enhance efficiency but also to optimize labor control.[4] By contrast, services are characterized by a three-way relationship: workers are supervised and directed not only by managers but also by customers. On the one hand, this triangular relationship provides opportunities for workers to autonomously exercise control over customers.[5] On the other hand, bureaucratic methods, tipping systems, and normative modes of control are used by customers to direct the efforts of workers.[6] Existing studies illuminate the complexity of power relations within service, but they rarely touch on issues of technological control, or more specifically, the ways in which technology might be used to coordinate relationships between management, workers, and customers.

Instead, scholars of service labor tend to focus their studies on affective labor—the ways in which workers produce emotive responses in customers by inducing or suppressing their own emotive responses.[7] In this effort, employers use a variety of techniques to control the social content of worker interactions with customers, including tipping systems,[8] requiring workers to recite preformulated scripts to customers,[9] altering workers' personality and interactive habits,[10] inviting customer commentary,[11] exerting control over workers' physical appearance,[12] channeling customer race, class, and gender aspirations,[13] or creating a work environment that allows workers to act without pretense in displaying their own authentic emotive responses to clients.[14]

However, it is widely assumed that, while manufacturing industries inevitably utilize machine technology as a way to pace and control labor, the forms of control used in interactive services are socially, not technologically, organized. Scant attention is paid to the role of machine technology in forming the disciplinary strategies to optimize service labor. Yet, with the development and increasing use of surveillance, data collection, and analysis technologies, it is becoming vital to investigate how these innovations shape control in the service workplace. Since the bulk of interactive work in consumer services cannot be overseen directly by managers,[15] these innovative technologies are frequently used as a form of impersonal surveillance.[16]

This research therefore addresses the lacuna in service industry studies and takes into account the ways in which technology affects conditions of labor control as well as the responses of workers to this control. I raise three specific questions: How does the use of technology organize interactive labor? How do technologies fit in with management's interactive service strategies? In service labor, how is technology used to coordinate control between customers, managers, and workers? Instead of concentrating on the ways in which technology is used to enhance efficiency or focusing on its use to maximize managerial control, I argue in this chapter that in some labor regimes technology is designed and used to facilitate customer control over workers.[17]

In order to understand the diverse regimes of labor control in a single Walmart—and how technology is used within each—I compare two types of workers subject to two different job regimes. Each regime lies at an extreme pole along a continuum of technological control. The first job regime, "techno-despotic" describes the labor practices of cashiers. Cashiers are employed directly by Walmart, and they are tightly controlled by various surveillance and pacing technologies that direct customers to supervise them. In contrast to cashiers, salespeople exercise a fair degree of autonomy on the retail service floor. These sales personnel are not employed directly by Walmart; they are hired and paid by Walmart's vendors. I term the set of labor practices that pattern their work "entrepreneurial hegemonic." These two regime terms derive from Burawoy's historical analysis of patterns of labor practice, which fall broadly into one of two patterns. The first is a despotic pattern that functions through coercion, using fines, penalties, and disciplinary structures to exercise control over labor. The second is a hegemonic configuration, defined by the absence of coercive structures of control and the presence of active worker consent to labor participation.[18]

This research is based on a total of three months of field study. The first phase involved two weeks of daily visits to two Walmart outlets in Kunming by the author and a research assistant, Lihua.[19] The visits lasted from one to four hours, during which we observed the retail environment and chatted casually with workers and managers. The second phase is participant-observation research. Lihua gained access to the retailer by applying for a job as a cashier. She was interviewed, hired, and trained, after which she worked as a cashier for eight weeks beginning in early 2007. This allowed her to make direct observations of the cashier labor process. She sent me field notes in Chinese via e-mail, and we discussed the fieldwork over an Internet phone system (Skype) about every two or three days she was in the field. Additionally, in the summer of 2007 I returned to the Walmart branches for two weeks to conduct further observational visits and to interview vendors and salespeople.

WALMART IN THE CITY OF ETERNAL SPRING (KUNMING)

As it faces restrictions on growth in the United States, Walmart is taking its "everyday low prices" (*tian tian pingjia*) abroad, preparing to develop its next major retail market in China. In 1996 Walmart established its first retail store in China. Since then its pace of expansion has been brisk. By April 2009 the company set up 121 supercenters, as well as two Neighborhood Markets, three Sam's Club outlets, and 101 Trust-Mart chain stores, employing more than seventy thousand workers. In terms of number of outlets, it still remains far behind its largest foreign competitor, Carrefour, which maintained 456 stores as of 2008.

Kunming is the provincial capital of Yunnan, located in China's southwest bordering Myanmar, Vietnam, and Laos. It is one of the country's poorest and least-developed regions. It is also the country's most ethnically diverse province. Major industries in Yunnan include tobacco production and mineral extraction.[20] As the "city of eternal spring," Kunming has become a magnet for domestic travelers, so that tourism is now a pillar of the local economy.

There are three Walmart outlets in Kunming, the first opening in 1999. In 2005, another outlet was founded in Yuxi City, a tobacco-growing and processing center, about fifty miles away from Kunming.[21] Part of Walmart's appeal to customers is that it is a U.S. company; American companies in China have a reputation for selling high-quality products. For this reason, Walmart explicitly promotes its exotic American image: workers are assigned English names displayed on badges pinned to their uniforms and the vast majority of products are labeled in both English and Chinese. Customers are also attracted by the fact that they can return defective items within thirty days, widely viewed as an American-imported practice. In spite of its American image, however, approximately 90 percent of products sold in stores are made in China. In the Kunming outlets, about 50 to 60 percent of products are from Yunnan. Most of these are not only locally produced but also locally branded. Walmart sources much of its merchandise from domestic vendors, independent suppliers who provide them with everything from fruit and vegetables to wine, toys, and clothing. Walmart negotiates with these vendors individually, and their local agents send shipments to each store. Some of these vendors also provide between two hundred and three hundred sales representatives to work on the service floor (see chapter 6). These workers, discussed at greater length below, stock shelves and promote their employer's goods to customers. They comprise a flexible supply of outsourced labor that Walmart management can also call on to handle a variety of tasks when needed. In short, inside the store there are two types of workers, those directly employed by Walmart and those employed by vendors, namely salespeople. These salespeople are controlled both by vendor managers and Walmart managers, but in general the latter do not exercise tight control over them, thus giving them a considerable degree of autonomy on the sales floor. In the following section, I describe the conditions of employment for workers directly employed by one of Walmart's Kunming branches.

WALMART'S DIRECT WORKERS IN KUNMING

About three hundred workers are directly employed by Walmart in a number of occupational posts: managers, cashiers, greeters, and stockpersons as well as just a few sales staff positioned on the retail floor. Produce workers and cooks in the fresh food department are also direct employees. Greeters stand watch at the entrances, incessantly welcoming customers through microphones that amplify and distort their voices. Greeters also check the receipts of exiting customers, so they act as a form of security. Stockpersons work in the warehouse storing and organizing the products circulating through the store, while produce workers maintain the aisles of fresh fruits and vegetables, continuously restocking the shelves.

Workers are typically urban residents; many are from small cities outside of Kunming. Most are between the ages of eighteen and twenty-four. Most have completed three years of technical high school (*zhongzhuan*). Some are still in school and most of these gain employment through Walmart's "work-study" program. The work-study program participants earn the same wages as other categories of new workers, but their hours are limited, and they are not eligible for full-time status or for the benefits associated with it.

New employees are initially hired as casual workers (*linshigong*), a typical strategy used by Walmart's U.S. branches. In the United States and China alike, full-time employees are legally entitled to insurance benefits. By hiring employees as casual workers Walmart limits expenditures on these benefits. Furthermore, by limiting their work to five-hour days six days a week, workers can be used flexibly throughout the day and assigned to posts when customer traffic is the highest. Casual workers are paid at an hourly rate of 5 yuan (US$0.60), amounting to 600 yuan per month. In 2007 the minimum wage in Kunming in 2007 was 540 yuan (US$73) per month for a forty-hour week, or 3.40 yuan an hour (about US$0.48).[22] Hence casual workers' earnings exceed the minimum wage. However, managers frequently fail to schedule these employees for a full thirty-hour week. And when customer volume is low, managers regularly require casual workers to end their shifts early. Hence, casual employees are often left with around 500 yuan each month, and sometimes less. These workers do not receive benefits, such as health insurance, although they do receive a free daily meal in the staff canteen. After three months of probation, casual employees have the option of becoming formal full-time workers, but many prefer to remain casual workers.

Full-time workers are guaranteed eight-hour days that yield a regular 760-yuan monthly salary (about US$70). Two-hundred yuan is deducted for insurance benefits (retirement, medical, housing subsidy, maternity leave, disability, and unemployment) so the take-home wage is 560 yuan. Take-home pay, then, is about the same for both casual and formal workers.

Why would anyone consent to full-time work? In addition to the insurance benefits, the advantage of full-time over casual work is that only formal full-time workers can be considered for promotion to a managerial position. Nevertheless, given the large deduction for insurance, full-time work is not an attractive option for many young workers. Indeed, since take-home wages are so low for full-timers, Lihua could not imagine why anyone would want to move to full-time employment, despite the benefits. After canvassing fellow workers she discovered that few were interested in going full time. Given their relatively young age (between eighteen and twenty-four), the benefits held little allure, and they prefer to have money in hand rather than benefits, which they might not use until sometime in the distant future. Workers older than twenty-five are more interested in becoming full-timers because they are moving into a life stage of family and marriage when they begin to utilize benefits like maternity, health, and housing subsidies. Most of the part-timers do not aspire to a managerial position in Walmart. Lihua encountered no one among the casual workers who aspired to full-time work. In fact, the similarities in wages made it quite difficult for managers to recruit the best of the casual workers into full-time positions. For example, a couple of weeks after Lihua began work with Walmart, the human resources managers pressured her to sign a full-time contract. In direct violation of the national Labor Law, they refused to give her a copy of the contract. After she insisted on having a copy in her possession, management allowed her to borrow a copy for three days. She declined the promotion, but management insisted she be transferred to full-time status. She held her ground and eventually they relented, allowing her to continue as a part-time worker. The wage system attracted younger, more readily controllable workers interested in casual work who would not mind being excluded from the ranks of full-time workers, since full-time labor held few attractions for them. But the system clearly also discouraged those workers managers thought to be promising from moving into full-time and, later, managerial positions.

Management monitored work hours strictly, often directing workers to punch out slightly before their shift was over. Workers were required to punch out even to use the restroom, and they were even forbidden to change out of their uniform before punching out. Workers were also urged to proceed immediately to their work post after punching in, otherwise, managers insisted, they would be "stealing" the company's time. Although management utilized every moment of workers' time on the job, they were careful that workers not put in any overtime, or work off the clock.[23]

The vigilance surrounding shift time contrasts sharply with Walmart's U.S. practices: reports are widespread of workers being forced to put in work time off the clock.[24] I can only speculate about the reasons behind the different employment practices between the two countries. The first and most obvious may be simply that wages are much higher in the United States, so management has more to gain by forcing workers into unpaid overtime. A second may be that fewer workers are employed directly by Walmart in China, since most of the service-floor labor is supplied by vendors, and they can be asked to perform a variety of tasks, including stocking shelves, collecting shopping baskets, and cleaning the store. If management needs extra labor, they can call on this "reserve army."

The labor conditions for casual workers lead to high labor turnover: within a month, Lihua was already training new cashiers because so many of the experienced workers had resigned. She spoke with a cashier who had worked at the store for less than two months; when she began working she had thirty co-workers in her training cohort; two months later, only three were still working. The unrelenting streams of disgruntled customers, long hours of standing, low wages, and a coercive labor regime proved intolerable for many workers. I now turn to a more detailed discussion of working conditions and labor strategies of control for cashiers at Walmart, Kunming.

GETTING A JOB AT KUNMING WALMART

For Lihua getting the job was fairly straightforward. She asked one of the greeters standing at the entrance of the store how to apply for a job and was directed to the personnel office on the fourth floor. After filling out a two-page application that required she provide the name of a "guarantor" (someone who could be held responsible if the employee steals or causes other damage to the employer), she submitted it and proceeded home to wait to be called for an interview. A few days later, she was summoned for the interview.

As she ascended the stairs to the fourth floor, Lihua passed numerous posters proclaiming Walmart slogans, such as "Happy Associate, Happy Customers," "Our Service: Smiling within Three Meters, Boundless Hospitality, Guaranteed Customer Satisfaction," and "Strive for Brilliance." Lihua waited in the training room along with six or seven other applicants, two of whom were men. After about an hour, a friendly assistant manager called her into the personnel office and apologized for the delay. She asked Lihua to introduce herself briefly and inquired about her educational background as well as what type of post she wanted. When Lihua responded that she would like to be a cashier, the manager warned her that the post was demanding and required the processing of seemingly endless lines of customers who often grumble at workers. Lihua assured the manager that she was fully prepared to face the demands of cashier work. The manager explained the terms of employment, wages, and hours and instructed her to arrive the following day for her first day of training, warning her not to be late. Within twenty-four hours, Lihua would begin working at Walmart.

Training to Be a Walmart Cashier

Walmart attempted to import its egalitarian ideology through its multiday training, required for each employee. However, while the ideology may resonate with a bygone Mao era radical collectivism (see chapter 5), it is clear that it is a thin veneer for an underlying regime of despotism. Labor is highly regulated by fines, penalties, and fear, with technological surveillance used to thoroughly recruit customers into direct supervision of employees.

As in Walmart outlets in the United States, motivational signs fill the wall space of the training room and employee areas. On one poster is written: "The Walmart Spirit" and three injunctions below it: "Serve Every Customer, Respect the Individual, and Strive for Excellence." Another poster lists rules on how to treat fellow workers. Yet another warns workers not to accept any kind of bribe from customers or companies, listing in detail what would constitute a bribe, which includes food, money, and travel. Another features a Walmart smiley face inside a stop sign, and read: "Stop. Don't forget to smile." Each slogan is given in English and translated into Chinese.

On the first day of training, Lihua and the other new employees were required to submit a pile of documents to management: ten small color photos, two health cards (confirming that the person has no infectious disease), an employment form, a temporary employee agreement, a signed "morality" statement, and a guarantor letter signed by a Kunming city homeowner, as well as a signed short-term contract. The paperwork represents the company's domain over a worker's body, as well as legal and ethical commitments. By requiring a guarantor, the company enlists the employees' personal, usually familial networks into regulating its staff members.

After accepting the new staff members' paperwork, the training manager taught the new recruits the special Walmart greeting. They were instructed to form a fist and exuberantly chant, "It's my Walmart." The new employees found the cheer ludicrous. Later, Lihua discovered that it is actually used only at the occasional large meeting, when managers would require that everyone shout it in unison.

Using managerial ideology imported directly from Bentonville (see chapter 5), the training managers seized every opportunity to persuade new workers of Walmart's dedication to an egalitarian ethic, instructing them in the three principles of "company culture": respect for the individual, customer service, and striving for excellence. Respect for the individual meant that each worker will be treated equally. How does Walmart actually put this ideal into practice? The training manager explained that the new employee badges displayed only their name and picture, but did not indicate their department. The manager stressed that this was evidence that the company treated everyone equally, as an associate rather than a member of a particular department. The company's official organizational chart, on display in the training room, inverted the typical pyramidal organizational hierarchy so that the general manager was placed at the bottom and workers or "associates" at the top. The manager underscored that the company treated every worker as an "associate" (*huoban,* meaning "working partner") The trainer explained that the term *associate* (used in the English-language materials) reflected the company's policy that employees are not merely wage workers but enjoy full partnership in the organization. However, despite the frequent use of "associate" in English materials to symbolically elevate the status of rank-and-file workers, in practice they are regularly referred to in Chinese as "staff" (*yuangong*) or "co-workers" (*tongshi*); the term *associate* is not even translated from English into Chinese. The term, popularized in the United States, has not yet taken on common usage in China's employment settings. Even the employee time sheets, which indicate the work number assigned to each employee in English as "associate number," still use "work number" (*gonghao*) in the Chinese translation.

As part of the effort to draw workers into adopting the goals of the company, management shares up-to-date performance indicators with them and ties their employment performance to branch revenue. In fact, management urges trainees to stay apprised of company performance by regularly consulting the information board in the staff locker room, where outlet revenue and revenue targets were posted daily. On one day in February 2007, revenues were recorded at 1,050,000 yuan. Based on that number, management created a sales target of 1,290,000 yuan for the following day. The revenue numbers fluctuate throughout the course of the week, but the sales target is always pegged higher than the previous day's sales total.

Training sessions also introduce workers to Walmart's basic rules of employment. Foremost among these rules is zero tolerance for romantic liaisons (*tanlianai*) among workers in the same department and with any sales representatives dispatched by vendors to negotiate with Walmart about items sold in the store. Trainers detail how exactly workers are to maintain the appropriate distance from vendor agents: workers are to refuse any gift or favor from a vendor representative and should never provide services to vendors. Cashiers were also not to settle bills with relatives and friends at their counters, so as to avoid any theft. The company's reputation for preventing *guanxi*, or networks, from influencing promotion and hiring decisions gives it a positive reputation among its workers, and many attribute this "fair play" to Walmart's American origin. So in this respect at least Walmart's egalitarian ideology had a positive impact on workers' attitudes toward the company. Overall, though, the company's egalitarian ideology is rarely practiced on the service work floor. In fact, it is largely disregarded. Despite an occasional gesture of support from lower-level managers, cashiers like Lihua rarely experienced a strong sense of egalitarianism at work.

At the training sessions, new workers are also taught the basics of good customer service. The trainer instructs employees to smile when within three meters of each customer. Cashiers are taught to state the total amount of cash each customer tendered and then state the total change required, and to return change using both hands, a signal of respect in China. Cashiers are also instructed to promote special products of the day to each customer.

Cashier trainees are urged to be vigilant about customer theft. In general, the company inculcated a routine suspicion of customers as potential thieves. Workers were trained to inspect systematically every box and package purchased, to ensure that no additional items were placed in them and that customers did not exchange cheaper items for more expensive ones. Underscoring the need for the utmost vigilance, managers used the acronyms "LISA" (look inside always) and "BOB" (bottom of the basket) to remind cashiers to check inside every box and inspect the bottom of every shopping basket; they also had to demagnetize all items that had security strips.

Despite its official egalitarian ideology, the company has developed an elaborate system of rules and penalties to enforce discipline among workers. These penalties are euphemistically called "coaching" and "guidance" (*zhidao*), but the rules and "guidance" in fact reflect a highly coercive work system. The training manager set out the penalty system for new employees: if a cashier defies a rule, for example by stealing money or products, accepting counterfeit currency, failing to recommend products, or failing to demagnetize a security strip, or if at the end of the day there is a cash discrepancy of more than forty yuan, the cashier is issued a pink slip.[25] If a staff member receives three pink slips in a period of six months, management offers "guidance," and this is recorded in the worker's file. There are four types of "guidance": first verbal, then written, followed by a request to return home, and finally, for the chronic or extreme offender, dismissal. Every month each worker's misconduct slips, numbers of suggestive-sale items sold, and scan rate are displayed publicly for everyone to see. Cashiers whose performance has been outstanding are rewarded with between 200 and 300 yuan (US$22–$33) and designated "five-star" cashiers, and they wear a special bright blue vest with stars for the month of the award.

At the end of two days of training, the trainees are tested on Walmart rules and regulations. Once the exam was completed, the training manager asked the trainees to swap tests to that they could correct each other's tests. Trainees took the opportunity to alter each other's answers so that everyone passed, with management seemingly turning a blind eye. After the test, trainee cashiers underwent two additional days of training, in which they role-played their tasks and shadowed experienced cashiers.

At no point during the training or at work did Lihua hear any mention of the trade union, which had recently been established in outlets throughout China (see chapter 9). During one of my store visits, I asked a manager if the national trade union had a branch at the store. He became visibly uncomfortable, responding that the company has a good, cooperative relationship with the union.[26] Hence, officially this Walmart branch has a union, but workers are not at all aware of its presence; the company's egalitarian statements, its declarations about worker empowerment, and its charismatic managerial ideology (discussed in chapter 5) do not trickle down to the service floor. On the contrary, the use of computer and surveillance technologies invites customers to exert control over service staff members. Workers occasionally viewed low-level managers as allies, but managers were also the ones who dispensed penalties when workers displeased customers.

THE LABOR PROCESS: TECHNO-DESPOTIC CONTROL

The first day that a trainee steps in her new role as a cashier is nerve-wracking. Long lines of easily irritated customers readily provoke anxiety among the new cashiers. Minor mistakes require managerial intervention, further lengthening the time that customers have to wait in line and inciting more apprehension among new trainees seeking to impress managers. Each shift begins and ends with money: managers place a bag of 700 yuan (US$90) in small change in each cash register at the beginning of the work shift. At the end of the shift, a manager counts the money. New cashiers are especially concerned about taking responsibility for the considerable sums of cash that they process during each shift.

After shadowing an experienced cashier for a few days, Lihua took over the register while a trainer looked on. Her field notes describe the fumbling of a neophyte workers, before the work tasks became sufficiently habitual:

> I made several mistakes. I often forgot how much change to give the customer. I closed the drawer before getting adequate change so my trainer had to ask another cashier for money to compensate. I felt so nervous... because I got it wrong, because I'm working with money... money is important in the market. If we make a mistake we need to call the Customer Service Manager (CSM); I don't want to call the CSM. I'm so scared of losing money.

Further considering the consequences of her mistake, Lihua reflected on the management's use of the term *guidance* as a euphemism for managerial intervention, "Guidance means that if you make a mistake someone will help you, not punish you; it makes me feel less nervous, more relaxed. So I think the company is very smart." But if the idea of managerial guidance provided some solace, there were plenty of sources of pressure on the service floor. I discuss those in the following section.

WORKING AS A WALMART CASHIER

Eventually, Lihua developed a work rhythm for her major task, which was to scan the bar codes of each product customers purchased. She soon learned the location of the bar code on each item, which sped up the checkout process and improved her scanning rate. She describes her checkout technique: "First I open the plastic shopping bag, using two hands, and use my right hand to scan, while using my left hand to demagnetize the product and to put it in the bag." Fellow workers eventually taught Lihua a technique to improve her scan rate: when there are no customers she could press the "off-duty" button on the register stop the scanning clock and enhance her overall scan rate. Although this function was built into the cash register, no trainer or manager ever pointed this out.

Workers are also aware of the security cameras looming over every cashier stand, another source of anxiety. Staff members generally assume that somewhere in the store multiple personnel scrutinize the work activity recorded by the cameras. But after she resigned Lihua discovered that the monitors are not "monitored." As part of the resignation process Lihua needed to collect a signature from a manager who was in the monitor room, which was part of the Loss Prevention Department (*fangsun xi*). She saw eight monitors with each screen divided into quadrants, each quadrant piped in video from a different camera. She was shocked to see only a single security worker in the room, and he was paying no attention at all to the screens. Instead, he was busily filling out paperwork. As Foucault has pointed out, the utility of technology designed to oversee discipline lies more in the *potential* for watching than in the actuality of observation.[27]

In addition to panoptic surveillance, management also keeps efficiency pressure on cashiers by maintaining high customer volume. Using register data that records variable levels of customer traffic throughout the day, management schedules workers to maintain the highest possible customer-to-worker ratio. Even when customers are fairly sparse, there are surprisingly long checkout lines, because during low-volume periods management rosters the minimum number of cashiers, opening just one or two checkout aisles. Cashiers sense the customers' mounting discontent when they are kept standing in long lines for more than five minutes or so. Lihua's field notes registered acute awareness of customers' soured faces, their muttered comments deriding slow cashiers, and body language silently broadcasting their annoyance. In this way, the seemingly endless checkout lines form a point of pressure by which management maximizes output from each worker.

Cashiers are formally required to scan at least 380 products per hour, although in reality few workers can maintain that rate. The fastest scanner, rewarded with the special vest and a 300-yuan bonus at the end of the month, scanned an average of 420 products an hour over one month. On average, workers scan around 300 products an hour, a rate Lihua managed to exceed by twenty as she became more skillful. Scanning is especially difficult when customers purchase large numbers of items. The machine is over sensitive, and there is a constant danger of scanning a single product multiple times. The scanner beeps to indicate that it has processed an item's price, but high levels of ambient noise from music, customers, and salespeople often drown out the beep, so it is all too easy to scan an item more than once.

In addition to coordinating high customer-to-worker ratios, management optimizes the labor of workers by requiring them to quickly perform multiple tasks within a single transaction. As a cashier, Lihua was to match each product that she scanned with a scan report on the screen, then demagnetize security tags (so that the customer would not trip the security alarm), bag the purchased items, receive the payment and return accurate change, check for counterfeit money if the customers used 50 or 100 yuan bills,[28] keep the amount of change disbursed as low as possible by asking customers for small change, be pleasant in her interaction with the customer, and recommend additional products. If a customer uses a credit or gift card the checkout process is slowed considerably.

With such a daunting number of tasks to complete quickly and efficiently, how do cashiers decide which tasks to prioritize? Workers seek to avoid any form of public humiliation, no matter how apparently slight, so they endeavor to minimize any actions that will trigger their counter's flashing signal light that immediately beckons a customer service manager (CSM). Hence they give priority to accurate scanning, demagnetizing products, and returning correct change. Workers give tasks that are unlikely to trip the "light of shame" low priority. Hence suggestive sales are often neglected. And interactive amenities (smiles, pleasantries, and the like) fall by the wayside, as managers do not enforce them. Cashiers are efficient, indifferent, and sometimes surly.

Under these conditions, cashiers are little inclined to recommend special products, even though they can earn an additional 300 yuan (US$36) for selling the most special products in a month. Everyday, managers assign employees ten items, such as beef jerky, laundry detergent, or sausage. These products are to be recommended to each customer. Some workers never recommend anything, even though they thereby risked a misconduct slip. Lihua tended to use discretion in recommending items, suggesting beef jerky to young people, for instance. Cashiers felt uncomfortable about suggesting items. Lihua noted: "When I recommend products, customers often frown, smile, or laugh at me. The customers at the back of the line will already have heard me repeat the suggestion several times, so they laugh at me."

A number of organizational and technological applications thus result in customers becoming agents of worker control. The sheer numbers of customers in line and their mounting impatience constitute a perpetual source of pressure for cashiers, not unlike that of an assembly line. After having waited for a considerable time, customers are not disposed to be pleasant. Once they reach the checkout stand, a sign appears inviting them to contact the manager if they are displeased with the service.

With little else to do, most customers monitor the checkout process closely and report when the cashier overscans and so overcharges them. Lihua reported a number of incidents in which the customer was overcharged. For example, she wrote:

> There was a guy who bought eight sausages, four each of two different kinds. One type scanned at 9 *mao*. The other sausages were 1 yuan. But the 1 yuan sausage scanned at 4 yuan. When I totaled the exchange, it was 14.5. Some customers add up the cost in their head. The guy said, "Why is the total so high? I didn't buy that much." He kept talking louder and louder, faster and faster. "This is your mistake...your mistake! I didn't buy that much stuff!" I was so nervous, because I knew I'd made a mistake. I took the sausages out of the bag to check them—to check the price and the bar code number.

Eventually Lihua gave up and turned on her light to alert the CSM, who directed the customer to the customer service desk to deal with the overcharge. While scanning too quickly compromises accuracy and can result in overcharging, scanning too slowly also created problems. Lihua noted: "If I scan too slowly, customers complain to each other loudly or give me a dirty look. They also complain when I take too long inspecting the new currency (for counterfeits)."

Furthermore, when customers trip the security alarm with items that have not been demagnetized, they are quick to inform management which of the cashiers was responsible, since they have in effect just been publicly accused of theft. Lihua recorded one among numerous such incidents:

> A customer bought a bicycle; it had a security tag on the front and I didn't notice it. I just scanned the soft tag. As the customer exited; he tripped the alarm. The greeter heard the alarm and checked out

the bike, asking the customer who checked him out. The greeter took down my name and reported me. I asked other cashiers what would happen; they said I would get a pink slip. The greeter brought the customer to my cashier stand to confirm that I was the one who had checked him out. The greeter held up the security tag and looked at me. I was so nervous and ashamed. I felt like I wasn't careful about this.

The company attaches security magnets to increasing numbers of items, including quite small things like batteries and light bulbs, which can easily be shoplifted. The growing numbers of security tags cause difficulties for the cashiers, adding one more checkout procedure and considerably increasing the likelihood of incurring a pink slip.

Serving slow and picky customers also proves to be a perpetual challenge for cashiers. Lihua found herself especially frustrated by elderly people who tended to frequent the store in the morning to take advantage of special discounts on food items. They all wanted to break large bills and were often very slow in getting their money out. Sometimes, impatient cashiers would "help" the elderly with their money, reaching over the counter and plucking the correct bills out of their hands. Lihua felt this "assistance" was disrespectful, though she heard of no customers complaining when cashiers did this.

A major obstacle to processing customers efficiently is the perpetual shortage of small change. Since few customers pay with credit cards, an enormous quantity of cash is processed through the cashier's stand. There is a chronic shortage of small change and customers are continually asked to offer the smallest bills possible. When cashiers are out of change, they have to interrupt the checkout process and press the bright, red checkout stand light to alert the Customer Service Manager to the problem. The difficulty can be compounded when, as occasionally happens, the CSM is not available or the store runs completely out of change. Lihua reported:

I was short of 1 yuan for a customer. I asked the customer to wait while I went to borrow the money from another cashier, but my colleague hadn't yet opened her drawer, so I had to wait. A customer started grumbling; she said that I shouldn't make the customers at the back of the line wait. I just told her what was happening. I then began to cash out the customers further back in the line. The customer who was owed the yuan waited quite a while and my light went on and on blinking, but the CSM didn't come, and the customer started to complain. She said, "I really don't want to wait." I told her that I was sorry, but my manager had gone to dinner and that I had no money. After that she checked her money and gave me 4 yuan, asking me to give her back 5 yuan. So I gave her 5 yuan after the drawer opened again, but I knew she was upset.

The chronic shortage of change encourages cooperation between cashiers, who often share their change with each other, but it also encourages them to demand, sometimes harshly, that customers provide small change.

Bagging the items bought is also a frequent source of tension. Customers can be very picky about how items are bagged, and some request extra bags. Sometimes plastic bags are in short supply, and management asks the workers to economize on them as much as possible. Lihua witnessed a particularly unpleasant incident during her training:

When I was watching the cashier check a customer out, she packed the products, separating them into different bags. The customer said, "I don't want to carry so many bags on the street, I just want one bag." The cashier answered that this is how she had been trained, so she was doing it correctly, adding that the company requires that food be separated into different bags. The customer responded in local dialect, "You little bitch [*xiao lan shi*]! You'll never attract a husband [*ni jia bu chuqu*]."

On another hand, another a customer insisted that fish and shrimp should have separate bags, saying, "It's as natural as putting men and women in separate categories."

Processing a constant stream of customers is utterly exhausting for the cashiers. Lihua notes: "After work I felt tired and hungry, and my neck hurt, and my leg hurt. We just stand for five hours, and we can't move, so it hurts." On holidays the stress is intensified. On Valentine's Day, "Fifteen customers waited for me while I cashed out. I began to sweat; it was suffocating, as if the air conditioning was broken. I started getting a headache." The boredom and pain of standing continuously in an extremely small, confining space for hours means that cashiers relish any opportunity to escape and walk around the store for a few minutes. When customers bring along items without a bar code, the cashiers have to find the product and check the price; these occasions offer a small opportunity for them to stretch their legs and roam around the store a bit. Such incidents occur three to five times a day and workers typically take their time, using fifteen to twenty minutes to excavate the number from store shelves. Credit card use also presented a chance to "steal some time," as Lihua often quipped. She notes,

> When we swipe credit cards, we have to wait for the machine to print, which takes about thirty seconds, so we can drink some water or stand or talk to another cashier. So when customers use a credit card I'm actually quite happy.

However, these occasional self-instituted breaks cannot do much to alleviate the coercive labor system administered to a large degree by unwitting customers. Unlike manufacturing work, in which workers are directly controlled by machines, the organization of technology at Walmart encourages and enables customers to exercise control over the cashiers. Technology is the primary factor mediating the customer-worker relationship.

WALMART'S INDIRECT WORKERS: OUTSOURCED LABOR

Compared to the army of highly disciplined, fast-paced cashiers, the sales labor force positioned on the service floor to manage and promote products enjoys a fairly relaxed pace of work. These workers learn how to duck out of sight of the surveillance camera, and they are only occasionally directly supervised by Walmart management. Hence these workers enjoy a large degree of autonomy on the retail floor: they answer cell phone calls from friends, chat with each other, try out each other's products, roam about the store at will and sometimes hang out with friends and relatives who come to the store to visit, with few disciplinary consequences.

These outsourced workers are subject to what I call an "entrepreneurial-hegemonic" regime. Control over sales workers is exercised principally through a commission system, which provides the sales force an incentive to promote the vendor's products. These workers are subject to diverse, yet fairly relaxed sources of oversight, and therefore enjoy a fair degree of autonomy. The diverse sources of oversight obscure the relationship between employer and control.[29]

At Walmart in Kunming, the vast majority of service-floor sales and cleaning staff on the service-floor (around two hundred in all) do not work directly for the retailer, but are outsourced. The cleaning staff for the three

Kunming outlets is contracted from a single company. The bulk of the sales labor force is also outsourced. Walmart allows its vendors to place product representatives on the service floor for a small fee (US$1.20 per worker per day). About a quarter of the vendors send salespeople to the branches. These workers comprise the retail floor sales force but they are recruited and paid by the vendors. The sales workers report daily to vendor representatives, either in person or, more frequently, by cell phone, and have periodic contact with vendor representatives delivering products.[30] The use of cell phones, owned privately by individual workers, requires that they take direction from employers and therefore constitutes one vehicle of labor control. These workers are also subject to some supervision and control by Walmart management. Given the relatively relaxed nature of this labor regime, it was quite easy for me as a researcher to hang out and strike up conversations with the vendors' workers when business was slow. At one point I even helped a worker distribute free samples of coffee.

This sales workforce is comprised mostly of migrants from the countryside or from small cities outside Kunming. These workers do not have urban residence permits. They find the sales jobs through newspapers or the Internet. The terms of their employment with vendors vary considerably: many earn commission based on their sales volume, while some earn a fixed monthly salary. These workers labor eight hours a day, six days a week. They can be assigned overtime by Walmart management during busy periods, which is compensated by offering them shorter work days during slack periods. These do not necessarily reflect conditions at other Walmart branches. For example, in Nanjing's Walmart some sales workers are reported to labor eight hour days, seven days a week, without time off.[31] More research is required to understand the full complement of work conditions for this outsourced labor force.

The majority of these workers are women; only about 25 percent are men. The workers' ages range from eighteen to forty-eight, so some of them are married and have families. The vendor salespeople promote products, often offering customers free samples. There is a gender division on the sales floor: men are usually assigned to demonstrate appliances like blenders, smokeless woks, and steam irons, while women hand out small food items and work in the makeup and personal hygiene departments. Some vendors rent space in open areas of the store, erecting large displays and counters and using the space to demonstrate their products. The salespeople perform simple package assembly and clean and stock shelves on the sales floor; they unpack, assemble, and package products in the aisles. Sometimes the aisles are blocked by piles of boxes. This work is directed by the vendors but Walmart management requires workers to organize and clean shelves for products sold by other vendors who do not provide sales representatives. A small handful of staff directly employed by Walmart also performs some of these tasks on the retail floor. These workers are not called "sales workers" (*chuxiaoyuan*). Rather they are regular staff members (*yuangong*). The produce department employs a number of Walmart workers who labor side-by-side with salespeople and continuously stock shelves throughout the day.

Compared to the workers directly employed by Walmart and subject to the the coercive, technology-driven labor regime already described, the vendor-employed salespeople enjoy more autonomy and are often better paid. Sales workers are monitored by surveillance cameras suspended every few meters on the ceiling. But the cameras are mostly disregarded, as workers carry on cell phone chats, informal conversations with visitors, and informal pow-wows among themselves, often directly beneath these cameras. During one visit, Lihua saw a worker reading a book that she had stashed under the basket of sanitary napkins that she was selling.

These workers have an ambiguous relationship to Walmart managers. Once on the service floor, they follow the directives of the vendors but they are also formally subject to the supervision of Walmart managers who occasionally require them to collect and clean shopping baskets or to stock shelves with products sold by vendors who do not send sales representatives. Walmart managers can discipline these sales workers for venturing from their post, talking on the phone, or socializing. But since the salespeople do not work directly for Walmart, managers cannot issue these workers pink slips and warnings. If there is a persistent and visible disciplinary problem with one of the sales workers, management's only option is to call the employing vendor to report the issue. Control is mostly exercised through an incentive-based system that guarantees workers varying percentages of total sales.

While cashiers are disciplined by the "stick" of pink slips, customer disapproval, and monetary penalties, the vendor-supplied sales labor force is controlled by the "carrot" of commission. Commission from the sales of each representative is calculated from daily sales receipts, delivered by Walmart to the vendor, which indicate how much product was sold during a worker's shift. Such sales receipts, then, report how well these workers have been promoting the vendor's products, and the workers fill out weekly sales reports based on the data collected by Walmart.

The terms of employment for salespeople vary, depending on the vendor. I talked to a woman who was shouting out the day's special on pig thigh, a local delicacy from Xuanwei. Her base salary was 900 yuan (US$110); if she sold over her quota she could make 1,400–1,600 yuan, with commission. Another worker selling walnut candy on the first floor earned a base salary of 600 yuan (US$80) and 1 percent of the revenue from products sold. There were exceptions to commission systems, however. A young woman selling "pudding tea" worked directly for the milk tea company. She spoke to me through her hygienic face mask as she frenetically assembled samples of tea in her rubber gloves, placing the tea power, sugar, and gelatin in small cups, which were being snatched up by customers faster than she could mix them. She would be rotated through different supermarkets every few weeks or months, working eight hours a day. For this she received a fixed salary of 700 yuan (US$90).

Why do the two labor regimes exist side by side? Each one serves very different purposes for Walmart management. Directly employing the labor of cashiers allows management to control and exact the maximum output from each worker. The use of vendor-supplied labor, by contrast, meets three needs. Most obviously, it reduces labor costs substantially and even provides some modest revenue through vendor fees. Use of outsourced sales labor also encourages competition among vendors, who devise all manner of attention-getting strategies, including distributing free samples, to boost sales. Finally, letting vendors organize their own sales injects an atmosphere of energy and buzz reminiscent of the traditional Chinese market, and customers can interact with sales staff who have considerable knowledge of the wares they sell. These rationales create the basis for a hegemonic labor regime that contrasts sharply with the despotic regime in the cashier aisles. Cashiers and salespeople work in the same space, but barely speak with each other. The sales workforce does not even eat in the staff canteen with the Walmart formal workers. They usually spend their lunch periods with other vendor salespeople in the employee backroom eating, talking, playing poker, and sometimes smoking. They are informally segregated from the Walmart direct workers, who each receive a free meal for each shift in the staff canteen. Hence, the labor forces are fragmented, each barely aware of the working conditions experienced by the other.

Conclusion: Technology, Control and Two Labor Regimes

The service-work literature focuses on the distinctions between technology-intensive manufacturing and socially organized service labor, rarely considering the multiple roles of technology in the service labor process. In my investigation I found two sharply contrasting labor regimes at a single retail Walmart outlet. One uses technology to coordinate customer control over workers, backed up by the disciplinary "stick" of managers ready to enforce rules and regulations with an armory of pink slips and monetary penalties. I term this regime "techno-despotic." The second uses a commission system as a "carrot" to exert indirect control. I term this regime "entrepreneurial-hegemonic." Why do two regimes emerge in a single store? How is technology used in the social organization of interactive work?

The regimes are the product of contrasting strategies of employment, direct and indirect. Direct workers are strictly regulated. Armed with customer volume data, managers appoint a minimum number of workers to process large numbers of customers, and mildly disgruntled customers keep cashiers on their toes. The negative emotions of customers, therefore, become a mechanism to enforce worker effeciency. Technological surveillance prevents customer theft but also allows for close monitoring of worker efficiency by both management and customers. Direct workers are taught about Walmart's charismatic managerial ideology of egalitarianism, detailed in chapter 5, but the ideology has little impact on them. On the contrary, they daily encounter highly coercive forms of discipline and control. Cashiers develop techniques to slow the pace of work but have few opportunities to directly contest the low wages and unsatisfactory work conditions.

While the scheduling and control of direct workers is designed to minimize labor costs, so too is the outsourcing of two hundred salespeople and cleaners to private companies. Outsourced sales workers perform incidental work for Walmart and were subject to a limited measure of control by Walmart managers. These workers did not undergo Walmart training and so were scarcely exposed to the corporation's ideology of egalitarianism. The ambiguity of their relationship to Walmart gave them little concern for the company's much vaunted corporate culture. Rather, their primary concern was to maximize commission by selling products, and they did this at their own discretion with a surprising degree of autonomy. The commission-based motivation helps Walmart push products, enhancing its revenue while at the same time eliminating the labor cost of sales workers. In contrast with the direct workers, whose labors were effectively channeled by data processing and monitoring technologies, sales workers showed indifference to the surveillance cameras stationed at regular intervals above their heads. Another form of technology central to their work, the cell phone, was used to stay in touch with their sales office but just as frequently was used to chat with friends and family who called regularly. For sales workers, communications technologies enabled their autonomy as much as it channeled their labor.

It seems that the appearance of China's state-sponsored trade union has little to do with Kunming's Walmart retail workers. The establishment of branches of the All-China Federation of Trade Union (ACFTU) in China's Walmart retail stores received widespread attention from the popular press. For the international trade union movement, this was indeed welcome news about a company that has been vehemently antiunion (see chapter 11). For a while the ACFTU mobilized grassroots support among Walmart retail workers to set up their own unions and choose their own union chairperson and committee members (see chapter 9). However, the situation at the Kunming Walmart showed that this drive from the top to organize Walmart workers does not reach all the way to southwestern China. Workers never encounter union representatives or any artifact of union presence, indicating perhaps that the company has been able to limit the presence and influence of the union, if it does exist. At this point, we can only conclude that there is sweating at the two ends of the supply chain (see chapter 1): both in the factories where migrant workers labor (see chapters 2 and 4) and at the retail end among direct workers.

PART THREE

Walmart Trade Unions

9 UNIONIZING CHINESE WALMART STORES

Anita Chan

The four chapters in part 2 of this book provide a varied picture of the lives and work conditions of Walmart employees, from a store's general manager down to a cashier. There had been no signs suggesting that Walmart employees at the stores would agitate to set up union branches on their own. Instead of organizing to make demands on Walmart they tended to take the exit option if dissatisfied. As will be seen in chapter 10, the turnover rates at the Walmart stores in China are extremely high.

The All-China Federation of Trade Unions (ACFTU) is widely thought to be "useless." It was a surprise, therefore, when, despite the lack of any prior push by employees, the ACFTU took on Walmart in 2006 and succeeded in setting up workplace union branches at twenty-two Walmart supercenters in China within the short space of four weeks. Walmart is famously antiunion and has successfully fought off unionization in North America. It was especially surprising, therefore, when Walmart capitulated to unionization in China. Equally surprising, the ACFTU achieved this through a technique it had not endeavored since the early 1950s—grassroots union organizing. Also almost unprecedented for China was that the first new union branches were democratically elected by employees. This chapter examines the emergence of these Walmart union branches, traces what has happened to them, and discusses whether they are sustainable and can carry out collective bargaining, one of the main tasks of genuine trade unions.

The chapter is based largely on the Chinese-language news media, supplemented by interviewing. To appreciate the usefulness of Chinese media reports, it is necessary to understand that the Chinese press today is no longer totally under state control. On their own initiative, newspapers cover stories and conduct probing investigative reporting that they consider newsworthy. For more than three years before the Walmart stores were unionized, the Chinese media had been following the jostling between the ACFTU and Walmart, shaping public opinion. At least some reporters adopted the following stance: Why should we Chinese give in to this giant corporation, which comes to China, throws its weight around, and openly defies the law of the land?

After analyzing eighty reports from Chinese newspapers and magazines on the initial emergence of the Walmart unions, it becomes obvious that in taking on Walmart the ACFTU successfully engaged in grassroots union organizing. A focus on how the first several union branches came to be formed within such a short period—only to have the unionization of Walmart subsequently undermined and derailed by the higher levels of the union and Walmart—provides intriguing insights into both Walmart's China operations and China's union officialdom. Despite the setbacks, as will also be seen, the ACFTU has recently taken on Walmart in collective bargaining. It is evident that, both in the initial unionization drive at Walmart stores and in the new drive for collective bargaining, reformist elements within the ACFTU are ready to push an active agenda when the opportunity arises.

Setting Up Unions from the Top

The prior experience of the ACFTU in establishing workplace union branches in foreign-funded enterprises had, until it encountered Walmart, been limited to one technique—from the top down. Whenever the ACFTU sought to establish a union branch at a foreign or private company, the official district-level union would seek management approval and cooperation to set up a branch. Once an agreement was struck, management and the local union would decide together on a midlevel Chinese manager to serve as the union chair, without a union election. After the fact, an announcement would be made to the employees about the formation of a new union branch, or in some cases, no announcement would have been made at all. More often than not, such a union branch does not even perform the traditional welfare functions that it fulfills in state-owned enterprises, where it holds occasional entertainment events, distributes gifts to the entire workforce during major festivals, pays visits to the sick and injured, hands out welfare relief, etc. There normally was no collective bargaining or other actions that we associate with unions.[1]

Innocuous as these so-called union branches might be, many foreign investors still do not want branches in their factories and stores. One reason is that no matter how subservient a union branch might be, managers often prefer not to provide any potential platform through which workers could have representation. Another is that, by law, management has to pay to the union branch a substantial sum—2 percent of the total payroll—to support union activities. Part of this goes to the upper levels of the union, and part is used to provide the above welfare functions.

For more than ten years, despite yearly quotas set by the ACFTU's upper levels to establish union branches in foreign-owned factories, when companies refused to cooperate the district trade union normally did not insist. Under the influence of the local government, the local union bureaucracy often did not want to scare off foreign investment. But over the past decade and a half, the ACFTU has undergone a decline in its national membership, as the numbers of state-owned enterprises decreased. From 1999 the ACFTU decided to offset this by expanding membership in the foreign-owned sector. Some reformist union leaders were disturbed by the international image that China, the world's factory, has become a gigantic sweatshop, and they particularly welcomed the new opportunity.

In 2004, the Chinese union federation selected Walmart as a special target.[2] The ACFTU was taking a leaf out of the global anti-Nike and anti-Walmart movements, targeting the most high-profile company: the reasoning was that if Walmart fell into line, other foreign companies in China that refuse to accept unions would have to follow suit.

During 2004–6, Walmart miscalculated in thinking it could use the same antiunion tactics in China that it does around the world. When Walmart refused to enter into discussions with the ACFTU and refused to let the ACFTU into its stores, as is the practice of Walmart worldwide, the ACFTU made a series of unprecedented moves. For the first time it openly threatened to take a foreign company to court for violating China's trade union law by barring the union. Walmart retorted that the law says joining a trade union is voluntary and that it is up to the employees to apply. Since none had, Walmart was not violating any law.[3]

The ACFTU had never engaged in grassroots organizing. Going among workers to agitate to form a union instead of asking management for permission was alien to ACFTU union officials, and the ACFTU was at a loss as to how to go about it. For a long period it persisted in seeking management's cooperation so that a union branch could be introduced in a top-down fashion. For instance, local union officials in the city of Nanjing made approaches to a Walmart store twenty-six times in two years but were not even granted a meeting with the store manager. This humiliating experience was repeated many times over in Walmart stores in other cities.[4]

Unionizing Walmart from the Bottom Up

The ACFTU chairman, Wang Zhaoguo, finally ordered that "the ACFTU has to send people to set up unions in Wal-Mart using all possible channels."[5] The ACFTU realized in the end that to achieve the mission of setting up unions, Walmart employees would need to come forward to apply to set up a workplace union, and that to accomplish this, the ACFTU would have to resort to grassroots organizing. The organization drive had to be underground outside the workplace just as unions have to in other countries when facing hostile management. The ACFTU had not used this organizing method since before 1949 when it tried to penetrate workplaces before the Chinese Communist Party took power. According to Chinese newspaper reports, in the spring of 2006 local union officials in several cities began approaching employees after-hours away from Walmart's premises and handed out literature to convince them of the benefits of a trade union branch. In early July, the union federation called a national meeting in Quanzhou City, Fujian Province, in order to coordinate the efforts.[6] Quanzhou had been selected to spearhead the drive, as the city had already achieved a 90 percent rate of unionization.

Several Chinese newspapers have reported in some detail on how the first Walmart branch was established at the Jinjiang Walmart store in Quanzhou at the end of July.[7] Ke Yunlong, a twenty-nine-year-old college graduate who supervised the store's meat-packing department, and two colleagues became enthusiastic about securing a trade union branch at their Walmart store. Secret communications began taking place between Ke and a special task force set up by the local union. To support Ke's efforts to convince his workmates, a union official rented and moved into a room near the store so that he could more easily meet at night with interested Walmart employees.[8]

According to clauses of the Chinese labor law, setting up a trade union branch and getting recognition for it is, legally speaking, as easy as ABC (in stark comparison to, say, the procedures set down in U.S. laws).[9] In China's trade union law, a minimum of only twenty-five signatures is needed to establish a branch at a workplace. Having secured the requisite number, the city-level union sprang a surprise on Walmart. A union committee was formed on July 28, 2006, at a meeting held from eleven in the evening until three in the morning. This was the only time employees from both night and day shifts could assemble. This unusual time and the secretive nature of the founding ceremony were firsts for the ACFTU.

At the meeting, seven executive committee members were elected, with Ke as the union chair. To underscore their determination and the solemnity of their commitment, the thirty members affixed their fingerprints to the application form, rather like the swearing-in ceremony of traditional Chinese secret societies. At 6.30 a.m. they declared the union branch formed and sang the Internationale beneath a banner that read, "Determined to Take the Road to Develop Trade Unionism with Chinese Characteristics!"[10] The ACFTU later declared the ceremony a "historic breakthrough" for China's labor movement, and there was a scramble across China to announce further Walmart union branches in rapid succession. Several branches were established within days after Jinjiang. They similarly resorted to secret founding ceremonies held after midnight, and the proclamations of their formation were sprung on Walmart the following day.

As soon as Walmart was informed of the new trade union branches in its stores, antiunion activities went into high gear. Big meetings were called at which, according to Chinese newspaper reporters, warnings were duly announced that those who join the union would not have their contracts renewed. Walmart also announced that it would not pay the union the 2 percent payroll union fees. It tried to discredit the ACFTU by accusing it of bribing employees to join the union and charged that the workers had not joined voluntarily, in violation of the Chinese trade union law.[11]

But within a week, it offered an olive branch in a 180 degree turnaround. It tried to co-opt the ACFTU to work together to achieve "harmony." Top Walmart regional executives invited themselves to the local Quanzhou trade union office, where they met with the Quanzhou General Trade Union deputy chair, Fu Furong, the official who had been overseeing the program of unionizing the Jinjiang union branch. Fu reported to the press that the meeting was cordial but there were still disagreements. He admitted many people were skeptical that the new trade union branches would accomplish anything and said that the most urgent task now was to "nourish and protect" (*kehu*) the new unions.[12]

He had good reason to express concern about the vulnerability of the new branches. Chinese newspaper reports have not mentioned any ACFTU or local union officials making any commitment to improve workers' conditions or salaries. Instead, the union officials were quoted using phrases such as "cooperation," "working with management," "no confrontation," "common purpose," "harmony," and "win-win situation."

COMING TO AN AGREEMENT

On August 16, 2006, ACFTU officials from Beijing met with Walmart's top executives in China at Walmart's headquarters in Shenzhen and signed a five-point memorandum. In an interview with a business magazine, Guo Wencai, the top ACFTU official in the "grassroots construction department" of the Beijing union headquarters, who was the brains behind the campaign, recalled as "tough" the negotiations that culminated in the memorandum. Walmart had wanted to control the union branches by inserting top management personnel into their preparatory committees and argued that management staff should be eligible to run for the union executive committee and for the trade union chair. In the end, it was agreed a preparatory committee would be composed of management, district union officials, and employees, although management representatives were to be capped at middle-management level and at 20 percent of the committee members.[13] The memorandum stipulated there subsequently would be a multicandidate election for the union committee, the union chair, and deputy chair, and the election would be organized by an official sent from the district union, not by management. Higher-level management personnel and their relatives were to be barred from becoming union members. District and city-level union officials would be allowed to conduct in-house training of employees about China's labor laws and the employees' labor rights, and to recruit new members. But the memorandum's final point seemed ambiguous: Walmart union branches will support management in exercising its management rights *in compliance with the law,* will mobilize and organize the employees to fulfill their responsibilities, and will cooperate on *an equal basis* with management in order to allow the enterprise to develop harmoniously.[14] The statement could be read as a concession by the ACFTU, but the emphasis on compliance with the law in management practices and sharing equal responsibilities and rights between the management and union counterbalanced the rhetoric about management rights and harmony.

The five-point memorandum was seen at the time as the ACFTU's template for setting up trade union branches in all foreign-funded enterprises.

Grounds for optimism lay in an editorial that appeared on the ACFTU website on August 16, the day the memorandum with Walmart was signed: "How Walmart Came to Change Its Attitude." The grassroots organizing experience had not been lost on some of the union leaders. The editorial was filled with self-confidence: the Chinese union has "cracked the world's toughest problem." In seeing this as a "world problem," the editorial contextualized the ACFTU as part of an international anti-Walmart movement. This excerpt captures the editorial's tone:

Setting up these unions encountered many ups and downs. It did not come about easily....It is a major breakthrough in creating something new that will definitely open up a new stage! The positive determining factors in the births of these Walmart union branches were the employees' aspirations, plus legal compliance. The guidance and assistance provided by the upper level unions fostered positive outcomes. It is a big departure from our previous method of setting up union branches by relying on persuading management to give support. Now instead we turn to propagating, inspiring, cultivating, and reinforcing employees' trade union consciousness, instigating and mobilizing their aspirations to join the union. Even in circumstances where employers are uncooperative and unsupportive, we still will set up our unions. In reality, in the past few years, in our work to establish trade union branches, particularly in foreign-funded and private enterprises, we encountered much passive resistance on the part of employers. It was enormously difficult. This successful experience in setting up Walmart unions is groundbreaking in that we have discovered a new line of thinking. It not only will influence other foreign and private investors to quickly abide by the law to allow unions to be established; it also brings to trade unionists a new mission. Following the new logic in setting up unions, new adjustments in union work will be needed, be it in methods, in organizational structure, ways of identifying backbone activists, down to how to use union funds.[15]

The ACFTU is not the monolithic structure it is often portrayed to be. Within the leadership, as exemplified by this national editorial, there are reformist union officials who understand the principles of grassroots organizing and are willing to push the limits, but they normally have been constrained and hamstrung by procapital forces within the Communist Party, the government, and the ACFTU itself. Notwithstanding this, the mid-2006 editorial expressed a belief that the ACFTU's confrontation with Walmart had opened up a means for reformers to operate in future. The well-publicized Walmart breakthrough also had set a legal precedent for Chinese workers to take on their employers and to demand and obtain union branches.

In one such case that erupted in 2006, a group of workers at a Danish-owned electronics factory elected their own union committee. Management fought tooth and nail against it, trying its best to fire the activists on the flimsiest possible grounds. Originally the workers gained public support from the ACFTU in Beijing, but soon afterward it withdrew support, leaving the union on its own to struggle against management and the district level union's harassment. Within a period of three years all of the labor activists were fired, the union branch was decimated, and the workers lost their case.[16] In another case, in 2007 a group of street cleaners in Shenzhen City went to the authorities to ask to set up their own union branch, and their wishes were granted.[17] These are isolated incidents, but such initiatives would not likely have been tolerated by the ACFTU had the Walmart union branches not been set up through bottom-up organizing, with so much fanfare and public endorsement.

REGRESSING TO TOP-DOWN UNIONIZING

Whatever the hopes of the reformers, the ACFTU has almost no experience of grassroots initiative, and many union officials habitually become nervous about any activities that are not top-down and controlled by themselves. Nor are they accustomed to, or comfortable with, organizing workers themselves, whatever the precedent set by the initial experiences with Walmart. Reformers within the ACFTU and some activist workers wanted to push in that direction, as the editorial and the scattered efforts to organize bottom-up union branches made clear, but the reformers were untrained and on unsure ground. Moreover, they were weak or nonexistent within the district-level union organizations in most parts of the country.

Thus, although the memorandum was to be used as a template for a nationwide drive to set up workplace unions in the foreign-funded factories, after the ACFTU's victory over Walmart in August 2006 the reformers' hopes were dashed. Once the memorandum was signed, the union branches that quickly sprang up at all of the remaining Walmart stores across the country were founded in a very different manner from the earlier batch. No longer did the union officials need to reach out to employees in confidence and persuade them to take the initiative to sign up. Instead, the branches were created in a top-down fashion with Wall-Mart's cooperation. The founding ceremonies were now held inside the store rather than at the local trade union office; and during work hours instead of after midnight.

Overall, in the nationwide drive to expand union membership at the foreign-funded factories, the signs were unfavorable. District unions were coming under pressure to fulfill quotas set by the national union leadership, and they typically were falling back on the top-down method in establishing union branches, or were turning to a truncated fast-track means of signing up new members. They needed to. Shanghai union density was targeted to reach 60 percent by the end of 2006, and 80 percent by the end of 2007. In 2005 Zhejiang Province claimed 70 percent union membership among the employed workforce, and it was scheduled to reach 80 percent by the end of 2006. How was that achieved? Zhejiang contains more than three thousand Taiwanese-funded factories alone, and as of 2005 two-thirds of these had no unions.[18] Even the top-down unionizing method takes time. The quotas became impossible targets if a genuine grassroots organizing method was used.

Even in the few places where bottom-up organizing was attempted, the picture was not what it seemed. This was the case with the ACFTU's next biggest target after Walmart—to "organize" Foxconn, a gigantic Taiwanese-owned electronics company that supplies Apple, Dell, Nokia, and many other brands from its factories in China. After the *Mirror* in the United Kingdom in mid-2006 exposed Foxconn's management practices at a vast factory in Shenzhen that produces the world's iPods, with workers forced to stand throughout their twelve-hour work shifts, the news media in China picked up the story,[19] and Foxconn employees began blogging to vent their anger. The Shenzhen city trade union responded by announcing that Foxconn, which employs more than 200,000 workers in the city, would be obliged to have union branches by year's end. Jumping the gun by one day, on December 31, 2006, union officials set up a table outside the largest plant, signed up 118 employees as union members, and handed them union cards on the spot.[20] According to *Shanghai Daily,*

A spokesman for Foxconn said the company had planned to set up its own trade union in January.... But the local was set up unilaterally by the general trade union of Shenzhen and not through cooperation with the company. "This is an innovative move," said the union official who represents the new local at Foxconn. "It'll help promote the protection of workers' rights in other foreign-funded and private businesses."[21]

However, our follow-up interviews a number of months later with Foxconn workers outside the factory compound revealed that workers had no knowledge about the union's existence. The Shenzhen efforts to set up union branches at Foxconn had been no more than a local union trying to fulfill quotas and chalking up "achievements" for the record.[22]

In contrast, at the Walmart stores a number of the branches had been established through genuine organizing and had elected their branch committees. But the party and government soon began to take steps to nip in the bud the potential for the new union branches to act independently. One means was to install a workplace party committee above the union branch in each Walmart store. The first two of these party committees were established simultaneously with the new union branches at stores in Shenyang in northwest China as early as August 2006, followed soon by two stores in Shenzhen in the south. The messages permeating the media reports stressed a "win-win situation," with an emphasis on stability and company development, on "reinforcing communication and mediation with the company and winning top management's understanding and support."[23] In these pronouncements, not a word was mentioned about protecting the rights of Walmart employees. An ordinary party member of a Shenyang Walmart store was quoted as saying, "The Party branch secretary told me that the criterion for assessing Party members' progressiveness is success in attaining better sales."[24] A new slogan for the Walmart party branches, "Construction of the Party to Facilitate Union Construction; Construction of the Union to Facilitate Party Construction," is telling.[25] The slogan's implicit message is that the party now plays the leadership role, not the union.

On December 15, 2006, five months after the ACFTU reformers' euphoria about the sudden emergence of grassroots Walmart trade union branches, a party branch committee was set up at Walmart's Chinese headquarters in Shenzhen. The founding ceremony was attended by top local party officials, with fanfare and media publicity and with the full knowledge of Walmart.[26] Tellingly, a search of the ACFTU-run newspaper *Workers' Daily* and of ACFTU websites revealed that these did not carry a single report about the new development. The union federation appears to have been unenthusiastic about the party's intrusion.

The manner by which they came into existence initially affected the operations of the Walmart union branches—those set up surreptitiously, with elected union committees, as against those that were set up from above by district level unions in partnership with Walmart management.

Those set up by secret elections before the memorandum was signed sometimes began making attempts to represent workers' interests. A search of Chinese websites and web blogs revealed Internet discussions among workers in at least three union branches where union members treated the union branch as their own and resisted being controlled by Walmart management or by the district unions or party committees.[27]

One of these was the Jiali Walmart store trade union branch in Shenzhen. Based on blog postings, for a while this branch was functioning with some independence, but the trade union chair had to resign and Walmart management quickly moved in and replaced him with its own person without an election. In October 2007, some workers in this store posted blogs calling out, "It's over! It's over! Come and save this Walmart trade union!" It is likely that Walmart was able to "reconquer" the branch with the tacit consent of the local party, which had moved into the store to set up a party branch in December 2006.[28]

A second union branch where members were struggling was the Hujing Store branch union in Shenzhen, which also initially had been set up secretly. It had been the second store in China and the first in Shenzhen City to have a union branch. At a time when joining the union and running for office was a risky undertaking, an ordinary worker stepped forward and got himself democratically elected.[29] The blog indicates that he and the elected accountant eventually became corrupt and embezzled trade union funds, and did nothing for the workers. According to blogs posted between February and March 2008, the members were now trying to get rid of them and to organize a new committee. An interesting point to note about this case is that the trade union members, having elected their representatives, insisted that the union branch heads be held accountable. The experience of electing union cadres of their own choice arguably created a sense that they have the right to dismiss these representatives when they did not live up to the expectations of their constituency. A few employees were in the midst of trying to organize an investigation committee and signature campaign to get rid of the head and the accountant, despite encountering enormous pressure from Walmart management during work hours. Within days, 150 branch members had already signed a petition. Dozens of employees contributed web comments lambasting the corrupt branch officers. As commentator No. 22 observed, "I just can't stand seeing this union organization of ours becoming like this. I can't stand watching them steal our money and spend it irresponsibly. All I want is to straighten this mess out for myself and for most of our members and to fight for the welfare and benefits that rightfully belong to us!"[30]

Another interesting case was the Bayi store union branch in the city of Nanchang, the capital of Jiangxi Province, which had been set up in clandestine fashion in the first half of August 2006. The chair elected at that time, Gao Haitao, persisted in battling Walmart management over one issue after another up to the latter part of 2008. Significantly, Gao had studied law on his own while supporting himself by working at Walmart part-time, and in 2005 he passed a nationwide examination in law but decided to stay on in Walmart as a full-timer. His legal knowledge became his main weapon when confronting Walmart. His efforts soon began to be recorded on the Internet by his supporters. Being required by the Trade Union Law to pay 2 percent of the total payroll to the workplace union as union activity fees, Walmart tried to retrieve this expense by skimping on bonuses and an annual holiday gift to workers, which provoked Gao to challenge Walmart. In two other instances, Gao fought management against unfair dismissals and succeeded. This was seen as so unusual by other workers that union branch membership jumped many fold. It is alleged in the blogs that Walmart tried one trick after another to control Gao. One attempt was to win over the city-level union, and then to create a so-called union working committee at the city level headed by a Walmart manager to override the workplace unions of the three Walmart stores in the city. Gao refused to go along with this and sought help from the ACFTU in Beijing, which supported Gao and overrode the decision of the city-level union to establish the committee. In September 2007, the store's deputy manager charged that Gao had spent union branch funds without members' permission while attending a union conference in Beijing. Half a year later Walmart fired the deputy manager. Gao leaped to his defense and helped him draft an application for arbitration, which resulted in the man's receipt of ninety thousand yuan in compensation. Gao's reputation rose another notch.

I have uncovered more than a hundred comments (including a few by supervisors and managers) from Walmart store employees all over China in support of Gao, hailing him as a genuine trade union leader. Some suggested that he should train the trade union chairs of all of the other Walmart stores. Many addressed him respectfully as "Chairman Gao" though he was not their union chair and was in fact just a young rank-and-file employee in one of the many stores. One blogger suggested that they start collecting funds to support Gao's efforts, and another wrote he was willing to contribute a hundred yuan a month of his cigarette money to start a union fund.[31]

In general, the blogs by Walmart employees are vehicles for self-expression, exchanges of information and ideas, and discussions about collective action. The comments made in the blogs by worker-authors bring out clearly that they do not totally dismiss the ACFTU. They can be disappointed and cynical about Chinese trade unions, but there is no mention of a desire to set up an independent trade union. The bloggers want the space to pursue their interests against management through existing legal and institutional structures.

COLLECTIVE BARGAINING BETWEEN THE ACFTU AND WALMART

The ACFTU prides itself that by 2007 it had signed 975,000 agreements nationwide with employers covering some 128 million workers.[32] The ACFTU understands that these agreements are no more than a statement of intent by management to comply to minimal labor standards. In the state-owned enterprises, where such contracts are common, they often are pro forma—written by management and ratified by a union branch head who is a management appointee.

Few private or foreign firms abide by a government directive to engage in contracts. To alter this situation, the ACFTU in 2008 launched a campaign, and once again used Walmart as a target. Despite having acceded to the establishment of union branches, Walmart remained resistant to the idea of signing collective agreements. More than a year earlier in April 2007, the Jinjiang Walmart store union, the first Walmart union branch in China, had requested a collective contract, but was ignored. It is not clear whether this was a local initiative or was initiated from Beijing, but the fact that the Jinjiang store was targeted is of some symbolic significance.

In 2008 the ACFTU put pressure on Walmart at a national level to enter into negotiations, as a nationwide campaign got underway to sign collective contracts at foreign-funded enterprises. Once again, Walmart was targeted in a well-publicized fashion, to serve as an example to other foreign firms. This time, the effort was a top-down exercise, in which the ACFTU was able to rely on the Chinese government's political backing.

The first Walmart store to sign a collective agreement was in the northern city of Shenyang in China's Liaoning Province. Why this particular union branch? Back in 2006, not only was a trade union set up in the Shenyang store but also simultaneously a Shenyang City Walmart Store Party Branch Committee. This was the first city-level Party Committee to do this vis-à-vis Walmart. It is therefore not surprising that the ACFTU sought to have the first Walmart collective contract signed at a store whose Party Committee is shored up by the municipal party and government. When the store unions are weak and most of them are under management control, this bureaucratic method of relying on external political weight was an obvious way to go.

According to a news report, the bargaining was quite tough. The union presented to management a draft of the collective contract on May 28, 2008. In the beginning management refused to negotiate, and there was a stalemate. On June 26 the union's lawyer sent a letter to management again formally requesting "collective consultation." On July 4 Walmart conceded that it would act in accordance with the law. After five rounds of "consultation," on July 14 the two parties held a formal collective consultation meeting. The highlights of the contract included issues of importance to workers: labor awards, a wage increase, paid leave, social security, and workers compensation. It was agreed that in 2008 there was to be an 8 percent or higher wage increase compared to 2007, and another 8 percent increase for 2009. It declared that henceforth collective consultation would take place in December of each year, and the Walmart basic wage would be higher than Shenyang City's official minimum wage. The contract terms were then approved by the store's Staff and Workers Representative Congress.[33] The agreement was to be the template agreement for all Walmart stores in China. Walmart and the ACFTU declared this a win-win agreement.

Examined closely, though, the content of the agreement is more a win for Walmart than for the ACFTU or for the workers. Most of the contract language favors management. The length of coverage is unusually long—five years with little possibility of adjustment. Most noticeable is the absence of any job classification system or salary schedule, as any agreement should spell out. Other missing provisions that are standard in most collective agreements around the world include the absence of any procedure for handling individual employee grievances or for resolving collective disputes over the interpretation of the agreement.[34]

Within a week after the Shenyang contract was signed, twenty stores in China signed very similar agreements. Playing to symbolic appeal, the second superstore at which the contract was signed was the Jinjiang store, followed by stores in Shenzhen, in the same order that the union branches had cropped up two years earlier.[35] In all cases, the Walmart store union chairs were given the template Shenyang contract to sign. Since most of the union chairs were essentially subordinate to and conciliatory toward management and since the very idea of collective agreements was entirely new to the union branch heads, every store branch complied without questioning, except for Gao Haitao of Nanchang Bayi store—the same branch union head who had previously resisted management and had built a national following. Gao detected some potential problems in the agreement and asked to have amendments included to ensure management could not subsequently dictate how all of the terms were implemented. But his request was ignored. Instead, another Walmart store union head in Nanchang city signed it in his stead. The city level union did not support him, nor did the ACFTU intervene as it had previously.[36] Gao resigned from Walmart in frustration in September 2008.[37]

Elsewhere, the management at a Walmart store in the city of Chengdu refused to sign and the city union had to organize a small street protest before the store complied.[38] By mid-September all 108 stores had an agreement. One of the deputy ACFTU chairpersons, Xu Mingde, emphasized that the campaign to have Walmart sign contracts would have an "emulative and demonstrative effect" for all foreign-funded workplaces in China.[39]

Even though it was widely reported in a number of local newspapers that Walmart employees would get an 8–9 percent pay rise in 2008, Gao Haitao was right that the terms in the agreement were too vague—and Walmart was able to get away with not honoring the wage increase immediately. Since the agreement did not specify the starting time of the wage increase, when store managers announced to store employees that they were covered now by a collective agreement, they simultaneously announced that the pay increase for management staff would begin in January 2009 and for ordinary workers in June/July 2009.

Were there any actual financial gains in the contract benefiting employees? For instance, at the time the contract was signed, did the 8–9 percent wage increase look likely to outpace the inflation faced by employees? It does not seem so, based on the high rate of inflation in 2007 and 2008—in which pork prices in June 2007 had already doubled since the beginning of the year, and the price of eggs increased by 51 percent. Food prices accounted for 33 percent of all consumer price index factors,[40] and accounted for an even higher proportion of the expenditures of low-income Walmart workers. Food prices continued to surge in 2008, with rice and other grains leaping in cost. At the time, an 8–9 percent wage increase seemed too low for these workers to stay abreast of the rising costs they faced. Within the past year they had already fallen behind by far more than 8–9 percent.

Notably, too, the 8 percent wage rise was not assured for individual Walmart employees since the contract stated that the increase is only an "average percentage," which means some employees can get a lot more at the expense of others.

Was the ACFTU aware of these problems? It is difficult to say. Perhaps it was, since the negotiations were described as being "tough." Presumably the terms were not totally dictated by Walmart. But Walmart is one of the world's most sophisticated multinational corporations with vast experience in negotiations, while the ACFTU has scant experience at a negotiating table and scant knowledge of international labor-contract practices. The ACFTU was also in a disadvantaged position. Even in the West, according to several seasoned American trade union negotiators, the initial contract agreements drawn up between unions and corporations tend to be weak. Granted this, in not coming to the aid of Gao Haitao, the only union chair who asked for changes and refused to sign the agreement, the ACFTU ultimately was willing to let Walmart call the shots.

Conclusion: Appraising the Unionization Effort

Whatever the setbacks, starting in 2006 the ACFTU had taken two big steps forward vis-à-vis Walmart. First, it had overcome Walmart's resistance and had succeeded in getting workplace union branches set up at all Walmart stores, and subsequently it had signed a collective agreement covering all of the employees in the stores. Unfortunately, having attained an initial breakthrough in its organizing drive in 2006, the ACFTU regressed to its past practice of top-down union organizing, and the collective agreement in 2008 was signed only with government and party backing. Consultation with workers was off the agenda. The ACFTU has made almost no efforts to help inexperienced union committees deal with Walmart's antiunion ploys, and indeed Walmart was allowed to control most of the branches.

But even if this exercise has been fraught with predictable problems, it has not been totally meaningless. The two initiatives have served an important function. The main purpose of the ACFTU's Walmart campaign, according to one of its deputy chairs, Xu Mingde, was to serve a legitimizing and demonstrative function. Union branches and collective contracts have been put in place, and they potentially will have favorable impacts in the future. Walmart henceforth faces collective bargaining over wages and conditions, and subsequent negotiations may not go as well for Walmart. The ACFTU is on a learning curve. In only a few countries in the world has Walmart needed to accede to collective bargaining, and the Chinese union federation has a stake in turning this to its benefit. The ACFTU's dealings with Walmart have created an opening for reformers within the union leadership, but they need to better understand how to negotiate collective contracts, and here Western unions are beginning to play a role. Unions in Germany and Scandinavia, in particular, have begun providing training sessions for Chinese unionists, in this and other forms of capacity building.

Sections of the ACFTU that are in the hands of reformers are particularly receptive to learning from foreign counterparts about organizing and collective bargaining, none more so than the Guangzhou Municipal General Trade Union. One development that reflects well on the Guangzhou municipal union's efforts is that in 2009 it hired Gao Haitao, the former Walmart store union chair who had repeatedly stood up to Walmart.

What, specifically, obliged Walmart to concede to unionization in 2006 and collective bargaining in 2008? On what basis might the union make gains in collective bargaining in the future? Any concessions by Walmart cannot be attributed to the independent power of China's trade union, which had weak links to the Walmart workforce and little experience. Instead, Chinese labor laws have become the fulcrum around which industrial relations revolve. All parties have used the laws to argue their positions. Walmart used the Chinese trade union law to refuse to let the ACFTU set up unions; and the ACFTU in turn used the procedures stated in the law to obtain employee signatures and set up union branches. The initial organizing of Walmart and, later, the collective contracts depended on clauses in the Chinese labor laws and the power of the Chinese state to enforce these.

In some respects this is in line with the situation in the United States vis-à-vis Walmart. Governments and legislation have become the only actors powerful enough to confront and dictate terms to the largest corporate entity in the world. Thus far, despite concerted efforts by American trade unions to organize Walmart employees, not a single trade union branch has been set up in the United States. On the other hand, several state and city governments in the United States, employing legislation and administrative powers, have acted to rein in the giant and to make it pay a higher minimum wage and contribute to medical care and pension funds. National labor laws in China are, in a number of aspects, stronger than in the United States, and reformers in the Chinese trade union federation, when they gain the capacity to act, can turn to the labor laws to oblige Walmart to come to the table. The question is whether, in the years to come, union reformers can muster sufficient power within the ACFTU to take charge of negotiations with Walmart over collective contracts, and whether, once there, they know how to play their hand. The next round of contract negotiations will be a test of this.

10 DID UNIONIZATION MAKE A DIFFERENCE?

Work Conditions and Trade Union Activities at Chinese Walmart Stores

Jonathan Unger, Diana Beaumont, and Anita Chan

In the wake of the unionization campaign described in the previous chapter, have the new union branches taken any form of action to improve working conditions at Walmart stores?

To address this question we sought out the help of an indigenous labor NGO (nongovernmental organization) in Shenzhen City, which sent researchers to three of the twelve Walmart superstores in the city to interview blue-collar employees. We also separately engaged the services of several researchers from the Beijing municipal union federation, who conducted interviews on our behalf with union branch committee members and junior managerial staff at all three Walmart stores in Beijing, as well as with relevant Beijing union officials. While information was sought in both cities regarding work conditions at the stores and the union branches' functions, the differences in the types of interviewees meant that the interviews in Shenzhen provided considerably more information about ordinary employees' work conditions and their knowledge of the union, while the interviews in Beijing revealed more about the formation and internal operations of the Walmart stores' branch unions.

WORK CONDITIONS AND UNION BRANCHES AT THREE STORES IN SHENZHEN

To appraise the situation in this large south China city where Walmart's China operations are headquartered, researchers from the labor NGO carried out investigations on our behalf between November 2006 and May

2007. In June 2008 they again visited two of the three stores to find out whether there had been new developments, and again visited one of the stores in July 2009. In between, they telephoned several of the employees periodically to elicit the latest news.

The stores are named after the districts in Shenzhen City where they are located—Xixiang Walmart, Buji Walmart, and Shekou Walmart. Xixiang Walmart and Buji Walmart are huge stores in the rapidly developing industrialized outer districts of the metropolis, in what is known as the Shenzhen Outer Zone. Shekou Walmart is in an exclusive suburb in the western part of the city, with leafy streets, expensive real estate, and a Western expatriate ghetto.

Shekou Walmart is financially the most important for Walmart. Business there is among the best of any Walmart store in China. It employs about 600 staff, including approximately 300 full-timers (60 of whom are part of the managerial staff), 150 part-timers, and 150 casual staff. At Xixiang Walmart there are approximately 500 staff, of whom 300 are full time, and the Buji store's numbers are similar.

During 2006 and 2007 the researchers went twenty times to the Buji and Shekou Walmart stores and four times to the Xixiang store. All interviews were conducted with shop-floor workers without the knowledge or permission of Walmart management or the trade union, and were carried out mostly outside the stores. The researchers found that these workers were generally quite hesitant to talk about any concrete details of their work or the union because they had been warned by management that they were not to release any information, especially about their wages, to outsiders and co-workers. Their wage slips are sealed and stamped "Confidential." Despite this, the researchers were able to find out enough information about wages and work conditions to piece together a picture.

The researchers gained information by seeking out acquaintances employed in the store and chatting with them and their co-workers. Sometimes they also posed as shoppers or inquisitive members of the public, and chatted with Walmart staff at restaurants, parks, and other public places after the workers finished work. At the Buji store, one of the researchers had an existing friendship with a woman working there, who provided a particularly detailed account of her experience with the union.

In June 2008, follow-up research was conducted at the Buji and Shekou stores on how the union branches were faring.

Working conditions at Walmart generally adhere to occupational safety and health regulations and other relevant regulations that apply to daily

Table 10.1
Number of full-time employees, part-time/casual employees, and brand marketing representatives
interviewed between August 2006 and June 2007

Store name	Number of interviewees	Number of full-time employees	Number of part-time/ casual employees	Number of brand marketing representatives
Xixiang	8	4	3	1
Buji	4	3	1	—
Shekou	16	9	·7	—
Total	28	16	11	1

work conditions. As one of the Chinese researchers remarked to us, "Walmart doesn't mind cheating workers, but doesn't dare cheat the government" in terms of material conditions at the stores. Walmart also pays workers on time, which is much welcomed by the stores' employees. Many of them are migrants from the countryside, and in previous jobs they often encountered serious problems of delayed payments and owed wages. Like all big companies, to low-paid workers Walmart symbolizes security, as they are aware of their vulnerability in the labor market.

The overwhelming problem facing Walmart employees was the low salary, and many of the interviewees complained about this. Shenzhen city is divided into an Inner and Outer Zone with different officially set minimum wages. As stipulated by national law, the minimum legal wages are calculated by the local government in keeping with the local cost of living. In the Shenzhen Inner Zone (which is mainly commercial) the legal minimum wage was 810 yuan (US$110) per month between June 2006 and June 2007, while in the Shenzhen Outer Zone (which is mainly industrial) the minimum legal wage was 690 yuan per month.[1] Walmart's full-time shop-floor employees in Shekou, located in the Inner Zone, received a base wage of 750 yuan, plus a 400 yuan housing subsidy and a 200 yuan bonus for good performance. Shop-floor employees in the Xixiang and Buji Walmart stores, which are located in the Outer Zone, were paid a base wage of 550 yuan a month, with the same 400 yuan housing subsidy and 200 yuan bonus. Walmart's pay structure was in fact illegal, because article 13 of the Shenzhen Regulation on Employee Wages stipulates that workers' base wage must be equal to or more than the legal minimum wage, independent of any additional bonuses or subsidies. The Walmart base wages of 750 yuan and 550 yuan per month are both lower than the official minimum wage, by 160 yuan and 140 yuan respectively.

The housing subsidy is not paid to store employees in cities with a considerably lower cost of living. Why is it paid in the form of a "housing subsidy" in Shenzhen, rather than simply paying the Shenzhen employees an additional 400 yuan in their wages? Making rents affordable for employees from out of town is not in fact the real purpose—interviews at Walmart's stores in Beijing reveal that employees who are locals living free-of-charge in their family homes and employees who are outsiders renting rooms in Beijing all equally receive the same "housing subsidy." Why then, in both Beijing and Shenzhen, does Walmart pay an illegally low base wage and then provide this extra money as a subsidy? In these two cities, paying employees this way appears to be a deliberate effort to avoid paying the full employer's contribution to the employees' social security premium, which is calculated as a percentage of the worker's wage. Thus Walmart gets away with only paying about half the legally required social security premium.

From Walmart's perspective, there are also other good reasons to manipulate the wage package by allocating close to half as a subsidy and bonus. First, since the subsidy and bonus are fringe benefits, Walmart does not violate the labor law in not adjusting them each year to catch up with inflation. Thus, when the official minimum wage in Shenzhen goes up every year, Walmart often adjusts only the base wage. Here is what the wage package of a full-time Walmart worker at the Buji store looked like in the years 2006–8.

In short, as seen in table 10.2, only 50 percent of the wage package in 2006 was being indexed for upward adjustment. The result was clear—a worker's wage package at the Buji store rose between 2006 and 2008 at only half the percentage rise of the legal minimum wage.

The Buji store was not unusual. Across China, the wages of workers at Walmart stores failed to keep pace with rises in the legal minimum wage. As shown in table 10.3, in five of the six other cities for which we have obtained

Table 10.2
Declining real value of workers' wage packages, Buji Walmart Store, Outer Shenzhen 2006–08 (yuan per month)

Year	Legal minimum wage	Base wage	Housing subsidy	Bonus	Wage package
2006	700	600	400	200	1200
2007	750	675	400	200	1275
2008	900	775	400	200	1375
Percent change, 2006–08	28.6				14.6

Table 10.3
Legal minimum wages and Walmart store wages in six Chinese cities, 2006–08 (yuan per month)

City	Legal minimum wage				Walmart's base wage				Housing subsidies			Bonus			Wage package			
	2006	2007	2008	Change (%)[a]	2006	2007	2008	Change (%)[a]	2006	2007	2008	2006	2007	2008	2006	2007	2008	Change (%)[a]
Nanchang	360	510	580	61.1	500	600	675	35.0	0	0	0	200	200	200	700	800	875	25.0
Quanzhou	600	650	760	26.7	700	765	855	22.1	0	0	0	200	200	200	900	965	1055	17.2
Nanjing	690	750	850	23.2	700	800	875	25	0	0	0	200	200	200	900	1000	1075	19.4
Daqing	390	620	680	74.4	850	900	975	14.7	0	0	0	200	200	200	1050	1100	1175	11.9
Wuxi	690	750	850	23.2	750	810	875	16.7	0	0	0	200	200	200	950	1010	1075	13.2
Luoyang	400	510	550	7.8	Not yet opened	560	645	15.2	N/A	0	0	N/A	200	200	N/A	760	845	11.2

Source: These data were collected on our behalf by a former Walmart store employee in March 2009, largely through e-mails from current employees who had access to store records. The local government data about minimum legal wages were acquired through the Internet.

[a] The minimum wage and wage percent change in Luoyang are for the single year between 2007 and 2008, whereas the percent change for other five cities cover the two years from 2006 to 2008.

information, the percentages by which the wage packages of Walmart employees increased were far outpaced by the percentage increase in the local legal minimum wage.

Even including the bonus and subsidy, Walmart employees' overall wage package was low by Shenzhen city's standards—not just because Walmart avoids keeping abreast of inflation but also because Walmart's working hours are short, since employees are not given any overtime work. Walmart's practice of not providing overtime is a big problem for its employees, who have difficulty making ends meet in a region where it is normal for assembly-line workers and service-industry employees to rely on overtime for about 30 to 40 percent of their wage package. Walmart avoids paying the legally required higher pay rates for overtime work, which are 1.5 times the normal hourly rate for weekdays and twice the normal hourly rate on weekends. If a Walmart worker has to work overtime, he or she either is told to "volunteer" to do the work for free (we will return to this later) or is given time off in lieu of overtime pay.

Another method that Walmart uses to cut back on the wage bill is to employ a large percentage of its workforce as part-time or casual staff, who receive lower pay and no subsidies. They work an average of four to six hours per day, six or more days a week. They are rostered during busy times, and their work schedule may change from day to day. A part-time female employee at the Buji store complained that she worked four hours a day, thirty days a month. For this she was paid 5.5 yuan per hour, which amounts to only 500–600 yuan take-home pay each month, even though she had only one full day of rest. She received one free meal each day. To make ends meet, she took up several part-time jobs and found that she rarely had any free time. At some stores, a new nonskilled employee like her has to work on a casual or part-time basis for a year before getting a chance to sit for an exam for promotion to full-time status.

Walmart imposes very detailed rules and disciplinary procedures, and closely monitors workers' compliance. Workers interviewed at both the Buji and Shekou stores complained that they work under enormous pressure. In this environment, many workers are focused on working hard and winning a promotion: for full-time staff, a promotion to low-level management; for part-timers and casuals, a chance to become a full-time Walmart employee. Many of these workers do not want to jeopardize their prospects by making a fuss about their own situation.

Several companies rent retail space from Walmart to sell their products in the Walmart stores, and they employ their own staff, who receive considerably higher salaries than do Walmart's employees. A salesperson for one of these companies at the Xixiang store claimed that she was making two thousand yuan per month, as well as ten thousand yuan in commissions per year. In the Buji store, another said that she earned up to ten thousand yuan per month! Though they work in close proximity to the Walmart workers on the shop floor, their take-home pay is far higher.

According to an interviewee, if an employee from a Walmart store in the Outer Zone is transferred to the Inner Zone, his or her wage does not increase in line with the latter's higher wage scale. This is clearly illegal, since it violates the minimum legal wage in the Inner Zone. It also makes it virtually impossible for these employees to meet the higher cost of living in the inner districts. At the same time, employees who had been transferred from the Inner to the Outer Zone claimed that they had seen their pay reduced.

Walmart might seem attractive to low-skilled workers looking for a service industry job, as the company presents a sophisticated face and is known as the world's largest corporation. However, the turnover rate of shop-floor employees is very high, suggesting employee dissatisfaction.

TRADE UNION BRANCHES

Has the arrival of trade union branches in these stores helped the staff in any way? The Xixiang and Buji Walmart unions were established covertly on August 4 and 8, 2006.[2] Xixiang was the second store in Shenzhen and the fourth in the whole of China to have a union branch. The Shekou store did not gain a union branch until early September, after the national memorandum had been signed on August 16, 2006. The previous chapter suggested that the memorandum was a critical watershed in how branches got organized, so we might expect the Xixiang and Buji trade unions to be different today from the branch at Shekou.

The Xixiang Walmart union branch was established as a result of secretive organizing, and the inaugural ceremony was held covertly at 1:00 a.m. with the support of the local and district trade union organizations. The elected chair was the twenty-four-year-old head of the store's electrical appliances department.

Three months afterward, in October 2006, one of the Chinese NGO staff members who conducted research for this chapter saw a female employee entering the home appliances department with several trade union recruitment forms. The employee gave these to several of the staff there, saying, "Fill them in. Our wages are really too low. We need the help of the union." Four workers filled in the forms. The researcher pretended that he was a curious customer and approached one of the workers who was filling in the form:

Q: Union? What's a union?
A: You don't even know what a union is?
Q: No.
A: Let me tell you. A union helps workers to defend their rights. It's a voluntary workers' organization.
Q: Oh, so you're filling in the form to join the union. Is it that everyone has to join?
A: No, not everyone. It's voluntary. If you want to join, you fill in the form.
Q: Are there membership fees then?
A: No need.
Q: Why is it only the guys who are filling in the form? How about the women?
A: Oh, women don't dare to. It's because they want to advance their careers. In any case we have no chance for a promotion.
Q: How many union members are there now?
A: I heard that there are more than a hundred.
Another worker joined the conversation:
A2: What's the function of the union? Well, if you come across bosses who don't pay you your wages, you can lodge a complaint.
Q: Do you have to go to trade union meetings?
A2: I'm not sure. But the union can organize the workers to go on an outing, or organize some entertainment activities during festivals, or hand out some goodies and benefits. If your factory doesn't have a union, you can go and apply to set one up. Then you might become the trade union chair. The employer will give the union an amount equal to two percent of the store's wages for union expenses. If the union has 200 workers or more, you can become a full-time union cadre.
A: Then where is this union money?
A2: With Huang Guoliang, the chairman. When the union needs money to do things or organize activities, he uses that money.
Q: Do you know how the union really works?

None of the workers present said they knew how the union operated.

In short, three months after the union was formally set up, the membership recruitment drive was still going on, and the union activist who was doing the recruiting appears to have seriously believed that the union would help to secure higher wages. Some workers thus had some knowledge about the trade union, but it is noteworthy that Chinese workers, unlike American workers, expect a union to organize social activities and give away festival gifts, much as Chinese trade union branches have done in state enterprises during and since the Maoist era.

Events at the Shekou store, where the union branch was established some three weeks after the memorandum was signed, unfolded quite differently. A staff meeting was called where one of the store managers announced that a trade union branch had already been created a week earlier. Employees were told that, if they wanted to join, they should speak to the store manager. Our researcher in January 2007 was able to talk to a few workers outside the store. Two of them were trade union members. According to the researcher's report:

> This Walmart trade union is an empty shell. The person who's really in charge of the union is the store's general manager. It seems the way this union works is different from the way unions work in our home town. [This researcher had once worked as a production-line worker in a state enterprise in Hubei Province]. Our unions back home have an elected trade union chair, a deputy chair, and several other executive committee members. But here the Walmart manager told the employees that the trade union branch's staff actually is located at the Walmart headquarters for China and that the branch chairperson is also over there. That means no one actually knows who the trade union chair is.

A full-time female worker said that she knew nothing about the union, and became a member only because her supervisor signed her up. Seven out of sixteen interviewees were union members, but only three of them had "actively" signed up. Two full-time workers who had not signed up thought that the only people interested in the union would be those who want to impress their managers and get a promotion. Another employee—a woman who was a low-level manager—described the union as "hollow": "What does this union do? It has nothing to do with us. After the union was set up, no one any longer mentions it, and there have been no meetings."

Despite the early enthusiasm at the Xixiang store, as of 2007–8 interviewees there and at the other two stores knew of almost no union activities. At Buji, during the mid-autumn festival in October 2006 the union gave each worker a box of small festival cakes. Buji was also the only store where interviewees could recall any instance of the union taking action on workplace problems. In 2006, the union had negotiated with the company to secure ten thousand yuan as workplace injury compensation for two workers who were beaten up by a customer. Walmart had initially refused to class the incident as a case of occupational injury.

At the Xixiang store, on May Day 2007 the union organized a basketball match and an outing to another Shenzhen district. The Shekou store similarly had an outing on May Day. However, these activities had also taken place before the union was established. At both stores the so-called union outing was still open to all employees, including part-timers, casuals, and the in-store marketing staff employed by vendor companies, all of whom are excluded from joining the union. The only difference now is that union members are not charged a tiny fee to take part.

This appears to be a well-thought-out policy on Walmart's part. The outings were listed as union activities but the participants knew that the company was responsible. By sidelining the trade union as the *actual* organizer of these traditional Chinese trade union activities, Walmart deprived the new trade union branches of the only credit they could claim for doing something for the workers. Handing out small gifts at festival times or organizing an outing may be the most innocuous of activities, but in the Chinese context these acts help employees to identify with the union, especially among low-paid workers who have almost no chance of spending a day out at a scenic spot and who do care about a box of festival cakes. Such workers, mostly migrants, envy state enterprise workers who bring home all kinds of gifts distributed by their unions during festivals. Walmart management well understands the potential significance of these benefits in the eyes of the workers and tries to deprive the union of this traditional function.

Of the three trade union branches, Xixiang's is the only one that deducts 5 yuan from union members' pay package every month. This is the union that, after having emerged secretly, continued to try to recruit members in the hope of strengthening itself. At the other two stores, interviewees who were union members expressed surprise at the fact no union fees were deducted or collected. We believe this could be another one of Walmart's ploys to try to downplay the presence of the trade union, or indeed to expunge the idea of trade unionism among its workers: when there are no union fees, there are no expectations of union activity. This explains why many of the interviewed workers tended to be confused about whether there even was a union branch at their store. One worker interviewed at the Buji store in July 2008, almost two years after a union branch was established there, observed that "with or without a union, it makes no difference." Even though interviewees were highly dissatisfied with their low wages, they had virtually no expectations of the union. Even the union branch that had been set up secretly at the Xixiang store in a democratic election no longer attempted to represent workers or to stand up to Walmart.

THE UNION BRANCHES AT THREE BEIJING SUPERSTORES

We have secured a thick pile of interview transcripts conducted on our behalf by several researchers associated with the Beijing Municipal Federation of Trade Unions in mid-2007 at three Beijing Walmart stores. Taped interviews were carried out with twenty-seven store employees at the Xuanwumen, Zhichun Road, and Jianguo Road superstores. At two of the stores, interviewees included the store's union branch head, and in all three stores a member of the union branch committee as well.

All of the interviews at the Walmart stores were prearranged through official channels. One consequence was that every one of the store employees who were interviewed had been selected by Walmart management. All but six of these twenty-seven interviewees held a junior or middle-level managerial post, usually as the supervisor of a section of the store or as a member of the store's human resources department. As would be expected, given that they were selected by Walmart, all but one felt positively about Walmart as an employer.

All of the twenty-one junior and middle-level Walmart managerial staff members—including the union branch heads and branch committee members—were young. The eldest was thirty-three, and most were in their mid-twenties. These Walmart stores had been recently established, and Walmart preferred to recruit its supervisory staff within a few years of their entry to the job market. Most were recent graduates of lesser-known provincial universities, where most often they had majored in management studies. Most were relatively new to Beijing. They were happy to be employed at an internationally significant company like Walmart. They had faith in the company's goodwill and looked forward to shaping their

Table 10.4
Interviewees' status at each of the three Beijing stores

Store name	Total number of interviewees	Number of junior/mid-level managers	Number of union members	Union head interviewed?	Number of other union committee members
Jianguo Road	7	7	4	Yes	1
Xuanwumen	15	11	10	Yes	1
Zhichun Road	5	3	2	No	1

careers there. They saw themselves very much as part of the Walmart management team. This was true of all of the union branch heads and committee members who were interviewed.

The researchers in Beijing also sought out officials from the urban trade union who had played a part in the establishment of the Walmart union branches. The trade-union structure is in line with Beijing's administrative divisions. The city is divided into eight large districts (*qu*), each containing about 2 million people, and each district is in turn divided into subdistricts (*jiedao*) containing approximately 100,000 residents. The researchers were able to secure interviews with the heads of the trade union federation in two of the large city districts that contain Walmart stores, as well as with the leading union official at each of the three city subdistricts in which the three Walmart stores are located.

The Selection of Union Branch Committees

Beijing was not among the areas which had sought to organize Walmart stores prior to the memorandum in August 2006 between Walmart and the national union federation. Nevertheless, during the following weeks the mission to establish union branches at the Beijing Walmart stores was regarded as so important, recalls the union head of one of Beijing's subdistricts, that three task forces were formed by the city-level union, one for each of the three stores, to push through the program. The chair of the Beijing city-level union came to hold strategy meetings every day with the district and subdistrict union leadership.

In these strategy meetings they anticipated that they would encounter resistance from store management. How should they go about reaching out to store employees? How could they get hold of the employee name lists? In the end, though, they fell back on the well-tested method of requesting an exploratory meeting with the store managers. The union head of the subdistrict containing the Xuanwumen store recalls that a meeting was granted, but a mere deputy store manager received the subdistrict union head, and told her that Walmart's China headquarters had instructed the store managers to be supportive and to help the union to set up branches. Thereafter, the union head communicated with the store's human resources department, rather than with the managers.

It might have been expected that in the weeks that followed, the union officials at the district and subdistrict levels would have followed the wishes of the city-level union federation, but that was not what occurred. The head of the union of another of the subdistricts noted proudly, "Each trade-union district has some independence." The lower levels of the union tended to be more pro-company than the city union federation, and they simply followed their own preferences in deciding what steps to take. The deputy head of the Haidian District Trade Union, where the Zhichun Walmart superstore is located, recalls:

> The city-level trade-union federation and the district trade union were in conflict.... The city-level union prepared application forms, and wanted to have the staff vote as though it was secret. We [the district-level trade union] felt it was necessary to cooperate with Walmart and seek its support. We wanted to be more accommodating to Walmart. We felt that we didn't need to act like an underground union.... We felt that in establishing union branches we ought to ... discuss and come to a consensus with the leadership of the store, and have mutual empathy, mutual support.... In establishing the store's union branch we [in the district level union] were able to coordinate and cooperate with the Walmart store's human resources department, and smoothly talked through it step by step. The city union put up posters soliciting candidates [for the store's union branch committee], but we disagreed. We wanted it all done within the store, and to let the store arrange which employees we spoke to. We let the store's human resources department choose the nominees, and we were in accord with the store management as to who among these nominees should be the union branch's chair.

The head of the trade union of the large Xuanwu District noted that his district union went a step further. The city-level trade union had provided awards of 100,000 yuan to each of the three trade-union districts that contained Walmart stores, but in his own district, his union office kept half of this amount, and passed on the other half to the Walmart management as a "start-up fund" (*qidong zijin*) for the company to use when it supervised the union branch's establishment.

The head of the union subdistrict containing the Xuanwumen store claimed that she played at least some role in selecting the nominees for the store's union branch committee. But the district and subdistrict union officials who oversaw the other two stores admitted frankly that they had simply handed all of the decisions on the composition of the union branch committees to the Walmart stores' management. Why did they do so? For one, their own concept of a union branch is that it should serve as a welfare arm of management in providing leisure-time activities for employees and charity to employee hardship cases. For another, the district and subdistrict unions come partly under the jurisdiction of the district and subdistrict government administrations, most of which were in awe of a large corporation like Walmart and were pleased to have a superstore in their territory. A substantial number of union officials at these levels had made their careers in these local governments, not in the trade union structure, and they were sensitive to the local government's wishes. Third, the local levels of the union were understaffed, and therefore preferred to relinquish to Walmart much of the work involved in setting up the branches. For instance, the union officer in charge of the subdistrict level of the union that was supposed to oversee the Xuanwumen superstore noted that her office has seven staff members, but six of these are there only part-time, and this is not their main job. She is the only full-time staff member. Until assigned to head the union subdistrict office, she had served in various other offices of the same city subdistrict government. Her subdistrict contains sixty full-scale enterprises, of which the Xuanwumen Walmart is the biggest. The Walmart superstore, she added, is quite important to the subdistrict government.

Despite having let the stores' human resources departments take over the lion's share of the responsibility for setting up the union branches, various levels of the union organization punctiliously went through the motions of introducing the union to employees through recruitment meetings, and subsequently held formal elections for the union committee as specified in union regulations. At the recruitment mobilization meeting held in the Jianguo Road store's employee canteen, the store management was in charge of keeping order and handing out union materials and application forms, and the store's general manager was the main speaker. However, at the other two Walmart stores the speeches at the recruitment meeting were presented by union leaders from the city level, and some of these introduced the union as safeguarding the workers vis-à-vis management. A member of the audience at the Xuanwumen store recalls, "We were told that the union protects the staff's interests and that the union will help defend their rights if these are violated—for example, if they don't get their wages." One participant recalled that at the Zhichun Road store, "We were told the union will provide funding and organize outings, and I understood the union is the workers' organization, and that if you join the union you can go to it, that if you encounter trouble you could seek it out. The union would resolve it, the union would speak for you." (She did not join, saying she was too busy.) Another member of the audience remembers that the speakers "said the union would enable employees to speak up." At the Xuanwumen store, two recruitment meetings were organized, one for each work shift. The head of the subdistrict union recalls,

We distributed union membership application forms and asked those who wanted to join to fill them in right there. We even circulated a piece of paper asking the employees to write down their names and mobile telephone numbers. The moment the store's human resources department saw this, they took away the list from us. Then they themselves made out an attendance list for us, and so we were not able to have a grasp of the situation.

The perception of the union presented by the city-level union speakers at the Xuanwu and Zhichun Road stores, that the union branch would defend employees, was nullified in the weeks that followed. As has been noted, the district and subdistrict levels of the trade union simply let the human resources departments at two of the stores entirely determine the nominees in the elections for the union branch committees.

The subsequent committee elections were merely a matter of eliminating a few of the human resources departments' choices. At the election meeting at the Jianguo Road store, the employees who had signed up to join the union were provided with a ballot sheet of eight preselected nominees, every one of them a middle-level manager, of whom seven were to be elected. The "election" consisted merely of a chance to eliminate one of the nominees. At the Zhichun Road store, seven union committee members were elected out of a list of ten nominees selected by the store's human resources department. This process of eliminating a few candidates from a preselected list has been standard election procedure in China from the days of Mao onward.

The Branch Committees' Operations

The new branch heads and union committee members had little idea of what they were supposed to do. The union branch head at the Jianguo Road store says that her training in trade-union work after her appointment was in Walmart's hands, and that it entirely concerned "Walmart's enterprise culture" and company policies. At the Zhichun Road store, the new branch committee participated in a single training session organized by the district union. At the Xuanwumen store, no training session of any kind was held.

In interviews, branch heads and committee members said that a lack of knowledge hampered their work. A couple of them noted that their conception of a union was based on their parents' employment at a state enterprise. One recalled that the trade union had given her parents small gifts at Chinese New Year; the other observed that "a union sometimes organizes things that are fun," and she foresaw the union branch "helping out employees facing emergencies through gifts of money, carrying out social activities, and giving little gifts to members." Neither the branch heads and committee members nor any other interviewee reported that their Walmart union branch had handled any case of an employee's workplace grievance. As a union member at the Zhichun Road store noted, "We'd originally been told [by speakers at the recruitment meeting] that you can go tell the union your problems, but it seems no one does so." The union branch head at the Zhichun Road store had initiated the only action of any kind that addressed a workplace problem at any of the three stores, and it was not the type of problem that normally involves a Western trade union. He was trying to obtain a secure parking place for the staff's bicycles and was talking with the subdistrict government about this.

Despite the recruitment-meeting speeches about defending workers, almost all of the interviewees perceived a union largely to be a sort of social club, and they judged its effectiveness in those terms. They thought that a union should organize occasional outings on staff members' days off, hold a party to celebrate the Chinese New Year, organize sports competitions, and the like. Interviewees who had not joined the union usually said it was because they were too busy with their work and often were too tired afterward to engage in organized social activities.

The three stores' unions were almost totally inactive even in arranging for social activities. One of the only concrete events involved the distribution by the Xuanwu subdistrict union of free movie tickets at the Xuanwumen store. At the Jianguo Road store, the branch made plans for an outing to the Great Wall, but—similar to what occurred in Shenzhen City—the company ultimately preempted the branch and itself organized an outing there. In several other cases, the Walmart store's human resources department added the union's name as a cosponsor of an activity that the company was providing, but (again like the stores in Shenzhen) all employees, union and nonunion members alike, could equally participate, and it was obvious to interviewees that these were not actually union-sponsored activities.

Union branch heads and committee members complained that a lack of funds was the major reason for the near-absence of branch-organized events. Up to mid-2007, Walmart's China headquarters had not provided the Beijing union branches with any of the 2 percent of the total wage bill stipulated by law for all unionized enterprises. For the Jianguo Road store alone, the unpaid funding already amounted to more than fifty thousand yuan. The head of the district union in the large Xuanwu District explained approvingly that the union federation needs to treat Walmart with kid gloves: "Walmart isn't the same as other foreign-invested enterprises. Walmart is a very significant transnational chain, and so we need to have a special policy in terms of it having to hand over funds." In the absence of any funds from Walmart, the Beijing-level union stepped into the breach and provided ten thousand yuan apiece to the three district unions overseeing the Walmart stores. Of this, five thousand yuan (US$720) was supposed to be handed down to each of the three stores' branch unions, but even this small amount was not forthcoming. The head of the Jianguo Road store branch reported that less than two thousand yuan had arrived from the subdistrict level of the union, and a branch committee member at the Xuanwumen store reported that no funding at all had reached his own branch.

Nor were any union membership fees (0.5 percent of a member's salary) being deducted and handed over by Walmart. Almost all of the union branch heads and committee members complained that their lack of funding stymied efforts to do anything. Walmart was obviously playing it extra safe. Despite having stacked the Beijing union branch committees with its own junior and middle-level managerial staff, Walmart was keeping the branches starved of funding and was itself still directly running the various social activities that in China are associated with unions. Walmart was quietly undermining even the low-key, entirely innocuous union branches that it itself had largely created and still controlled.

Nor have the higher levels of the union reached out directly to store employees. Even after the establishment of the branch at the Jianguo Road store, the subdistrict union never initiated any contacts with the store's staff members. It had contact only with branch committee members, and even then generally only with the branch chair, while the store union itself had very little contact with its own members. In interviews with both ordinary union and nonunion members, they all responded that they did not know who the union chair is.

The branch committee members put in relatively little effort. A committee member at the Xuanwumen store noted, "Besides the fact that there are no funds, we committee members are too busy to put in much time. My regular work has to take precedence over my union work," and the store provided no time off for the latter. At the Zhichun store, the committee of seven members met once a month, but within the first half year of its establishment three of its members had already left—one had been promoted out of the store, and two had quit Walmart. They had not been replaced.

In the absence of funding, a committee member at the Jianguo Road store said that *all* that the branch does is seek to recruit new members, and it has no other function. However, the number of members was dropping at all three stores. The Jianguo Road store had signed up ninety members at that initial mobilization meeting, but within half a year the branch was down to seventy members. The Xuanwumen store branch initially had seventy-three members, but it had now declined to fifty. The reason for this is the high employee turnover rate at Walmart stores—a committee member at the Zhichun Road store who is a department head estimated a 30 to 40 percent annual turnover rate at the store. An official in the human resources department of the same store said that many ordinary employees quit because of low salaries—which are lower in Beijing than in Shenzhen. After deductions, he said, as of mid-2007 store workers took home only about eight hundred to nine hundred yuan (US$110–$125) a month, plus any overtime pay;[3] and an official in another store's human resources department estimated the take-home pay was eight hundred yuan. The pay was so low that the Walmart stores in Beijing relied largely on migrant workers from other parts of China to fill the blue-collar jobs. A department head at the Zhichun Road store noted that only one out of the twenty-two workers in his section was from Beijing, and he noted that many of the migrant workers stay at the Walmart store only until they can find a better-paying job. The union branch committees faced the task of repeatedly informing new intakes of workers about the branch's existence.

When asked about the initial recruitment meetings, several interviewees favorably recalled the speeches of higher-level union officials about the union protecting the rights of employees. However, not one of the branch heads or branch committee members subsequently perceived this to be one of their roles, nor did the five local district and subdistrict union officials who were interviewed. In their hands, at best the union would serve as a social club, a dispenser of small gifts, and a source of charity for individual hardship cases. Only one interviewee had developed a vision that a union ought to play a proactive role on behalf of workers by helping them to raise their consciousness and by organizing them to defend their rights. A twenty-four-year-old university graduate who said he had not bothered to join the branch union confided,

> What I hope is that the union will care about employees who have real needs....The union ought to give training to the employees to improve their consciousness [*yishi*]. The employees don't have a consciousness about the laws, and don't understand government policies, etc., and we need the union to publicize these. The social security umbrella is used chaotically. The employees' rights need to be protected by the union. The employees need to be organized.

Collective Contracts

In 2008, the national government and the national union federation finally pushed forward one role for the union to play at Walmart that is commonly associated with genuine trade unions: collective bargaining. As observed in the previous chapter, the first Walmart store to sign a collective contract was in the northern city of Shenyang.[4] The third Walmart store to sign one was, coincidentally, the Buji superstore in Shenzhen that is one of this chapter's case studies. The branch union chair at Buji signed a contract with a high-level Walmart human resource manager on behalf of sixteen regional Walmart stores on July 24, 2008. Later in the afternoon a ceremony was held to formalize the collective contract, attended by officers of the Shenzhen City Federation of Trade Unions and of the union branch of the Walmart Headquarters for China that is located in Shenzhen City. It was claimed in a major official newspaper that the city trade union had previously consulted with Walmart workers, who had reportedly nominated forty-eight trade union chairs, officials, and representatives, of whom ten were allegedly elected as collective consultation representatives by secret ballot. It was reported in the newspaper that there were two rounds of bargaining. Agreement of a contract was reached on July 12, 2008, and on July 22 and 23 a Walmart trade union congress was allegedly convened to approve the contract, which covers more than eight thousand employees. It was reported in the official press that five and a half thousand employees (66 percent) voted affirmatively for a 9 percent increase in wages for the remainder of the year and into 2009. In an interview the city trade union chair told a reporter that initially the union asked for a 12 percent wage increase, but failed to achieve this.[5]

In light of our knowledge of what has transpired in union affairs since 2006 at six of the Walmart stores, including the Buji store, we hold serious doubts about the reported consultation process. Most of the employees at the superstores did not even know the identity of their own store's union chair, let alone know who were the union committee members, so how could the workers possibly nominate forty-eight trade-union representatives from the sixteen Walmart stores? And since most of the trade union chairs and committee members in these stores are management staff appointed by Walmart, how meaningful could the union congress exercise possibly be?

Nor can much credence be given to the supposed vote of approval by some fifty-five hundred Walmart employees. Workers at the Buji store told our researchers in 2008 that they were simply informed about the outcome of the collective bargaining in a thirty-minute meeting and were asked at the meeting to provide their pro forma assent, but they were not given an opportunity to read the contract draft's contents. According to a Buji store worker, management announced at the meeting that the 9 percent raise would begin in 2009, not the latter half of 2008. Although Walmart was not bothering to honor the collective contract, employees were not aware of this because the contract was not shown to them.

The contractual promise in mid-2008 of a (delayed) 9 percent increase was low, compared to raises being offered elsewhere in Guangdong. In March 2008, the Guangzhou City Labor and Social Security Council declared that the city's employees should be given a minimum increase of 12 percent for the coming year.[6] In Shenzhen itself, in the face of a rapidly rising consumer price index, the legal minimum wage was raised in July 2008 by 17.6 percent in Inner Shenzhen and by 20 percent in Outer Shenzhen, yet the inclusion in the contract of a (delayed) 9 percent increase at the Walmart Buji store that same month was hailed as a success. At the time, it appeared that Walmart's employees in Shenzhen were being short-changed.

In the event, what the signatories to the contract could not foresee was that, several months later in the autumn of 2008, the United States and Europe would be stricken by a banking-sector meltdown and ensuing recession. The export industries of Shenzhen consequently suffered deep cutbacks in purchase orders and financial losses starting in the latter part of 2008, and the Shenzhen city government responded in July 2009 by freezing the following year's legal minimum wage at the 2008 level. But Walmart, having signed a contract in Shenzhen guaranteeing a 9 percent wage rise, granted the raise in July 2009. An employee of the Buji store who was interviewed that month reported that she had just received a 150 yuan increase in her wage package, in line with the promised 9 percent raise.

Union Representation of Mid-level Store Management: A Niche Role

Walmart's retail business had expanded rapidly in China, and by April 2009 the country contained 121 supercenters, 3 Sam's Club outlets, 2 Neighborhood Markets, and 101 Trust-Mart chain stores. Walmart employment in the retail sector reached more than seventy thousand. But the company had overexpanded and was now finding its profit margin squeezed. In early 2009, plans were in progress to demote or fire ten thousand employees, including about twenty-five hundred of the stores' managerial staff. Walmart moved to force out most of the latter through a stratagem, ordering them to transfer to stores in other parts of the country. Transferring or demotion, the company told them on April 10, 2009, were their only alternatives to resignation. *China Daily* quoted a mid-level manager at one store: "The company actually wants us to leave, because few will find the first two options acceptable."[7]

As this chapter has noted, the union branch committees at the Beijing and Shenzhen stores, and elsewhere in China, were stacked by Walmart with junior and middle-level managerial staff. Other mid-level staff at the stores loyally signed up as members of the tame branch unions that had been shaped by the stores' human relations departments. As a result, they comprised much of the branches' constituency, as well as the leadership. Now, in the face of company efforts to maneuver them out of their jobs, groups of mid-level managers from the stores, their jobs threatened, approached the city-level unions for help. The director of the law department of the municipal union in Changchun, the capital of Jilin Province, told *China*

Daily, "We invited the general managers of four chain stores in the city to our office immediately and expected them to negotiate with the [junior store] executives on equal terms. We don't think it right for the company to announce such a decision without consulting the employees." It was, she said, the first time that her trade union had become involved in Walmart's internal affairs. The city union also contacted its counterparts in several other cities, including Shenzhen, and these city-level unions began operating in coordination. Walmart quickly backed down. The director of the law department of the Changchun union said that three mid-level store management staff "came to my office this morning and told me the plan was shelved and they've resumed their work." A spokesperson of the Shenzhen union spoke of his union's "positive role in helping settle the dispute."[8] The union had for the first time successfully acted like a genuine trade union—although, ironically, on behalf of managerial personnel.

In the first sentence of this chapter we asked whether the union branches at the stores have taken actions to improve work conditions, and the answer to date is very obviously "No." In this case, it was the city-level unions that acted, and that had clout. Nonetheless, despite the very discouraging experiences at the six Walmart stores in Shenzhen and Beijing, Walmart has begun to face in China what it has always dreaded elsewhere in the world: union representation. While the branch unions within the Walmart stores are in the company's pocket, Walmart has only limited influence at the city and national levels of the union federation, and there is potential at those levels for the union to take the corporation on. The remaining question is whether or not the city and national levels of the union will, in future, decide to take up the gauntlet for ordinary Walmart store workers, and not just for managerial staff. Will the national union organization take a tougher stance on wages and work conditions on behalf of store workers in the next round of collective bargaining? Will city-level unions take concerted action if store workers, rather than managerial staff, come asking for help? Only time will tell.

11 WORKERS AND COMMUNITIES VERSUS WALMART

A Comparison of Organized Resistance in the United States and China

Katie Quan

In the preceding chapters, we have seen that Walmart is driving a worldwide economic race to the bottom, and that China is a critical part of that strategy. The authors have demonstrated that the effect of "Everyday Low Prices" in China is to drive sweatshop labor down to ever lower levels, control supply chain logistics using new technology, and replicate retail management policies in a tightly regimented culture.

While some regard Walmart as the "template" for corporate success, others see it as the "poster child" for unethical, unbridled capitalism. In New Dehli in February 2007, demonstrators burned "Walmart" in effigy in front of the Indian Parliament, as legislators debated the elimination of protections for small retailers from foreign competition.[1] In 2006, a British union called for a general strike against Asda Walmart for refusing to bargain in good faith with union workers in its stores and distribution centers.[2] And in the United States in the past decade, unions and community organizations have mounted dozens of grassroots campaigns to stop Walmart from locating in their communities and forcing wages down or small businesses to close. Campaigns like these seek to limit Walmart's ability to impose its race to the bottom agenda and have become part of a growing citizens' movement for corporate ethics, social responsibility, and decent standards.

However in China, reception to Walmart has been mixed, depending on who you are and how you see your long- and short-term interests. Workers face abusive labor practices (as documented by Pun and Yu in chapter 3 and Chan and Siu in chapter 4) and suppliers deal with relentless pressure to lower their prices (see chapter 2), yet the Chinese government continues to encourage businesses like Walmart to expand in China. The All-China

Federation of Trade Unions (ACFTU) was originally blocked from Walmart, but after a national campaign involving clandestine and confrontational organizing, it now seeks a harmonious relationship with the retailer.[3] Even disgruntled individuals like Edward and Li Shan who quit Walmart management because they disliked the corporate culture still regard themselves as "Walmart people" (see chapters 5 and 7).

In this context there is growing evidence of organized resistance to Walmart in China. This is particularly true in the field of labor rights, where the ACFTU has successfully challenged Walmart's antiunion policies, but where the question of what quality of union will take hold is being watched with much interest (as explored by Chan in chapter 9). As we shall see from additional information provided in this chapter, there is also news of unrest in Walmart's supply chain factories, where some workers have organized to strike and form unions. This growing collective agency bears careful examination, because if Chinese workers succeed in pushing back against Walmart's race to the bottom, this could change power dynamics throughout its global supply chain.

This chapter will provide an overview of labor struggles against Walmart in both the United States and China, compare their characteristics, and provide suggestions for strategic linkages. My information comes from field observation of Walmart's manufacturing and retail practices in China and the United States, as well as secondary materials available in hardcopy and online. My analytical framework is influenced by previous experience as a garment worker, labor organizer, and participant in the global antisweatshop movement.

WALMART ORGANIZING IN THE UNITED STATES

In the United States, for nearly two decades a loose network of labor and community groups has been pushing back against Walmart's corporate agenda. Unions have attempted to organize workers in Walmart stores, while others have demanded that Walmart be environmentally responsible, or have blocked Walmart from locating in their communities unless it adopts fair business practices and existing community living standards. In many instances, labor and community groups have worked together in coalitions to bring maximum pressure against Walmart. Today polls show that an increasing number of Americans have a negative view of Walmart.[4]

Although most of these organizing efforts have been initiated by citizens groups, their efforts have been greatly helped by "organizing hubs" that have sprung up in the past decade to centralize and disseminate information about various struggles through websites, use e-mail to alert thousands about the latest Walmart misdeeds, provide curriculum for students and toolkits for organizers, and sponsor other programs and research. Key among these is Walmart Watch,[5] a group founded by the Service Employees International Union (SEIU), and Wake-up Walmart, a similar group founded by the United Food and Commercial Workers Union (UFCW).[6] These hubs have effectively brought together local activists with no previous relationship to each other, elevated the visibility of small efforts that would otherwise have gone unnoticed, and become a useful information portal for researchers and policymakers.

A full discussion of all types of organizing efforts against Walmart is beyond the limits of this chapter. Therefore I will focus only on labor and community organizing, because these two arenas represent the most visible collective resistance to Walmart in the United States

Labor

In the United States, one of the most important critiques against Walmart has been about its low wages and substandard working conditions. A 2004 report by the Democratic staff of the U.S. House Committee on Education and Labor (the Miller Report) found that Walmart's wages were between US$8 and $10 per hour and health care insurance cost workers two-thirds of the premium. Because of this high cost of health care relative to wages, less than half of Walmart's workforce was insured by the company's health plan. The total compensation package to Walmart workers was 20 percent lower than other workers in the retail industry.[7] Later as a result of negative publicity, Walmart was forced to improve health benefits to its full-time workers.[8]

Not only are Walmart workers compensated below industry standard, they face numerous other violations of labor law. In 2005, the U.S. Department of Labor found twenty-four counts of child labor at Walmart, where children were operating hazardous chainsaws and cardboard balers. While shocking, this was actually better than the 1,371 findings of child labor in 128 Walmart stores in 2004, and 1,436 findings of child labor in 20 stores in 2000.[9] As for women workers, in February 2007 a federal court affirmed certification of a group of California women who filed a class-action lawsuit covering 2 million past and present female Walmart employees. Their suit alleges that Walmart engaged in sex discrimination in pay and promotion, and it retaliated against the women for complaining. Still working its way through the court system, this is the largest employment discrimination lawsuit in U.S. history.[10]

Such reliance on low-skilled jobs that pay low wages and benefits to gain higher profits is known among American economists as a "low-road" business strategy. It contrasts with a "high-road" strategy that mobilizes resources and upgrades labor skills for a high-quality, high-productivity, and highly paid workforce.[11] American unions are proponents of high-road strategies because it has been shown that they lead to a large middle class and a thriving business climate.[12] This framework helps to provide a policy rationale for improving the conditions of working people in low-income communities.

Many workers in the United States have attempted to form unions to improve their conditions, but Walmart is staunchly antiunion, a fact that it claims with pride.[13] When managers hear of workers wanting to unionize, they have been instructed to refer to the company's toolkit on how to fight unions and count on the company to mobilize extensive resources to obstruct unionization.[14] According to the Miller Report, "Walmart's labor law violations range from illegally firing workers who attempt to organize a union to unlawful surveillance, threats, and intimidation of employees who dare to speak out."[15] A 2004 International Confederation of Free Trade Union report to the World Trade Organization reported at least sixty complaints filed against Walmart at the National Labor Relations Board since 1995,[16] and a 2007 Human Rights Watch report unequivocally concluded: "Walmart has translated its hostility towards union formation into an unabashed, sophisticated, and aggressive strategy to derail worker organizing at its US stores that violates workers' internationally recognized right to freedom of association."[17]

Not only do Walmart's low-road practices affect its employees, but they cause a downward drag on the wages of workers in the surrounding region. A University of California, Berkeley, report found that when Walmart enters a job market, wages and health benefits go down.[18] Other studies have shown that Walmart's presence has reduced employment and earnings for retail workers,[19] and may have fewer community benefits than Walmart claims after all impacts are considered.[20]

An example of this downward pull on wages is the 2004 southern California grocery strike. In 2000 wages and benefits averaged US$18.25 per hour, and unionized grocery store workers enjoyed a middle-class standard of living. However at that time Walmart began to open supercenters to compete in the retail grocery market by selling food products in addition to its traditional stock of dry goods, and paying half the wages and few of the benefits of unionized workers.[21] At the bargaining table in 2001, union grocery owners pleaded to the union that they needed deep wage and benefit reductions concessions in order to compete with Walmart, and the union conceded.[22] Three years later at the bargaining table, the employers demanded further concessions, but southern California union members decided to draw the line and voted to strike.[23] After a two-month union strike and employer lockout, a settlement was reached that established a lower wage tier for new employees and greatly reduced health benefits.[24] Now only 66 percent of the workforce was eligible for health coverage, down from nearly 100 percent. Three years later in 2006, this change in eligibility rules, along with a turnover rate that increased from 19 percent to an unprecedented 32 percent, contributed to a precipitous drop in health care coverage among unionized retail grocery employees from 94 percent to 54 percent.[25] Though negotiations in 2007 restored some eligibility for benefits and eliminated the two-tier wage system, half of the workforce was now in the lower tier and much damage had already been done to lower working standards.[26] Working conditions were now well on the way toward converging with Walmart's low standards.

Community Coalitions

In addition to declining labor conditions, many American communities have become concerned that Walmart's business practices also lower living standards and lead to taxpayers subsidizing Walmart. Studies have shown that "big box" retail stores (where goods formerly found in separate stores are now for sale under one roof) push small and medium-sized stores out of business and do not generate as much revenue as locally owned businesses.[27] A 2005 report by the University of California, Berkeley, Center for Labor Research and Education found that Walmart paid wages so low that many employees qualified for public assistance, costing California taxpayers US$86 million per year.[28] The Miller Report concluded, "While charging low prices obviously has some consumer benefits, mounting evidence from across the country indicates that these benefits come at a steep price for American workers, U.S. labor laws, and community living standards."[29]

Resistance to this lowering of living standards comes in many forms,[30] but some of the most contentious are "site fights." In these campaigns, citizen groups attempt to block Walmart from locating in a community unless Walmart negotiates community benefits agreements (CBAs) that establish terms for building and operating Walmart stores. The aim is to protect local businesses and the local tax structure, preserve environmental and health standards, or otherwise ensure that local living standards are not compromised by Walmart's setting up shop in the community.

An example of a site fight can be found in Inglewood, California, where Walmart attempted to locate in 2003. Walmart appealed to the community on the basis of job creation, which initially resonated with the largely African American community where the unemployment rate was high and the poverty rate was 22.5 percent. Inglewood's African American mayor supported Walmart, as did prominent black leaders like John Mack of the Urban League who said, "I'd rather have a person on somebody's payroll, even if it isn't at the highest wage, than on the unemployment roll."[31] However on the other side, a large coalition of unions and community organizations that included the Los Angeles Alliance for a New Economy mounted an aggressive campaign to block Walmart from locating there, enlisting the support of noted civil rights activists such as the Reverend Jesse Jackson. Jackson's message to Inglewood residents was similar to the one he would later deliver in his hometown of Chicago:

> Some may say "these jobs are better than no jobs," and are attracted to Walmart's promise of "jobs and low prices," especially in these times of high unemployment and the need for community economic development. But a closer look at Walmart exposes it as a Confederate economic Trojan horse. On the outside, it looks like a show horse. But open it up and what do you see: jobs at welfare level wages; jobs without health care benefits; jobs without the right to organize; a Walmart that forces out local small business and throws their workers into the unemployment lines.[32]

This message proved effective. On April 6, 2004, Inglewood residents voted 61 percent to 39 percent to reject Walmart's entry to the community, sending a clear message to Walmart that they wanted quality jobs, not low-wage jobs.

Another example of a community struggle against Walmart can be seen in the Maryland Fair Share effort. In 2004, the state of Maryland spent US$350 million a year on health care costs for the uninsured, who were forced to get medical care through public poverty programs, which created a tax burden on state taxpayers. This burden was largely caused by Walmart, because of the four largest employers in the state, Walmart alone was not paying its share of employee medical coverage. A statewide coalition of religious, business, labor, and community groups formed the Maryland Health Care for All! Coalition and launched a grassroots campaign, uniting eleven hundred organizations to support a bill that required all for-profit employers with ten thousand or more employees to contribute at least 8 percent of payroll to either health care for its employees or a new Fair Share Health Care Fund that would augment federal medical funds for the poor. The bill passed both houses of the state legislature by wide margins. Walmart actively opposed this bill, and on May 19, 2005, the governor vetoed the bill, with a Walmart vice president at his side. Seven months later, the legislature voted to override the governor's veto. But subsequent legal challenges led by Walmart ended in the defeat of this bill.[33]

These examples illustrate the grassroots movement of workers and community groups that has come together to fight Walmart for better working conditions and defense of living standards. These campaigns use traditional methods such as unionization, filing lawsuits, and passing legislation, but they also increasingly use new tools like community benefits agreements that engage firms like Walmart in negotiating with community groups about the terms of store construction and operation. Labor unions have become key actors in many of these struggles, taking on a role that goes beyond the workplace to the community. Unions also provide resources that link various struggles against Walmart into an online network that brings together local struggles into a campaign that is much greater than the sum of its parts.

WALMART ORGANIZING IN CHINA

According to official Chinese news reports, the number of labor lawsuits increased 95 percent from January 2008 to 2009, and nearly tripled in the southern coastal areas where export processing is located. This increase is attributed partially to the global economic crisis that led to many factory closures with backpay due, as well as implementation of the Labor Contract Law in January 2008, which many employers violated by firing long-term employees or refusing to give them employment contracts. By the end of the first quarter 2009, the rate had slowed to 59 percent more lawsuits than the same quarter the year before, for a total of 98,568 cases.[34] Though this spike of lawsuits was temporary and did not continue at the same rate, it is one indication of a workforce that is increasingly aware of its rights and unafraid to exercise them.

Not only is the number of disputes high, but according to some analysts there has been a significant change in the quality of these labor disputes. According to one Hong Kong-based watchdog group, in the past most worker complaints involved basic grievances such as obtaining unpaid wages; however, in recent months a number of large-scale industrial work actions and strikes have involved negotiations for improved wages and labor rights.[35] This signifies a higher quality of collective action because it requires that the workers have a higher degree of consciousness about their rights, the organizational capacity to confront and negotiate with their employers, and the vision to build improved conditions incrementally in future negotiations. Other examples of this higher quality of labor dispute can be found in the nationwide strike wave of early 2010, where for example, nineteen hundred workers at the Honda transmission plant in Nanhai (near Guangzhou) won a wage increase of 25 percent before returning to work,[36] and twelve hundred workers at Toyota's Denso auto parts plant in nearby Nansha won an eight-hundred yuan compensation increase to their monthly base salary of about twelve hundred yuan.[37] According to union officials who were taken by surprise at the strikes, the workers at Nanhai Honda had been planning the strike for two months before they pushed the emergency button that shut the line down, and two hundred workers from the Nansha Denso plant had a "meeting" in a restaurant two days before the strike to plan it.[38] While these types of disputes have not yet led to a fully mature collective bargaining system, they indicate a growing sophistication among Chinese workers about exercising their rights.

Examples of this qualitatively new level of labor activism can also be found in labor struggles at Walmart. In preceding chapters, we got a picture of working conditions in Walmart stores (see chapters 5, 8, and 10), and a detailed account of the unionization of China's Walmart stores (see chapter 9). In fact, a scan of Chinese language reports and internet blogs reveals dozens of other labor disputes inside Walmart stores,[39] such as a case involving fifty-five workers at Walmart's procurement center in Shenzhen who were not paid daily overtime as required by law, but rather had been given time off when work slowed down. In August 2007 the workers were asked to sign overtime pay waivers, and those who refused to sign it were not allowed to work overtime. This unfair treatment sparked an angry confrontation where workers staged a two-day sit-in at the company's conference room demanding backpay for overtime work and equal treatment. Both the issue of lost overtime pay and rights to overtime are issues that workers in China have rarely raised in the past (see chapter 4). Moreover these workers had the confidence and organization to actually sit in at the company headquarters for two days straight and confront their employers while still employed.[40]

Besides Walmart procurement center workers like those mentioned above, and retail store worker activists like Gao Haitao who worked directly for Walmart (see chapter 10), there are the millions of workers who work indirectly for Walmart in its vast supply chain system, and some have managed to organize for better working conditions. For example, there is a high-profile lawsuit filed in Los Angeles in 2005 by the International Labor Rights Forum on behalf of Walmart workers in six countries including China on violations of labor law,[41] and one filed in 2004 by several hundred south China toy workers who were poisoned by cadmium, a toxin that is banned in the United States but was used to make batteries in toy factories that produced for Walmart among others. In the latter case, Walmart once again revealed its antilabor streak by filing a suit against a Hong Kong human rights groups in retaliation for helping the workers.[42] Nevertheless, through a group of dedicated workers and labor activists, the workers have received 1 million yuan in compensation from their employer so far and are continuing to pursue strategies to get reimbursed for the full cost of their medical care.[43]

Much lower in profile are the many cases of labor organizing that go unreported, or are reported only in the Chinese press. In one dispute involving a Walmart supplier, two hundred workers in a toy factory called Tai Qiang in Shenzhen were harassed and defeated in their attempt to form a union. According to a 2007 report by a Hong Kong–based group called Students against Corporate Misbehavior (SACOM), in 2004 the workers formed a club called the "Compassion Group" inside the factory to "collect books and to voluntarily contribute funds to buy stationary, periodicals, and other objects for entertainment." Some time later the members of this Compassion Group decided to form a union to "better build a bridge linking the workers and the management, create a balanced bilateral labor-capital relation, and uphold a platform of dispute resolution through consultation and negotiation." The employer retaliated by firing the leaders. Although the local ACFTU affiliate sent a representative to the scene, a union that was not supported by the workers was installed. When the workers wrote a letter to Walmart asking it to "assume responsibility for these violations in order to safeguard the international reputation and image of your corporation," Walmart refused to respond.[44]

Perhaps the most widely reported case of labor organizing in a Walmart supplier was the 2004 strike of ten thousand workers at the Japanese-owned

Uniden phone manufacturing plant outside of Shenzhen. This strike was the fifth at the factory since it was established in 1987. For eight days the mostly women workers stopped working to demand higher pay and benefits, better dorm and restroom facilities, and the right to form their own union. Scuffles with the police took place, and some strike leaders "disappeared." According to a twenty-two-year-old worker from Hunan, "There were some minor scuffles and, shortly after that, the policemen backed away and just blocked the entrance. So we staged a sit-in." In the end the workers went back to work with the promise of being allowed to have union representation; however Uniden put in new management that later reneged on that promise.[45]

These examples illustrate the bold steps that an increasing number of migrant workers in Walmart's suppliers are taking to stand up for their rights and organize unions. They have a keen sense of self-dignity and justice, believe that "in unity there is strength," and some believe that unions will improve their conditions. Unfortunately these workers have not received any support from the ACFTU, and any gains that they may make through bargaining or striking are not likely to be embedded in lasting, legally enforceable contracts.

A handful of these migrant worker activists have been trained by labor nongovernmental organizations (NGOs) that have stepped into the void left by the ACFTU to provide legal services and labor rights training to migrant workers. Across China there are several dozen of these labor NGOs, and many are concentrated in southern China where Hong Kong human rights activists began to do outreach in the 1990s. Over the past two decades, it is mainly through the work of these NGOs that the world has come to know about horrendous labor conditions in China's export zones. Unfortunately labor NGOs operate in a politically undefined area: theoretically allowed to exist by law but often denied by local governments permission to register as such, they are often harassed and intimidated by the local security bureau because they are seen as potentially political provocateurs. This political repression greatly limits their ability to carry out large-scale public activity involving labor.

It should also be noted that the labor struggles for better conditions and representation in the supplier factories described are not directed at Walmart but at their factory owners and managers. The linkage between poor work conditions with Walmart and the global supply chain is made by labor advocates, not by the workers themselves. The workers' ability to see beyond their own immediate conditions is still limited.

As for resistance to Walmart by local communities or grassroots organizing of "site fights," the Chinese context is of course quite different from America. Chinese citizens do organize to protest around land issues; for example, there is a high degree of both rural and urban civil protest of inadequate government remuneration of expropriated land.[46] However there has not been grassroots citizen organizing against the location of Walmart or other "big box" stores in the community. Where Walmart has been blocked from locating in certain cities the reason may stem from its inability to negotiate a land lease, or lease-free agreement, tax subsidies, or other favorable terms;[47] or it may be that a local government denies permission because it would not bring in any tax revenue, as Walmart would pay taxes to the city where its headquarters is located per Chinese law.[48]

As we saw in the earlier section of this chapter, American campaigns have been greatly aided by academic research that supports a high-road theoretical framework. However in China, similar academic discourse has not yet emerged. There is a critique of current economic policies that have led to widening income disparity, and in the past two years these voices have become so strong that the government and even the ACFTU have recognized this as a problem. Other labor scholars have shown the need for unions to implement collective bargaining and allow rank-and-file workers to elect their leaders, and with the recent strike wave showing how out of touch with the rank and file unions are, this line of thinking has gained momentum. However relatively little mainstream academic work has been done to critique existing low-road policies that have led to the extreme labor exploitation currently found in China, especially among migrant workers, or to propose alternative economic theories and policies that would narrow income inequality and ensure labor rights.

NEED FOR DIALOGUE AND JOINT ACTION

The characteristics of collective resistance to Walmart differs greatly in the United States and China. In the United States, union organizing in stores has been unsuccessful, and unions have instead focused on linking with community groups to advocate high-road policies affecting wages and benefits for communities. By linking local anti-Walmart campaigns, unions hope to build a social movement for economic and social justice with Walmart as the poster child for what is wrong with low-road capitalism.

In China unionization of Walmart stores has been successful, but given the experiences of activists like Gao Haitao, it remains to be seen whether union leaders will be elected by the rank and file, and whether the local store unions will be given the political space to act in the best interests of the union members. We have seen that there are many labor disputes in Walmart supplier factories, and in a few of them workers have demanded to form unions. At the moment there is no evidence that the ACFTU will actively attempt to unionize workers in Walmart's supplier factories as it did in the stores a few years ago, or to link labor organizing with any other civil society organizing or economic policy.

In spite of these differences, both types of collective resistance to Walmart in the United States and China are essentially about redistribution of economic wealth and balancing power in the workplace and community, and it would strengthen all workers if American workers made linkages with Chinese labor. While those linkages were difficult in earlier decades when there was little evidence of grassroots labor organizing in China, now that Chinese workers are becoming more sophisticated about strikes, collective bargaining, and building a system of industrial relations that leads to greater income equality, these linkages can now be built on the basis of mutual respect, solidarity, and collaboration.

One of the biggest obstacles to this engagement is the U.S. labor movement's long-standing policy of isolating and boycotting the ACFTU because of its dependence on the Chinese Communist Party, and its role in violating the human rights of labor activists.[49] In the mid-2000s the SEIU broke with AFL-CIO policy and began to hold talks with the ACFTU on a range of issues, from organizing and collective bargaining to Walmart. In fact, SEIU supported a tour of Chinese trade unionists to the United States that is said to have strongly influenced the ACFTU's decision to target Walmart for organizing.[50] In August 2009 Change to Win, the breakaway labor federation that the SEIU and other unions cofounded, signed a historic agreement with the ACFTU that pledged to advance "exchanges around creating green jobs in China and the United States, joint research on global companies operating in the United States and China, bringing workers from global companies together to share experiences with labor's involvement in the economic recovery and practices in organizing, and developing trade policies that will advance workers' interests."[51] However since then Change to Win has been rocked with internal disagreements and leadership changes, and its new leadership has not given any indication of moving forward with building relationships with the ACFTU. In 2009 the AFL-CIO also elected new leadership, and there is no indication that its current policy towards the ACFTU will change.

American labor economists have also accused China of causing massive job loss in the United States through unfair trade policies and manipulating its currency. Environmentalists decry the skyrocketing carbon footprint of China's industrializing cities, and consumer groups point to poisoned baby formula and dog food as evidence of pervasive fraud. All of these issues, and many more, are valid concerns that will have to be addressed in the course of step-by-step engagement. However they should not deter us from entering into dialogue and developing the relationships that will help to resolve these concerns and to move forward in the interests of all working people.

In the absence of formal union-to-union relations, there is a possibility of people-to-people relations. In the 1960s when diplomatic relations did not exist between China and the U.S. governments, people-to-people "ping pong diplomacy" proved to be an important way to thaw icy relations and build ties between the citizens of the two countries at a grassroots level. Today, more exchanges between workers groups and community organizers might build understanding and lead to collaboration on programs that could pave the way for formal relations. Another strategy might be to have academic exchanges that provide research and training support for labor and community organizers. Topics of mutual concern might include collective bargaining strategies, sustainable economic development, coalition building in civil society, and so forth.

If China is critical to Walmart's manufacturing and sales strategies, then labor and community groups who are organizing against Walmart need to have a China strategy. Knowing what is going on with collective resistance to Walmart in China is the first step. The next step is to develop relationships and act collaboratively.

NOTES

Introduction

1. Walmart ranked no. 1 in the 2010 Fortune 500 list of the world's largest corporations. Its revenues of $408,214 million far exceeded the revenues of the world's second largest corporation, Royal Dutch Shell, which recorded $285,129 million. (*Fortune Magazine*, July 26, 2010).

2. John Dicker, *The United States of Wal-Mart* (New York: Penguin, 2005).

3. Nelson Lichtenstein, *The Retail Revolution: How Wal-Mart Created a Brave New World of Business* (New York: Metropolitan Books, 2009).

4. A vast list of sources containing the term "Walmartization" will appear when Googled.

5. http://design.walkerart.org/worldsaway/Terms/Walmartization/.

6. Two unions—the Service Employees International Union (SEIU) and United Food and Commercial Workers Union (UFCW)—separately founded websites, Wal-Mart Watch and Wake-Up Wal-Mart, to monitor and disseminate information on Walmart's practices in the hope of organizing a grassroots movement against the giant. Walmart counterattacked by hiring a group of high-powered political consultants to ward off bad press. Ronald Reagan's image-meister and one of Bill Clinton's media consultants headed a counteroffensive public relations team at Walmart's headquarters in Bentonville, Arkansas, reportedly from a "war room," and frenziedly diverted daily barbs. "A New Weapon for Wal-Mart: A War Room," *New York Times*, November 1, 2005.

7. Jennifer Bair and Sam Bernstein, "Labor and the Wal-Mart Effect," in *The World's Biggest Corporation in the Global Economy: Wal-Mart World*, ed. Stanley D. Brunn (New York: Routledge, 2006), 109.

8. Thanks are due to the International Centre for Excellence in Asian and Pacific Studies at the Australian National University and to the Panta Rhea Foundation in the United States.

9. Two such reports from the middle of this century's first decade are Lan Xin-zhen, "Wal-Mart Presence: Can the Retail Giant Maintain Its Success in China?" *Beijing Review,* August 4, 2005, 30–33; and Zhao Linmin, "The Toy Industry: The Low-Wage Industry" (in Chinese), *Nanfang chuan* (Southern Window), December 1, 2005, 34–37.

10. The conference was cosponsored by the Contemporary China Centre of The Australian National University and Beijing University's Research Center on China's Workers.

11. Dorinda Elliott, "Wal-Mart Nation," *Time* magazine, June 19, 2004.

12. Robert J. S. Ross and Anita Chan, "From North-South to South-South: The True Face of Global Competition," *Foreign Affairs* 81, no. 5 (2002): 8–13.

13. *Business Week,* in a long and well-researched cover story, shows how auditing of corporate codes in supplier factories is a sham. "American importers have long answered criticism of conditions at their Chinese suppliers with labor rules and inspections. But many factories have just gotten better at concealing abuses." Dextor Roberts and Peter Engardio, with Aaron Bernstein, "Secrets, Lies, and Sweatshops," *Business Week* (U.S.), November 27, 2006.

14. Associated Press, "CEO Says Wal-Mart Needs Low-Cost Imports," *New York Times,* October 12, 2007.

15. Tanim Ahmed, "RMG Set for Walmart Boost," bdnews24.com, www.bdnews24.com/details.php?id=152958&cid=2; also see "Walmart Plans Major Boost for Bangladesh RMG" and "Bangladesh Needs Comprehensive Apparel Zone: Walmart Chief," http://www.priyo.com/news/2010/feb/06/35189/. Both of these web news sources similarly reported an association leader stating after the meeting that the Walmart executives "made it quite clear ethical issues were not important to them. All they care about is their profit and their share price."

16. Aradhna Aggarwal, Mombert Hoppe, and Peter Walkenhorst, "Special Economic Zones in South Asia: Industrial Islands or Vehicles for Diversification?" http://www.siteresources.worldbank.org/INTEXPCOMNET/Resources/Walkenhorst,_Special_Economic_Zones_in_South_Asia_Industrial_Islands_or_Vehicles_for_Diversification.pdf/.

1. WALMART'S LONG MARCH TO CHINA

1. Author's interview with Bentonville resident Hillary Claggart, April 29, 2005, Bentonville; Jeff Glasser, "Boomtown, U.S.A.," *U.S. News and World Report,* June 25, 2001, 17–20; Anne D'Innocenzio, "Wal-Mart Suppliers Flocking to Arkansas," *The State,* September 21, 2003, 1.

2. Joseph Y.S. Cheng, *Guangdong: Preparing for the WTO Challenge* (Hong Kong: Chinese University Press, 2003); Michael Enright, Edith Scott, and Ka-mun Chang, *Regional Powerhouse: The Greater Pearl River Delta and the Rise of China* (Singapore: John Wiley, 2005); Joe Studwell, *The China Dream* (London: Profile Books, 2005).

3. Author's interview with port official at Yantian International Container Terminal, Shenzhen, September 9, 2005.

4. David Dollar, "Why Does One Country Draw More Investment Than Another?" *YaleGlobal*, October 10, 2003, http://yaleglobal.yale.edu.

5. Philip Goodman and Philip Pan, "Chinese Workers Pay for Wal-Mart's Low Prices," *Washington Post*, February 8, 2004, 1.

6. Glenn Porter and Harold Livesay, *Merchants and Manufacturers: Studies in the Changing Structure of Nineteenth-Century Marketing* (Chicago: Ivan R. Dee, 1971); Sven Beckert, "Merchants and Manufacturers in the Antebellum North," in *Ruling America: A History of Wealth and Power in a Democracy*, ed. Steve Fraser and Gary Gerstle (Cambridge: Harvard University Press, 2005), 116–17.

7. Richard S. Tedlow, *New and Improved: The Story of Mass Marketing in America* (New York: Basic Books, 1990), for studies of Coca Cola, Sears, A&P, and the automobile companies.

8. For an overview of the supply chain literature, see Jennifer Bair, "Global Capitalism and Commodity Chains: Looking Back, Going Forward," *Competition and Change* 9, no. 2 (June): 129–56; Frederick H. Abernathy, John T. Dunlop, Janice Hammon, and David Weil, *A Stitch in Time: Lean Retailing and the Transformation of Manufacturing—Lessons from the Apparel and Textile Industries* (New York: Oxford University Press, 1999); Gary Gereffi and Miguel Korzeniewicz, eds., *Commodity Chains and Global Capitalism* (Westport, CT: Praeger, 1994), 95–122; author's telephone interview with former Bain and Company consultant, November 15, 2005.

9. "Wal-Mart, P&G Link Up for Efficiency," *St. Louis-Post Dispatch*, February 14, 1989; Constance Hays, "What's Behind the Procter Deal? Wal-Mart," *New York Times*, January 29, 2005; Howard Davidowitz quoted in Jeremy Grant and Dan Roberts, "P&G Looks to Gain Strength through Unity," *Financial Times*, January 31, 2005, 25.

10. Edna Bonacich with Khaleelah Hardie, "Wal-Mart and the Logistics Revolution," in *Wal-Mart: The Face of Twenty-First Century Capitalism*, ed. Nelson Lichtenstein (New York: New Press, 2006), 163–88.

11. Brooks Blevins, *Hill Folks: A History of Arkansas Ozarkers and Their Image* (Chapel Hill: University of North Carolina Press, 2002), 147–78; Ben Johnson, *Arkansas in Modern America, 1930–1999* (Fayetteville: University of Arkansas Press, 2000), 200–202.

12. Bob Ortega, *In Sam We Trust* (New York: Random House, 1998), 86–90; and see also the favorable but revealing account in Sandra Vance and Roy Scott, *Wal-Mart: A History of Sam Walton's Retail Phenomenon* (New York: Twayne, 1994), 44–47.

13. Mary Jo Schneider, "The Wal-Mart Annual Meeting: From Small-Town America to a Global Corporate Culture," *Human Organization* 57, no. 3 (1998): 295.

14. Don Sonderquist, *The Wal-Mart Way* (Nashville: Thomas Nelson, 2005), 59–60.

15. Schneider, "The Wal-Mart Annual Meeting," 295.

16. Soderquist, *The Wal-Mart Way*, 45.

17. David Chidester, *Authentic Fakes: Religion and American Popular Culture* (Berkeley: University of California Press, 2005); Kimon Sargeant, *Seeker Churches: Promoting Traditional Religion in a Nontraditional Way* (New Brunswick, NJ: Rutgers University Press, 2000); Christian Smith, *American Evangelicalism: Embattled and Thriving* (Chicago: University of Chicago Press, 1998); Zig Ziglar, *Secrets of Closing the Sale* (Grand Rapids: Fleming H. Revell, 2003).

18. Wal-Mart Stores, *Sam's Associates Handbook*, 3, in Vertical File, Food and Service Trades Department, AFL-CIO.

19. Jack Kahl, *Leading from the Heart: Choosing to be a Servant Leader* (Austin: Greenleaf, 2004), 107–9. Kahl was for many years owner and CEO of Manco, which supplied duck tape to Walmart.

20. Thomas O. Graff and Dub Ashton, "Spatial Diffusion of Wal-Mart: Contagious and Reverse Hierarchical Elements," *Professional Geographer* 46 (February 1994): 19–29; "About Wal-Mart: Senior Officers," http://www.walmartstores.com.

21. Brent Schlender, "Wal-Mart's $288 Billion Meeting," *Fortune*, April 18, 2005, 97.

22. Major Van Hart (retired), "Logistics: The Art of Doing War," http://www.chuckshawks.com/logistics.htm.

23. Marc Levinson, *The Box: How Shipping Made the World Smaller and the World Economy Bigger* (Princeton: Princeton University Press, 2006), 171–88; Bahar Barami, "Productivity Gains from Pull Logistics: Trade-offs of Internal and External Costs," paper presented at the Transportation Research Board Conference on Transportation and Economic Development, Portland, Oregon, September 22–25, 2001.

24. Thomas Friedman, *The World Is Flat: A Brief History of the Twenty-First Century* (New York: Farrar, Straus and Giroux, 2005), 128.

25. Sam Walton and John Huey, *Sam Walton, Made in America: My Story* (New York: Doubleday, 1992), 83–4.

26. As quoted in John Huey, "Wal-Mart: Will It Take Over the World?" *Fortune* 119, no. 3 (January 30, 1989), 52.

27. "Chain Begins Servicing Own Racks"; "Vendor Rep Move Stirs Debate," *Discount Store News*, June 15, 1992, 68, 135.

28. "Vendor Rep Move Stirs Debate."

29. Walton and Huey, Walton: *Made in America*, 308.

30. Gary Hamilton, "Remaking the Global Economy: U.S. Retailers and Asian Manufacturers: Hearing on China and the Future of Globalization," report presented before the U.S.-China Economic and Security Review Commission, May 20, 2005, http://www.uscc.gov/hearings/2005hearings/hr05_05_19_20.php.

31. Dana Frank, *Buy American: The Untold Story of Economic Nationalism* (Boston: Beacon Press, 1999), 131–38.

32. Ibid., 136.

33. "Wal-Mart Campaign Brings Jobs," *Arkansas Democrat-Gazette*, March 14, 1985; Michael Barrier, "Walton's Mountain," *Nation's Business*, April 1988.

34. "Wal-Mart Boasts 'Made in USA,'" *Discount Store News,* June 15, 1992, 127.

35. Ortega, *In Sam We Trust,* 206; Stacey Duncan, "Merchandising Profiles: What It Takes to Make a Conversion," *Wal-Mart World* 19, no. 6 (June 1989): 22.

36. Duncan, "Merchandising Profiles," 22.

37. Sam Hornblower, "Wal-Mart in China: A Joint Venture," on PBS *Frontline* website, *Is Wal-Mart Good for America?* http://www.pbs.org/wgbh/pages/frontline/shows/walmart/.

38. Bill Bowden, "PREL CEO Says Wal-Mart's Policy Is No Sweat," *Northwest Arkansas Business Journal,* June 25, 2001.

39. Ortega, *In Sam We Trust,* 206.

40. Michael Barrier, "Walton's Mountain," *Nation's Business,* April 1988, 64.

41. "Wal-Mart Boasts 'Made in the USA,'" 127.

42. Caroline Mayer, "Wal-Mart Flies the Flag in Import Battle; Prods U.S. Producers With Favorable Terms," *Washington Post,* April 21, 1985.; Farris Fashions, Inc. and Amalgamated Clothing and Textile Workers Union, Southwest Regional Joint Board, Cases 26-CA-14258 and 26-RC-7323, September 30, 1993, 550; Richard Hurd, *Assault on Workers' Rights* (Washington, DC: Industrial Union Department, AFL-CIO, 1994), 39; author's telephone interview with Joan Suarez, former regional director for ILGWU, August 30, 2005; author's observations, Brinkley, Arkansas, June 5, 2006.

43. Robert E. Scott, "The Wal-Mart Effect: Its Chinese Imports Have Displaced Nearly 200,000 U.S. Jobs," June 26, 2007, Economic Policy Institute at www.epi.org.

44. Anthony Bianco, *The Bully of Bentonville: How the High Cost of Wal-mart's Everyday Low Prices Is Hurting America* (New York: Doubleday, 2006), 187.

45. Hornblower, "Wal-Mart in China"; Bowden, "PREL CEO."

46. "Wal-Mart: 2005 Report on Ethical Sourcing," at Walmart website, http://walmartstores.com/Sustainability/7951.aspx.

47. Kyle Johnson and Peter Kinder, "Wal-Mart Stores, Inc.," Domini 400 Social Index Decision Series, no. 3 (May 16, 2001); Molly Selvin, "Wal-Mart Faces Suit by Labor Group," *Los Angeles Times,* September 14, 2005.

48. Author's interview with Billy Han, Students and Scholars against Corporate Misbehaviour (SACOM), September 14, 2005, Hong Kong; author's interview with Dick Ambrocio, Reebok production manager, Zhuhai, September 8, 2005.

49. Author's interview with Tom Mitchell, *South China Morning Post,* September 17, 2005, Hong Kong.

50. Author's interview with Brent Berry.

51. Hornblower, "Wal-Mart in China."

52. The Hindu Business Line, January 7, 2005.

53. Witness how in 2007 Mattel had to recall more than a million toys made by a Chinese supplier that were contaminated by lead paint. David Barboza and Louise Story, "Dancing Elmo Smackdown: In China, Mattel Toys Go through the Wringer

to Ensure Safety," *New York Times,* July 26, 2007, C1, C10; David Barboza, "Owner of Chinese Toy Factory Commits Suicide," *New York Times,* August 14, 2007.

54. Associated Press, "Nike Ventures into Discount Shoe Business," *Clarion-Ledger,* April 23, 2005.

55. Author's interview with Tiger Wu, September 12, 2005, Dongguan.

56. The best statement of Walmart's view is offered by CEO Lee Scott, "Wal-Mart and California: A Key Moment in Time for American Capitalism," Speech at Los Angeles Town Hall, February 23, 2005, at www.walmartfacts.com.

57. David Barboza, "China Inflation Exacting a Toll Across the U.S.," *New York Times,* February 1, 2008.

2. OUTSOURCING IN CHINA

1. In 2005 and 2006, Langsha had supplied products worth US$3 million and US$2.5 million respectively for Walmart, and from January to July in 2007, it had received further orders worth US$2.2 million.

2. Tian Aili and Li Suwan, "Zhongguo Zuida Waqi Langsha Zhongzhi Yu Wo'erma Hezuo, Cheng Dingjia Taidi" (Largest Chinese sock manufacturer Langsha says goodbye to Walmart's low price orders"), *Diyi Caijing Ribao* (First Finance Daily), July 19, 2007; Zhou Yiguang and Liu Zhengzheng, "Langsha: Bushi Wo'erma Fangqi Wo, Shi Wo Fangqi Wo'erma" (Langsha: I abandon Walmart rather than have Walmart abandon me), *21 Shiji Jingji Baodao* (21 Century Economic Herald), July 21, 2007.

3. There is a special forum for news reports and discussions about Walmart and Langsha at www.sina.com.cn (the largest Chinese-language infotainment web portal), http://finance.sina.com.cn/blank/qygc57walmart.shtml.

4. Available at http://finance.sina.com.cn/blank/qygc57walmart.shtml/. Up to February 25, 2008, 3,477 persons had contributed opinions about the case.

5. Hedrick Smith, "Who Calls the Shots in the Global Economy?" *PBS Frontline,* November 16, 2004, http://www.pbs.org/wgbh/pages/frontline/shows/walmart/secrets/.

6. Li Suwan, "Wo'erma Zhong Xiang Langsha Ditou, Fangzhiye Dui Dijia Caigou Shuo Bu" (Walmart concedes to Langsha, Chinese textile industry says no to low-price purchase), *Diyi Caijing Riba* (First Finance Daily), December 9, 2007.

7. The NGO is Students and Scholars against Corporate Misbehavior (SACOM), www.sacom.org.hk.

8. I was unable to interview any Walmart staff. In November 2005, through an introduction from one of my friends, I got to know a woman working in Walmart's outsourcing center in Shenzhen and made several calls to her, but she was very sensitive about being interviewed and was unwilling to share her experiences of working with Walmart's suppliers, because this was regarded as commercial inconfidence. She told me that Walmart's employees were not allowed to be interviewed.

9. I double-checked that these factories were producing merchandise for Walmart from publicly available information or their annual reports on the Internet and from my interviews with their workers.

10. In September 2007, Walmart changed its slogan from "always low prices" to "save money, live better." But the spirit of "always low prices" is still the most important business strategy for Walmart in its relationship with both its customers and suppliers.

11. Sam Hornblower, "Wal-Mart in China: A Joint Venture," *PBS Frontline,* November 16, 2004, www.pbs.org/wgbh/pages/frontline/shows/walmart/secrets/wmchina.

12. Anita Chan, "A 'Race to the Bottom': Globalization and China's Labor Standards," *China Perspectives* 46 (2003): 41–49.

13. In 1985, Sam Walton, the founder of Walmart, said Walmart would be firmly committed to the philosophy by buying everything possible from suppliers who manufacture their products in the United States. It was called Walmart's "Buy American" program.

14. Xu Yaqing, "TCL Huikao Wo'erma" (TCL meets audit of Walmart), *IT Jingli Shiji* (IT Management World), June 5, 2007, http://www.ceocio.com.cn/12/93/124/104/12801.htm.

15. Li Guangshou, "Wo'erma: Heigongchang De Haohuoban" (Walmart: Partners of underground factories), *Shimin* (Citizen), January 2008.

16. All eight factories are in Guangdong Province. Five of them are in Shenzhen, two in Dongguan, and one in Chenghai. I visited all the factories in Shenzhen and Dongguan and interviewed their workers. Some of these factories had business relationships with each other. Although I did not visit the toy factory in Chenghai, I interviewed its owner (Mr. Wang) on April 26 at the Canton Fair.

17. The factory is one of the manufacturing centers of a multinational corporation founded in Korea in the 1980s. The corporation has registered several companies in the United States, Hong Kong, and China, and it has been listed on the Hong Kong Stock Exchange since 2001. It has factories in Shenzhen, Shanghai, and Suzhou in China, as well as in Vietnam. Its business partners include brands such as Disney, Warner Bros, SEGA, and Banpresto, as well as mass market retailers such as Walmart, KOHL's, Costco, Target, and IKEA. Ninety percent of its products are stuffed plush toys. In its business with Walmart, besides the traditional stuffed toys it has also manufactured infant products such as rattles and bedding. This information is based on the company's website.

18. The internationally important Canton Fair, also called the China Import and Export Fair, has been held twice a year, in spring and autumn, since it was inaugurated in 1957.

19. Ying Zhou, "Dao Wo'erma Zongbu Qu" (Going to Walmart Headquarters), *IT Jingli Shijie* (IT Management World), June 20, 2007, http://www.ceocio.com.cn/12/93/124/100/13088.htm.

20. Xu, "TCL Huikao Wo'erma"; Zhou, "Dao Wo'erma Zongbu Qu."

21. Xu, Chunmei, "Wo'erma Yu Zhigou, Zhongguo Gongchang Shuo 'No,'" (Chinese factories say no to Walmart's direct buy), *Zhongguo Jingying Bao* (China

Business), November 14, 2007. Buyers generally do not pay suppliers immediately but settle their payments at a time negotiated in their contracts. (Walmart has a good reputation of paying on time.)

22. Li, "Wo'erma: Heigongchang De Haohuoban."

23. Author's discussion with some of Walmart's supply factories in the Internet forum (www.tianya.cn) in August 2007; Xu, "Wo'erma Yu Zhigou, Zhongguo Gongchang Shuo 'No.'"

24. Except for well-known brands (e.g., Langsha and TCL), the names of people and factories in this chapter are pseudonymous.

25. This company has more than ten contracting factories in China and also has a sales office in New York.

26. Author's telephone interview with the garment trader in Nanjing, March 19, 2005.

27. Author's interview with a toy supplier on April 26, 2005.

28. Walmart Stores Inc., "Corporate Facts: Wal-Mart by the Numbers," www.walmartfacts.com/FactSheets/Corporate_Facts.pdf.

29. For example, Misha Petrovic and Gary G. Hamilton, "Making Global Markets: Wal-Mart and its Suppliers," in *Wal-Mart: The Face of Twenty-First Century Capitalism*, ed. Nelson Lichtenstein (New York: New Press, 2006), 107–42; and Charles Fishman, *The Wal-Mart Effect: How the World's Most Powerful Company Really Works—and How It's Transforming the American Economy* (New York: Penguin, 2006), 102–3.

30. Some scholars think that modern logistics have contributed to a global race to the bottom to supply Walmart. See Edna Bonacich and Khaleelah Hardie, "Wal-Mart and the Logistic Revolution," in *Wal-Mart: The Face of Twenty-First Century Capitalism*, 163–88.

31. Author's interview with Mr. Hua on April 16, 2006 at the Canton Fair.

32. Author's interview with Mr. Liu on May 28, 2007.

33. For example, Ni Lijuan, "Wo'erma: Xiangshuo Aini Burongyi" (Walmart: It is hard to say 'we love you'), *Zheshang Zazhi* (Zhejiang Business), January 2005, http://biz.zjol.com.cn/gb/node2/node138665/node264826/node265122/node289305/userobject15ai3846678.html; Li Mingwei, "Gongyinglian Xianjing: Wo'erma Zhongguo Baoli Jiemi" (The trap of the supply chain: Behind the high profit of Walmart from China), *21 Shijie Jingji Baodao* (21st Century Economic Herald), December 30, 2003.

34. Author's interview, April 16, 2006 at the Canton Fair.

35. Author's interview with Mr. Hua, April 16, 2006.

36. Author's interview with apparel suppliers, April 16, 2006 at the Canton Fair.

37. Author's interview with suppliers at the Canton Fair; Mingwei Li, "Gongyinglian Xianjing: Wo'erma Zhongguo Baoli Jiemi."

38. "Quota restriction" in the textile and apparel industry also influences subcontracting in a similar way.

39. Author's interview, April 26, 2005.

40. The information is based on the website of the government of Chenghai, http://www.gdchenghai.gov.cn/chts/tscy.htm.

41. Hua Liu, "Langsha, Wo'erma Yu Zhongxiaolong: Caogen Shengtai Xiade Quanqiu Chanyelian" (Langsha, Walmart, and Zhongxiaolong: Global production chain in the grassroots environment), *21 Shiji Jingji Baodao* (21st Century Economic Herald), August 23, 2007. More information about Datang and its sock industry can be found at www.zhuji.gov.cn/countrystreet.jsp?catalog_id = 200403030000011&childcatalog_ id = 200403030000082 and www.datangsock.com/.

42. Walmart Stores, "Ethical Standards Program," http://walmartstores.com/ media/resources/r_2726.pdf.

43. National Labor Committee, "Made in China: the Role of U.S. Companies in Denying Human and Workers Rights," May 25, 2000.

44. Peter S. Goodman and Philip P. Pan, "Chinese Workers Pay for Wal-Mart's Low Prices," *Washington Post,* February 8, 2004.

45. National Labor Committee and China Labor Watch, "Wal-Mart Sweatshops Toys Made in China," and "Blood and Exhaustion: Behind Bargain Toys Made in China for Wal-Mart and Dollar General," December 2005.

46. China Labor Watch, "Wal-Mart, Made in China," December 6, 2006, www. chinalaborwatch.org/php/web/article.php?article_id = 1835.

47. Jianqiao Lei, "Gongyingshang Duifu Shehui Zeren Shenhe: Mao Zhuo Laoshu Youxi Yanxiuban"(Suppliers deal with CSR audits: Training workshops in a game of cat and mouse), *Nanfang Zhoumo* (Southerly Weekend), December 15, 2005.

48. There is a very long posting on Walmart in a trade business forum (http:// bbs.fobshanghai.com/) started on April 21, 2006, and updated over the following four years. The latest update I viewed was on August 15, 2010. In a business Internet forum, a posting followed by 50 comments can be regarded as lengthy; this entry on Walmart had received 1,024 comments when last viewed (http://bbs.fobshanghai. com/viewthread.php?tid = 156271&extra = &page = 1).

49. Many NGOs, including China Labor Watch, National Labor Committee, International Labor Rights Fund, and Human Rights Watch, have released reports on the labor standards of Walmart and its suppliers.

50. Dexter Roberts and Pete Engardio, "Secrets, Lies, and Sweatshops," *Business Week,* November 27, 2006.

51. This was a common view expressed during many of my interviews with suppliers in 2005–6. See also similar views expressed on postings in an Internet forum: www.tianya.cn/new/techforum/Content.asp?idWriter = 6727781&Key = 664191875&id Item = 141&idArticle = 553306 on May 6, 2006.

52. Walmart also admits that high-risk violations of its ES program are often found in undeclared subcontractor factories; see Walmart Stores, "2006 Report on Ethical Sourcing," http://walmartfacts.com/reports/2006/ethical_standards/docume nts/2006ReportonEthicalSourcing.pdf.

53. The factory-produced toys for Disney, Walmart, Toys "R" Us, Woolworths (UK), and GP Toys (Italy). The general manager explained that around 80 percent of its products were for Disney, 50 percent of which were sold to Walmart's stores directly.

54. Pun Ngai, "Global Production, Company Codes of Conduct, and Labor Conditions in China: A Case Study of Two Factories," *China Journal* 54 (July 2005): 101–13.

55. This was the case, for instance, at a factory that I encountered during my field work in July 2005 in Dongguan, Guangdong Province, which was producing toys for Walmart.

56. Walmart requires that working hours should meet whichever is the more stringent, local law or Walmart's Standard, which says: "Suppliers' employees shall not work more than 72 hours per 6 days or work more than a maximum total working hours of 14 hours per a continuous 24 hour period. Supplier's factories should be working toward achieving a 60-hour workweek.... Employees should be permitted reasonable days off (at least one day off for every seven-day period)," Walmart's "Standards for Suppliers," http://walmartstores.com/media/resources/r_2727.pdf. In China, the labor law is more stringent than Walmart's requirement on working hours—40 hours per week and 36 hours of legal overtime per month. However, in practice, Walmart usually uses its own standards in implementing the ES program.

57. Author's interview with workers from a Walmart toy factory in Shenzhen on October 9, 2005.

58. Author's interview on October 14, 2005.

59. Author's telephone interview with the garment trader in Nanjing on March 19, 2005. Mr. Liu from the craftwork industry made a similar comment.

60. Walmart Stores, "2005 Report on Ethical Sourcing," http://walmartstores.com/Files/05_ethical_source.pdf.

61. Ibid.

62. Ibid.

63. Author's interview with suppliers at the Canton Fair and by telephone during 2005–2006. Some suppliers also expressed similar views on the Internet forum at http://cache.tianya.cn/techforum/content/141/547045.shtml.

64. Author's interviews with workers from two Walmart toy factories on September 29, October 9, and December 13, 2005, and at a Walmart blanket factory on February 10, 2006. See also reports from labor NGOs such as China Labor Watch and National Labor Committee, "Wal-Mart Sweatshops Toys Made in China," "Blood and Exhaustion: Behind Bargain Toys Made in China for Wal-Mart and Dollar General," December 2005.

65. Author's interview with two women workers on November 17, 2005. They worked at a Japanese electronics factory producing telephones for Walmart. One of the workers only saw the poster on her way to the toilet on the day of the audit. The other had never heard of it.

66. Walmart Stores, "2006 Report on Ethical Sourcing."

67. Yiguang Zhou, "Wo'erma Zhongguo Dingdan Ruijian Sicheng" (Walmart reduces 40 percent of purchase orders in China), *21 Shiji Jingji Baodao* (21st Century Economic Herald), July 17, 2007; Ping'e Zou, "Wo'erma Caijian Zai Hua Caigou Jin'e, Zhongguo Gongyingshang Hen Shoushang" ("China's suppliers are severely hurt by Wal-Mart cutting procurement," *Meiri Jingji Xinwen* (Everyday Economics News), July 18, 2007.

68. See Yue Zhao, "Dongguan Qiye Daobi Chao Diaocha: Mingying Qiye 50 Qiang Jinwoniu Mianlin Pochan," (The investigation of the shutdown of factories in Dongguan: Jinwoniu, the top 50 private enterprises facing bankruptcy), *China News,* July 17, 2008, http://news.163.com/08/0717/08/4H1QQAKE000II24J.html; Meng Chen, "Yige Dongguan Gongchangzhu de Jiushu" (The salvation of a factory owner in Dongguan), *Shidai Zhoubao* (Time Weekly), January 8, 2009.

69. Ruohan Wang, "Wo'erma Wuyan Xia" (Under the eave of Wo'erma), *Huaqiu Qiyejia* (Global Entrepreneur), August 5, 2010.

70. Wu Lijuan, "Wo'erma Mingque Quannian Zhuti: Jiangjia"(Walmart confirms its annual theme: Reducing prices"), February 13, 2009, www.eeo.com.cn/eeo/jjgcb/2009/02/16/129373.shtml.

71. Purchasing B2B News, "Walmart Revamps Global Sourcing Strategy," February 1, 2010, www.canadianmanufacturing.com/purchasingb2b/news/industrynews/article.jsp?content=20100201_085202_9480; Karen Talley and Kate O'Keeffe, "Wal-Mart, Li & Fung Sign Sourcing Deal," January 29, 2010, http://online.wsj.com/article/SB10001424052748704878904575031173584170054.html.

3. Walmartization, Corporate Social Responsibility, and the Labor Standards of Toy Factories in South China

1. "Toy Markets Uncertain of Year's Profits," *Global News Wire—Asia Africa Intelligence Wire,* December 23, 2005.

2. "Toy Exports up 42% in 1st 11 Months of 2005," *Global News Wire—Asia Africa Intelligence Wire,* January 19, 2006.

3. "Bigger and Better: The Continued Growth of China's Toy Industry," *Playthings,* October 1, 2006.

4. "Toy Exports up 42% in 1st 11 Months of 2005."

5. Available at http://www.childec.com.cn/exec/news%5C2006%5%CNews62%5C2322335.shtml.

6. Ibid.

7. Anita Chan, *China's Workers under Assault: Exploitation and Abuse in a Globalizing Economy* (Armonk, NY: M. E. Sharpe, 2001); Ching Kwan Lee, "From Organized Dependence to Disorganized Despotism: Changing Labor Regimes in Chinese Factories," *China Quarterly* 157 (1999): 44–71; Pun Ngai, *Made in China: Women Factory Workers in a Global Workplace* (Durham, NC: Duke University Press, 2005).

8. Pun Ngai, "Global Production and Corporate Business Ethics: Company Codes of Conduct Implementation and its Implication on Labour Rights in China," *China Journal* 54 (2005): 101–13; Sum Ngai Ling and Pun Ngai, "Paradoxes of Ethical Transnational Production: Codes of Conduct in a Chinese Workplace," *Competition and Change* 9, no. 2 (2005): 181–200.

9. Pun Ngai and Yu Xiaomin (2008), "When Wal-Mart and the Chinese Dormitory Labour Regime Meet: A Study of Three Toy Factories in China," *China Journal of Social Work* 1, no. 2 (2008): 110–29; Jenny Wai-ling Chan, "Chinese Migrant Workers in Action: Bringing Wal-Mart to Corporate Responsibility," *Social Policy* 36, no. 1 (2005): 32–36.

10. Available at http://www.toy-tia.org/content/navigationmenu/toy_industry_association/Publications_Resources1/Toy_Industry_Fact_Book/TIAFactBook01-02.pdf; "Playing safely: ICTI CARE Process a Win-Win Situation," *Playthings,* December 1, 2005.

11. Eric Clark, *The Real Toy Story Inside the Ruthless Battle for America's Youngest Consumers* (New York: Free Press, 2007).

12. Eric Johnson, "Learning from Toys: Lessons in Managing Supply Chain Risk from the Toy Industry," *California Management Review* 43, no. 3 (2001): 106–24.

13. Ibid.

14. Available at: http://www.toy-tia.org/content/navigationmenu/toy_industry_association/Publications_Resources1/Toy_Industry_Fact_Book/TIAFactBook01-02.pdf; "Playing Safely"; Toy Industries of Europe, "Toy Industries of Europe: Facts and Figures, 2006," http://www.tietoy.org/Portals/28/TIE%20Facts%20and%20Figures%20brochure%202006.pdf.

15. Available at http://www.ita.doc.gov/td/ocg/outlook05_toys.pdf.

16. Clark, *The Real Toy Story.*

17. Ibid.

18. "Merchants of Mirth: The Top 25 Playthings Retailers," *Playthings* 104, no. 11 (2006): 22–26; "Playthings Top 25," *Playthings* 103, no. 11 (2005): 19–22; "Top 25 Toy Retailers," *Playthings* 102, no. 10 (2004): 9; "The Ranking: Top 15," *Playthings* 101, no. 1 (2003): 19; "The 'A' List," *Playthings* 99, no. 12 (2001): 38–44; "Playthings Top 50," *Playthings* 97, no. 9 (1999): 38–45.

19. Clark, *The Real Toy Story.*

20. Ibid.

21. "China's Toy Industry Feels Growing Pains," *USA Today,* December 21, 2006.

22. http://www.toy-tia.org/content/navigationmenu/toy_industry_association/Publications_Resources1/Toy_Industry_Fact_Book/TIAFactBook01-02.pdf; "Playing Safely."

23. "Toy Makers Uncertain of Year's Profits."

24. "The Hidden Downside of Santa's Little Helpers," *Irish Times,* December 21, 2002.

25. Hong Kong Christian Industrial Committee, "How Hasbro, McDonald's, Mattel, and Disney Manufacture Their Toys," 2001, 14–15, http://www.cic.org.hk/download/CIC%20Toy%20Report%20Web%20eng.pdf.

26. Available at http://www.sa-intl.org/index.cfm?fuseaction=Page.viewPage&pageID=505#cblist.

27. Available at http://www.toy-icti.org/info/care_process.pdf.

28. "Playing Safely."

29. Available at http://www.icti-care.org/.

30. Dara O'Rourke, "Outsourcing Regulation: Analyzing Nongovernmental Systems of Labor Standards and Monitoring," *Policy Studies Journal* 31, no. 1 (2003): 1–29.

31. Jill Esbenshade, "Codes of Conduct: Challenges and Opportunities for Workers' Rights," *Social Justice* 31, no. 3 (2004): 40–59.

32. "Wal-Mart: Vendors in Charge of Ethical Production," *Arkansas Democrat-Gazette,* April 5, 1998.

33. Available at http://walmartstores.com/Files/FactoryCertificationReport 2003.pdf.

34. For a deeper discussion of the problems of internal monitoring, see "A Life of Fines and Beating," *Business Week,* October 2, 2000.

35. Shareholder activism against sweatshop labor abuses at Walmart's overseas supplier factories can be traced back to the late 1990s when Walmart investors headed by the Interfaith Center on Corporate Responsibility filed a proposal at the company's 1997 annual meeting calling for independent monitoring of labor conditions at Walmart's supplier factories. In 2001, a larger coalition of Walmart shareholders put the proposal back on the table at the company's annual meeting. See "Group Targets Wal-Mart to Monitor Sweatshops," *St. Louis Post-Dispatch,* April 21, 1997; and "Bentonville Coalition Pressures Wal-Mart on Factories," *Arkansas Democrat-Gazette,* January 24, 2001. The Domini Social Equity Fund, the largest mutual fund aimed at social responsibility, dumped all its 1.2 million Walmart shares when sweatshoplike working conditions at the Chun Si Enterprise Handbag Factory in Zhongshan, Guangdong, were uncovered by *Business Week* in 2000. See "Wal-Mart Stockholders Address Sweatshop Issues," *Arkansas Democrat-Gazette,* May 27, 2001.

36. "Bentonville Coalition Pressures Wal-Mart on Factories."

37. "Wal-Mart Stockholders Address Sweatshop Issues."

38. "Wal-Mart Approach to Ethics Goes Global," *Arkansas Democrat-Gazette,* March 7, 2006.

39. Walmart's "Standards for Suppliers" states: "Employees shall not work more than 72 hours per 6 days or work more than a maximum total working hours of 14 hours per calendar day (midnight to midnight)." Available at http://walmartstores.com/Files/SupplierStandards.pdf.

40. Clark, *The Real Toy Story.*

41. At these two factories, about 80 percent of production workforces are young women aged between 18 and 30 years old, coming from China's rural inland provinces of Hunan, Hubei, Sichuan, Jiangxi, and Henan.

42. Available at http://walmartstores.com/Files/SupplierStandards.pdf.

43. The monthly wage of 991 yuan is calculated by the following wage formula: base wage (480 yuan) + 1.5 RHW (4.3 yuan) 60 overtime hours at night from Monday to Friday (3 hours 5 days 4 weeks) (258 yuan) + 2 RHW (5.74 yuan) 44 overtime hours on Saturday (11 hours 4 weeks) (253 yuan). The monthly wage of 1,197 yuan is calculated as 580 ÷ 480 991 yuan.

4. MADE IN CHINA

1. Taken from *The Free Dictionary* website, http//encyclopedia.thefreedictionary. com/sweating+system.

2. For instance, see "The Proletariat," in Friedrich Engels, *The Conditions of the Working Class in England,* chap. 7 (Oxford: Basil Blackwell, 1958).

3. Sheila Blackburn, *A Fair Day's Wage for a Fair Day's Work? Sweated Labour and the Origins of Minimum Wage Legislation in Britain* (Hampshire: Ashgate, 2007), 1–3.

4. "Sweating System," Fifth Report from the Select Committee of the House of Lords, *Proceedings and Appendix* (Sessional no. 169), vol. 17, no. Cxlii, May 5, 1890.

5. Sidney and Beatrice Webb, *Problems of Modern Industry,* new ed. (London: Longmans, Green, 1920), 139–40.

6. Nellie Mason Auten, "Some Phases of the Sweating System in the Garment Trades in Chicago," *American Journal of Sociology* 6, no. 5 (March 1901): 602–45.

7. Thanks are due to Xue Hong for helping to draw up the first draft of the questionnaire, which benefited from her familiarity with work hours and wages in supplier factories.

8. The surveyors were staff members of two indigenous Chinese labor NGOs who are very knowledgeable about the work conditions of migrant workers.

9. At best, we could only estimate each sampled factory's number of workers by taking the mean of the answers provided by respondents from that particular factory.

10. The weight for each factory, say, for garments, when used for making comparisons with toy factories is calculated as follows: Weight used for particular garment factory equals the *estimated workforce provided by worker respondents from that garment factory* divided by the estimated *total* workforce provided by workers for all sampled garment factories.

11. The exchange rate at the time when data was collected for this chapter was roughly US$1 to 8 yuan.

12. Anita Chan, Richard Madsen, and Jonathan Unger, *Chen Village: Revolution to Globalization* (Berkeley: University of California Press, 2009), chap. 15.

13. Our survey findings on hourly wages and monthly work hours are consistent with the most updated reports by China Labor Watch. China Labor Watch has conducted investigations from April to June 2009 of two Walmart shoe supplier factories. The investigations discovered that some workers made only 3.48 yuan per hour (US$0.51 per hour) and worked 77 hours per week (308 hours per month). This means that the wage level of 2009 fell between our garment and toy wage levels, which means there was no increase in wages, consistent with figure 4.1 in this chapter. This report is available at http://www.chinalaborwatch.org/20090727walmart.htm.

14. This percentage is an estimate. Since only managers can provide precise figures on gender, we could only ask worker informants to estimate the gender ratio in their own factories. We then averaged out the estimates for each factory, and then again took the average for all the sampled factories.

15. We have anecdotal evidence that the same shift in the gender ratio is also found in the shoe industry. In one enormous factory in Fujian that produces for an international brand, where one of us collected data in 2003, the male–female gender ratio stood at 30:70. By 2007 it had become 50:50.

16. This finding is consistent with a report by China Labor Watch, which conducted an investigation from April to June 2009 at two Walmart shoe supplier factories. The report revealed that some workers made only 3.48 yuan per hour (US$0.51 per hour) and worked 77 hours per week (308 hours per month). This means that the 2009 wage level of these toy workers fell between our garment and toy wage levels of a few years earlier. The report is available at http://www.chinalaborwatch.org/pro/proshow-123.html.

17. An interesting research project would be to see whether older workers and male workers are as productive as the young female workers who have been so sought after by management. If "older" workers and men are found to be as productive, then the findings would go against the (discriminatory) stereotype that young women workers are, by definition, more productive.

18. Diana Beaumont and the Shenzhen Workers' Self-Help Association, "Child Labour in China's Informalized Urban Industrial Sector," *Asian Labor Update*, January–June 2008, 12–17; "Small Hands: A Survey Report on Child Labor in China," *China Labor Bulletin*, Research Report 3, http://www.china-labour.org.hk/en/files/share/File/general/Child_labour_report_1.pdf.

19. Zhou Yiguang, "Wal-Mart's Orders in China Will Fall by 40 Percent: A Wal-Mart Chinese Regional Office Spokesperson Said This Number Still Needs to Be Confirmed", 21st Century Financial News (in Chinese), July 18, 2007.

20. Zhou Yiguan and Liu Zhengzheng, "Langsha: I Am Abandoning Walmart, Not That Walmart Is Abandoning Me," 21st Century Financial News (in Chinese), July 21, 2007.

21. Xue Liang and Huang Jian, "Shenzhen's Minimum Wage Adjustment Plan Will Be Released Soon: Standards May Not Be Adjusted Upwards," *Nanfang ribao* (Southern Daily) (in Chinese), June 28, 2007.

5. Corporate Cadres

1. For more on the relationship between employees and customers, see Eileen Otis's chapter in this volume.

2. Fiona Moore, *Transnational Business Cultures: Life and Work in a Multinational Corporation* (Burlington, VT: Ashgate, 2005), 2.

3. Nelson Lichtenstein, "'The Man in the Middle': A Social History of Automobile Industry Foremen," in *On the Line: Essays in the History of Auto Work,* ed. Lichtenstein and Stephen Meyer (Urbana: University of Illinois Press, 1989).

4. Michael Bergdahl, *The 10 Rules of Sam Walton: Success Secrets for Remarkable Results* (New York: Wiley, 2006); Michael Bergdahl, *What I Learned from Sam Walton: How to Compete and Thrive in a Wal-Mart World* (New York: Wiley, 2006); Robert Slater, *The Wal-Mart Decade* (New York: Portfolio, 2003); Don Soderquist, *The Wal-Mart Way: The Inside Story of the Success of the World's Largest Company* (New York: Nelson Business, 2005); Sam Walton, *Sam Walton: Made in America* (New York: Bantam, 1993).

5. David J. Davies, "China's Celebrity Entrepreneurs: Business Models for 'Success,'" in *Celebrity in China,* ed. Louise Edwards and Elaine Jeffreys (Hong Kong: Hong Kong University Press, 2010), 262–94.

6. A former store general manager provided these salary estimates corresponding to each grade in the summer of 2008 when the exchange rate was about seven yuan to one U.S. dollar. The salary ranges include bonuses and cost of living increases for large cities.

7. Unless otherwise noted, all translations are my own.

8. Allen W. Batteau, "Negations and Ambiguities in the Cultures of Organization," *American Anthropologist* 102, no. 4 (2001): 726–40.

9. I spoke with Rick, a comanager of an urban American Walmart store during two store tours and an extended conversation in the early spring of 2008.

10. Nelson Lichtenstein, ed., *Wal-Mart: The Face of Twenty-First-Century Capitalism* (New York: New Press, 2006), 18.

11. Bethany Moreton, *To Serve God and Wal-Mart: The Making of Christian Free Enterprise* (Cambridge: Harvard University Press, 2009).

12. Walton, *Sam Walton: Made in America.*

13. Slater, *The Wal-Mart Decade.*

14. Ibid., 54–55.

15. Ibid., 45.

16. Here I have summarized the words to the cheer from Slater's longer narrative description of the call and response. Slater, *The Wal-Mart Decade,* 47–48.

17. The similarity between representations of Sam Walton in Walmart's corporate culture and representations of Mao Zedong are examined in the context of ideal organizational structures in an earlier essay. In addition, that essay recounts a myth circulated among some managers at Walmart, China, that Sam Walton's corporate

culture was inspired by Chairman Mao's thought. See David J. Davies, "Wal-Mao: The Discipline of Corporate Culture and Studying Success at Wal-Mart China," *China Journal* 58 (2007): 1–27. Li Shan in chapter 6 of this volume describes a "cultural competition" between employees based on details of Sam Walton's life as similar to portrayals of the Cultural Revolution in contemporary Chinese film.

18. See Jianhua Zhang, *Xiang Jiefangjun Xuexi: Zui You Xiaolv Zuzhi De Guanli Zhi Dao* (Learn from the PLA: The path to the most efficient organizational management) (Beijing: Beijing Chubanshe, 2005).

19. Foucault, Michel. *Discipline and Punish: The Birth of the Prison* (New York: Vintage, 1995).

6. A Store Manager's Success Story

1. The authors would very much like to thank Edward, a former Walmart store general manager who agreed to the hours of interviews that provided material for this chapter during the summer of 2008. The recordings were subsequently transcribed and edited. Wherever possible, names and locations have been altered for anonymity.

2. For a description of the formal presentation of store culture, store management hierarchy, and a discussion of some issues of management style, see Davies, chapter 5. Bethany Moreton's book, *To Serve God and Wal-Mart: The Making of Christian Free Enterprise* (Cambridge: Harvard University Press, 2009), provides a comprehensive historical summary of the development of Walmart's management culture in the southern United States.

3. The previous chapter examines the way that Walmart's corporate management culture creates incentives for this "voluntary" extra work—and provides an interpretive lens for management to see volunteerism as entirely genuine rather than possibly the result of the coercion created by the culture.

4. At Walmart China all employees have English working names. Among managers it is common to call each other by their English names, even in Chinese conversation. For an insightful examination of English naming practices at foreign corporations, see Laurie Duthie, "The Chinese Meaning of English Names: Shanghai's Business Professionals and Western Naming Practices," *China Study* 2 (fall 2005): 49–73.

5. Eileen Otis discusses the experience of these vendor-provided workers in more detail in chap. 8.

6. See chap. 5 for a translation of this policy and Walmart's cultural emphasis on purity of service.

7. Anita Chan provides an insightful account and discussion of unionization of Walmart in China in "Organizing Wal-Mart in China: Two Steps Forward, One Step Back," *New Labor Forum* 16, no. 2 (2007): 91–101.

8. The managerial hierarchy of a Walmart store is described in chap. 5.

7. Practicing Cheer

1. As young people in China have become more and more computer savvy, blogs have become a popular medium of communication.

2. This was observed by Wu Ling, a graduate student at Beijing University who wrote her master's thesis on Walmart.

3. Walmart China employees wear red polo shirts and are therefore known as "red collar" workers.

4. Anita Chan, *Children of Mao: Personality Development and Political Activism in the Red Guard Generation* (Seattle: University of Washington Press, 1985), 60–69.

5. David Davies, "Wal-Mao: The Discipline of Corporate Culture and Studying Success at Wal-Mart China," *China Journal* 58 (2007): 1–27.

6. This was also observed by Wu Ling.

7. For the significance of this memorandum, see chapter 9.

8. Also called street-level trade unions (*jiedaoji gonghui*).

9. The translator met with Li Shan in Shanghai in August 2008 to discuss his blog and learn more about his experience working at Walmart.

10. Around US$1.20. *Kuai* is a common vernacular term for the Chinese RMB or yuan. When Li Shan started his diary in mid-2005, one RMB was worth around US$0.12.

11. Because of the importance of rice and noodles in the Chinese diet, some people believe that meat alone cannot fill one's stomach.

12. The word *cheer* was written in English in the original blog.

13. According to Walmart China's English website, "The Sundown Rule means we strive to answer requests by sundown on the day we receive them."

14. Marshall is the English name of the store general manager. As noted in chapter 6, all Walmart employees are given an English name (or use the one they already have) and everyone addresses each other using given names.

15. A British retailer.

16. The word *policy* was written in English in the original blog.

17. Li Shan is referring to the "campaigns" of the Maoist era, which were run by edict and had goals that no one could question. Those who failed to participate or show enthusiasm could be penalized.

18. China's first Walmart trade union branch was established on July 29, 2006, at the Jinjiang location in Quangzhou City, Fujian Province.

19. "Glorious Years" ("*Guanghui suiyue*"), a song by popular Hong Kong group Beyond.

20. Lao She (1899–1966). A major figure of twentieth-century Chinese literature best known for his works *Camel Xiangzi* and *Teahouse*.

21. GfK Group is a German market research company with operations in China and other countries.

8. Working in Walmart, Kunming

1. As Davies (chapter 5) points out, store managers exercise purchase discretion for less than half of the products they sell. Walmart's store managers have substantially less power over what goods are sold at each of their stores when compared to managers of other retail chains in China, but it would seem that Walmart store managers use whatever limited purchasing discretion they have to buy goods adapted to local tastes, especially in the food departments.

2. There are two exceptions. One is the study of transitions in clerical work after the introduction of word processors and other forms of mechanization; Harry Braverman, *Labor and Monopoly Capital: The Degradation of Work in the Twentieth Century* (New York: Monthly Review, 1998). Another is Leidner's analysis of the routinization of labor at McDonald's fastfood restaurants. In this work, though, technology is seen as a backdrop and the author focuses on the company's attempt to control workers' "words, demeanor, and attitudes," mostly through scripting interactions; Robin Leidner, *Fast Food, Fast Talk* (Berkeley: University of California Press, 1993), 83.

3. Arlie R. Hochschild, *The Managed Heart: Commercialization of Human Feeling* (Berkeley: University of California Press, 1983).

4. Richard Edwards, *Contested Terrain: The Transformation of the Workplace in the Twentieth Century* (New York: Basic Books, 1979).

5. Linda Fuller and Vicki Smith, "Consumers Reports: Management by Customers in a Changing Economy," *Work, Employment, and Society* 5, no. 1 (1991): 1–16; Leidner, *Fast Food, Fast Talk.*

6. Fuller and Smith, "Consumers Reports"; J. J. Sallaz, "The House Rules: Autonomy and Interests among Service Workers in the Contemporary Casino Industry," *Work and Occupations* 29 (2002): 394–427; Marek Korczynski, Karen Shire, Stephen Frenkel, and Mary Tam, "Service Work in Consumer Capitalism: Customers, Control, and Contradictions," *Work, Employment, and Society* 14, no. 4 (2000): 669–87.

7. Hochschild, *The Managed Heart.*

8. Sallaz, "The House Rules."

9. Leidner, *Fast Food, Fast Talk.*

10. Ibid.; Eileen Otis, "Beyond the Industrial Paradigm: Market-Embedded Labor and the Gender Organization of Global Service Labor in China," *American Sociological Review* 73 (2008): 15–36; Cameron L. Macdonald and Carmen Sirianni, "The Service Society and the Changing Experience of Work," in *Working in the Service Society,* ed. Cameron Lynne Macdonald and Carmen Sirianni (Philadelphia: Temple University Press, 1996), 1–26.

11. Fuller and Smith, "Consumers Reports."

12. Heidi Gottfried, "Temp(t)ing Bodies: Shaping Gender at Work in Japan," *Sociology* 37 (2003): 257–76; Lan Pei-Chia, "The Body as a Contested Terrain for Labor Control: Cosmetics Retailers in Department Stores and Direct Selling," in *The Critical Study of Work: Labor, Technology, and Global Production,* ed. Rick Baldoz, Charles

Koeber, and Philip Kraft (Philadelphia: Temple University Press, 2001), 83–105; Otis, "Beyond the Industrial Paradigm."

13. Otis, "Beyond the Industrial Paradigm"; Christine Williams, *Inside Toyland: Working, Shopping and Social Inequality* (Berkeley: University of California Press, 2006).

14. Steven H. Lopez, "Emotional Labor and Organized Emotional Care: Conceptualizing Nursing Home Care Work," *Work and Occupations* 2 (2006): 133–60.

15. Macdonald and Sirianni, "The Service Society."

16. Otis, "Beyond the Industrial Paradigm."

17. Edwards, *Contested Terrain*.

18. Michael Burawoy, *Manufacturing Consent: Changes in the Labor Process under Monopoly Capitalism* (Chicago: University of Chicago Press, 1979). Burawoy and Anne Smith describe a third type, "hegemonic despotism," which combines the first two in "The Rise of Hegemonic Despotism in United States' Industry," *Prokla* 58 (1985): 139–53.

19. The research assistant asks not to be named, so I use the pseudonym of Lihua to identify her. Lihua was a college student who grew up in Kunming. She was trained to collect ethnographic data and spoke Mandarin, as well as the local dialect, fluently. Her status as a researcher was unknown to the employer or to fellow employees.

20. Nescafé has developed a brand of Yunnan instant coffee. Furthermore, the outlets contain a local pharmacy, Jianzhijia. Pharmaceuticals is a major growth industry in Yunnan.

21. Walmart donated 200,000 yuan (about US$25,000) to the city for dam construction.

22. China Labor Watch, "Wage/Unemployment Standards in Selected Provinces/Municipalities/Cities," http://www.chinalaborwatch.org/2007wagestand.html.

23. This stands in sharp contrast to this volume's chapters on management by Davies (chapter 5) and Davies and Seeman (chapter 6). While workers' overtime was strictly limited by managers, managers seemed to be encouraged to volunteer for long hours of overtime work. I would explain this by pointing to an aspirational divide separating workers and managers. Most workers were part-time and did not expect to work at Walmart for an extended period. In fact, labor turnover seemed quite substantial. According to Davies, managers aspired to long-term employment and advancement within Walmart. And they had internalized corporate cultural principles. Walmart has more to gain and less to lose by using the "voluntary" overtime of the managers that is often off the clock, rather than pay rank-and-file cashiers to work overtime. In fact, for this reason managers may be more exploited than workers.

24. See Ellen Rosen, "How to Squeeze More Out of a Penny," in *Wal-Mart: The Face of Twenty-First-Century Capitalism,* ed. Nelson Lichtenstein (New York: New Press, 2006), 243–60.

25. Disciplinary action covers three general areas: procedures, attitude, and behaviors. A severe disciplinary reality belies the support and mentorship connoted by the language of coaching and guidance. Workers in U.S. Walmart stores have noted similarly harsh uses of this system of discipline. See Josh Smith, "My First Coaching," *Working at Wal-Mart*, February 8, 2006, http://workingatwal-mart.blogspot.com/2006/02/my-first-coaching.html.

26. This may indicate that the union presence in outlets organized relatively late after Walmart accepted the union may only be nominal. See Anita Chan, "Organizing Wal-Mart: The Chinese Trade Union at a Crossroads," *Japan Focus*, September 8, http://japanfocus.org/products/details/2217, for an analysis of the ACFTU's organizing efforts.

27. Michel Foucault, *Discipline and Punish: The Birth of the Prison*, trans. Alan Sheridan (New York: Vintage, 1979).

28. Workers are instructed to look for a water ink image, then feel the bill for a small protrusion on a section of Mao Tse-tung's collar, and then finally to listen to the sound that the bill makes when crumpled. Counterfeit bills are very common in China, and if the cashier mistakenly accepts one, the penalty is severe.

29. This analysis of sales workers relies on substantially less intensive data than has been collected for the cashiers. As mentioned earlier, I collected interview and observational data on sales labor, but did not directly participate in this work. My conclusions about this arena of labor are therefore not supported by the kind of detail from the case study of cashiers, but my many and varied observations as well as subsequent discussions with Walmart personnel from other stores convince me they are valid.

30. There are three types of salespeople working for vendors—underground (*hei tuixiaoyuan*), part-time, and long-term. Long-term salespeople are permanently assigned to a single Walmart outlet. They wear Walmart badges and some wear aprons with the company emblem. Part-time salespeople rotate through different stores, both Walmart and other firms. There are a number of people in street clothes who vend wares at the store without the permission of the retailer and without paying the vendor fee, but there is little that managers can do to thwart these salespeople; they are considered customers and are not in fact breaking any national laws, so management cannot force them to leave.

31. Wu Xiaoyu, "365 Days: Wal-Mart Workers Go to Work Every Single Day," *Nanjing News*, May 22, 2008, http://www.njnews.cn/z/ca966389.html.

9. Unionizing Chinese Walmart Stores

1. Anita Chan, "Labor Relations in Foreign-funded Ventures," in *Adjusting to Capitalism: Chinese Workers and the State*, ed. Greg O'Leary (Armonk, NY: M. E. Sharpe, 1998), 122–49.

2. New China News Agency (in Chinese), November 24, 2004.

3. Beijing Chinese News (in Chinese), November 24, 2004; David Barboza, "Walmart Bows to Trade Unions at Stores in China," *New York Times,* November 25, 2004.

4. Number One Financial Daily (in Chinese), August 6, 2006.

5. Xi Xiande and Wu Jinyong, "'Attack Wal-Mart" (in Chinese), *Zhongguo renli ziyuanwan* (Chinese Human Resources Network), September 5, 2006, http://book. hr.com.cn/content/139877.htm.

6. ACFTU website, http://www.acftu.org.cn/template/10002/index.jsp, August 17, 2006.

7. It was broadcast on Chinese television on July 31, 2006; Chinese Economic Management News (in Chinese), August 6, 2006.

8. Business Affairs Weekly (in Chinese), September 5, 2006.

9. Mark Dudzic, Larry Cohen, and Joshua B. Freeman, "Debate: The Crisis of Workers' Rights," *New Labor Forum* 14, no. 1 (spring 2005): 59–78.

10. Number One Financial Daily (in Chinese), August 3, 2006.

11. Chinese Economic Management News (in Chinese), August 7 and 8, 2006.

12. Number One Financial Daily (in Chinese), August 11, 2006; ACFTU website, August 11, 2006, http://www.acftu.org/template/10004/file.jsp?cid=181&aid=41372.

13. Business Affairs Weekly (in Chinese), September 5, 2006.

14. *Gongren ribao* (Workers' Daily) (in Chinese), August 19 and 21, 2006.

15. ACFTU website, August 16, 2006, http://www.acftu.org/template/10004/file. jsp?cid=222&aid=41801.

16. For a lengthy report on this case see *Globalization Monitor,* http://www. globalmon.org.hk/en/about-gm/; also see "Workers Fight to Save their Union Activist," *China Labor News Translations,* October 16, 2008, http://www.clntranslations. org/article/35/workers-fight-to-save-their-union-activists. I am one of the two coeditors of *China Labor News Translations.* The other coeditor is Diana Beaumont, coauthor of the next chapter.

17. "Cleaners Want to Set Up a Union to Protect Their Rights" (in Chinese), Southern Metropolitan, April 28, 2007.

18. *Guangzhou ribao* (Guangzhou Daily) (in Chinese), August 8, 2006; Beijing Commercial News (in Chinese), August 22, 2006.

19. An investigative report by two journalists from *China Business News* (in Chinese, June 15, 2006) confirmed the story and added details about workers blacking out from fatigue. In early July, Foxconn filed a lawsuit against the two journalists, demanding 30 million yuan (US$3.75 million). The company slashed its defamation claim to just one yuan (12 cents) in August and dropped the lawsuit in September.

20. http://www.sina.com.cn, January 1, 2007; South China Metropolitan News (Chinese), January 1, 2007.

21. *Sanghai ribao* (Shanghai Daily) (in Chinese), January 3, 2007.

22. In June 2008 the ACFTU embarked on another organizing campaign—to establish union branches at every one of the Fortune 500 companies that operate

facilities in China. Calling the campaign a "100-day focused action," local unions all over China would have to set up unions in 10,000 workplaces. Without a doubt, these are ineffectual and management dominated. On this Fortune 500 campaign, see www.clnttranslations.com, August 20, 2008.

23. In December 2006, searching the Web, I found ten Chinese reports on the establishment of these party branches.

24. *New China Web*, August 25, 2006.

25. This slogan appeared in a report on the setting up of the party branch in Shenyang in September. *Gongren ribao* (Workers' Daily) (in Chinese), August 22, 2006.

26. "New at Wal-Marts in China: A Communist Party Branch," *International Herald Tribune,* December 18, 2006; Shenzhen Special Economic Zone News (in Chinese), December 16, 2006; *People's Daily Online,* December 16, 2006.

27. "The Emergence of Real Trade Unionism in Wal-Mart Stores," *China Labor News Translations,* May 4, 2008, http://www.clntranslations.org/article/30/draft.

28. Luohu District Government website, "Party Branch Begins to Function: Workers with Party Membership Now Have a Home" (in Chinese) (date unknown), http://www.szlh.gov.cn/main/zfjg/jdbsc/lh/gzdt/41346.shtml#.

29. Available at http://finance.sina.cn.

30. "The Emergence of Real Trade Unionism in Wal-Mart Stores."

31. Ibid.

32. "108 jian woermadian jianli gonghui qiye quanbu qianding jiti hetong" (108 Wal-Mart Store Unions Have All Signed Collective Agreements), *Guangming ribao* (Guangming Daily), October 3, 2008.

33. "Wal-Mart Has Signed a Collective Contract on Wage Increases, Etc.," (in Chinese), *Huashang chenbao* (Chinese Business Morning News), July 15, 2008, http://nes.liao1.com/newspages?200807/2527492.html. Also see "Wal-Mart in Pay Deals with Chinese Unions," *Financial Times,* July 24, 2008.

34. A detailed discussion of the problems related to this agreement is in "The Bad and the Good of the Wal-Mart ACFTU Collective Agreement," May 18, 2009, http://www.clntranslations.org/article/38/wal-mart-contract.

35. "Quanzhou woerma qianding jiti hetong: jinjiangdian gonghui cong jianhui zouxiang jianzhi" (Collective Agreement of a Quanzhou Wal-Mart Store: Jinjiang Store's Trade Union on the Road from Setting Up a Union to Setting Up a System), *Fujian ribao* (Fujian Daily), July 24, 2008.

36. "The Bad and the Good of the Wal-Mart-ACFTU Collective Agreement."

37. A long interesting report from China's best news magazine, *Nanfang zhoumo* (Southern Weekend) on Gao's conflict with Walmart and his resignation is in *China Labor News Translations,* September 22, 2008, http://www.clntranslations.org.

38. For example, "Woerma zairong qiye yu zhigongdaibiao qianding jithetong: yuangong gonzi jiang dedao zhishao 8% zengzhang" (Wal-Mart Signed a Collective Agreement with Workers' Representatives at the Jirong Enterprise: Staff Wages Go up at Least 8 Percent"), Sichuan Ribao (Sichuan Daily), September 15, 2008.

39. "Quanzong fachu tuidong Woerma qianding jiti hetong 'zongdongyuan,'" *Gongren ribao* (Workers Daily), August 15, 2008.

40. "The Power of Pork: Rising Pork Prices Have Jacked Up the Consumer Price Index, Leading to Worries of Inflation," *Beijing Review*, June 28, 2007, 32.

10. Did Unionization Make a Difference?

Thanks to Feng Tongqing, Wu Ling, and Gai Haotao for collecting some of the data in this chapter.

1. The minimum wage standard in Shenzhen is announced each July.

2. "Woerma yuangong chengli dierge gonghui" (Walmart Workers Set Up the Second Union), http://tw.aboluowang.com/news/data/2006/0806/article_4662.html.

3. Walmart gives store employees a bonus at year's end that is the equivalent of obtaining 13 months of pay per year, so the store workers who lasted the full year can be considered to have obtained about 870–980 yuan per month.

4. This drive for collective contracts at Walmart was discussed in *Chinese Labor News Translations*, May 18, 2009, http://www.clntranslations.org/article/38/wal-mart-contract. Two of the authors of this chapter, Diana Beaumont and Anita Chan, are the coeditors of the website.

5. "Shenzhen woerma yu 8,500 yuangong qianding jiti hetong" (Shenzhen Walmart and Over 8,500 Workers Signed a Collective Contract), *Nanfang ribao* (Southern Daily), July 25, 2008, http://news.xinhuanet.com/fortune/2008-07/25/content_8764743.htm.

6. "Wage Increase Will Soon Surpass Average GDP Increase," (in Chinese), *Guangzhou ribao* (Guangzhou Daily), March 27, 2008, http://gzdaily.dayoo.com/html/2008-03/27/content_147902.htm.

7. *China Daily*, April 21, 2009 (in English). All of the information in this and the next paragraph derives from this article and from *China Daily*, April 15, 2009.

8. *China Daily*, April 21, 2009.

11. Workers and Communities versus Walmart

1. A. Gentleman, "Indians Protest Wal-Mart's Wholesale Entry," *New York Times*, August 10, 2007, http://www.nytimes.com/2007/08/10/business/worldbusiness/10Wal-Mart.html.

2. C. Buckley, "Asda Centres Face 5-day Strike," *The Times*, June 23, 2006, http://business.timesonline.co.uk/tol/business/industry_sectors/retailing/article678265.ece.

3. A. Chan, "Organizing Wal-Mart in China: Two Steps Forward, One Step Back for China's Unions," *New Labor Forum* 16, no. 2 (2008): 93–95.

4. Harris Interactive, March 8, 2008, "The 9th Annual RQ: Reputations of the 60 Most Visible Companies: A Survey of the U.S. General Public," in Walmart Watch, http://walmartwatch.com/img/documents/harris_interactive_report.pdf.

5. http://walmartwatch.com/.

6. http://www.wakeupwalmart.com/.

7. G. Miller, "Everyday Low Wages: The Price We All Pay for Wal-Mart," U.S. House of Representatives, Democratic Staff of Committee on Education and the Workforce, February 16, 2004 (Miller Report), http://wakeupwalmart.com/facts/miller-report.pdf.

8. Y. Q. Mui, "Wal-Mart Says It Will Improve Health Benefits," *Washington Post*, February 24, 2006, http://www.washingtonpost.com/wp-dyn/content/article/2006/02/23/AR2006022301857.html.

9. Child Labor Coalition, "Child Labor Advocates Call Wal-Mart Settlement Disastrous," February 16, 2005, www.stopchildlabor.org/pressroom/wal-martsettlement.html.

10. http://www.Wal-Marclass.com/Wal-Martclass casedevelopments.html.

11. World Bank, "Local Economic Development," http://web.worldbank.org/WBSITE/EXTERNAL/TOPICS/EXTURBANDEVELOPMENT/EXTLED/.

12. For examples of how American labor is promoting the high road for economic development, see http://www.cows.org/pdf/rp-highperform.pdf; for job training, see http://www.workingforamerica.org/documents/whatwedo.htm; for green jobs, see http://www.goodjobsfirst.org/pdf/gjfgreenjobsrpt.pdf.

13. *Store Wars: When Wal-Mart Comes to Town*, directed by M. Peled, Public Broadcasting System (2001).

14. Walmart, "Wal-Mart: A Manager's Toolbox to Remaining Union Free: Confidential," available at: www.reclaimdemocracy.org/walmart/antiunionman.pdf.

15. Miller Report.

16. International Confederation of Free Trade Unions (ICFTU), "Internationally Recognised Core Labour Standards in the United States: Report for the WTO General Council Review of the Trade Policies of the United States," 2004, http://www.ituc-csi.org/report-for-the-wto-general-council,5295.html?lang=en.

17. Human Rights Watch, "Discounting Rights: Wal-Mart's Violation of US Workers Rights to Freedom of Association," April 30, 2007, http://www.hrw.org/en/reports/2007/04/30/discounting-rights.

18. A. Dube, T. W. Lester, and B. Eidlin, "Firm Entry and Wages: Impact of Wal-Mart Growth on Earnings Throughout the Retail Sector," August 6, 2007, University of California, Berkeley, Institute for Research on Labor and Employment, http://escholarship.org/uc/item/22s5k4pv.

19. D. Neumark, J. Zhang, and S. Ciccarella, "The Effects of Wal-Mart on Local Labor Markets," Institute for Local Self-Reliance, 2007, www.newrules.org/retail/neumarkstudy.pdf.

20. Civic Economics, "The Andersonville Study of Retail Economics," February 2005, http://www.civiceconomics.com/Andersonville/html/reports.html.

21. P. Dreier and K. Candaele, "A Watershed Strike," *The Nation*, November 10, 2003.

22. Interview with B. Carpenter, president, UFCW Local 1179, January 2003.

23. J. Bair and S. Bernstein, "Labor and the Wal-Mart Effect," in *Wal-Mart World: the World's Biggest Corporation in the Global Economy*, ed. S. D. Brunn (New York: Routledge, 2006), 106–9.

24. K. Jacobs, A. Dube, and F. Su, "Declining Health Coverage in the Southern California Grocery Industry," University of California, Berkeley, Center for Labor Research and Education, January 2007, http://laborcenter.berkeley.edu/healthcare/grocery_industry07.pdf.

25. A. Dube and K. Jacobs, "The Impact of Health Benefit Reductions in the Unionized Grocery Sector in California," University of California, Berkeley, Center for Labor Research and Education, 2007, http://laborcenter.berkeley.edu/retail/heatlh_benefit_grocery07.pdf.

26. J. Hirsch, "Grocery Union Fought for Unity," *Los Angeles Times,* July 24, 2007, http://articles.latimes.com/2007/jul/24/business/fi-grocery24.

27. See K. Stone and G. M. Artz, "The Impact of 'Big-Box' Building Materials Stores on Host Towns and Surrounding Counties in a Midwestern State," American Independent Business Alliance, August 5, 2001, http://www.amiba.net/assets/files/pdfs/Studies/stone_home_improvement_center_study.pdf; and the Institute for Local Self-Reliance, "The Economic Impact of Locally Owned Businesses vs. Chains: A Cast Study in Midcoast Maine," September 2003, http://www.newrules.org/retail/midcoaststudy.pdf.

28. A. Dube and K. Jacobs, "Hidden Cost of Wal-Mart Jobs," University of California, Berkeley, Center for Labor Research and Education, August 2, 2004, http://laborcenter.berkeley.edu/retail/walmart.pdf.

29. Miller Report.

30. For an interesting example of a lawsuit claiming predatory pricing against Walmart by a pharmacist in Conway, Arkansas, see http://www.momandpopnyc.com/campaigns/Wal-Mart/articles/Predatory%20Pricing/Conway,%20BusHorizons,%209.1995.pdf.

31. A. Chaddha, "Good for the 'Hood?'" *ColorLines: News for Action,* July 2007, http://www.colorlines.com/archives/2005/07/good_for_the_hood.html.

32. *Black Commentator,* "Wal-Mart Threat Fuels New Urban Politics; Wanted: A Plan for the Cities to Save Themselves," May 20, 2004, http://www.blackcommentator.com/91/91_cover_cities_pf.html.

33. M. Barbaro, "Maryland Sets a Health Cost for Wal-Mart," *New York Times,* January 13, 2006, http://www.nytimes.com/2006/01/13/business/13walmart.html.

34. *China Daily,* "Labor Disputes Jump 59% in China during Q1 of 2009," April 24, 2009, http://chinachallenges.blogs.com/my_weblog/2009/04/labor-disputes-jump-59-in-china-during-q1-of-2009.html.

35. *China Labour Bulletin,* "Going It Alone: The Workers' Movement in China (2007–2008)," July 9, 2009, http://www.clb.org.hk/en/files/share/File/research_reports/workers_movement_07_08.pdf.

36. China Labor News Translation, "Honda Strike and the Union," http://www. clntranslations.org/article/56/honda.

37. Xinhua News Service, "Guangzhou Nansha Denso Raises Wages by 800 Yuan and Resolves Strike," June 27, 2010, http://finance.ifeng.com/news/20100627/ 2349078.shtml.

38. Author's interview with Kong X., October 13, 2010, deputy chair, Guangdong Confederation of Trade Unions.

39. "Guanyu 1008dian HRM he GM tuifan gonghui zhuxi er jinxing xin xuan-ju" (Incident Regarding Store #1008 HRM and GM Overthrowing Union Chair and Holding New Elections), *Tieba Baidu* (Baidu search engine), October 28, 2010, http://tieba.baidu.com/f?kz-682463135. Author's translation.

40. L. Chen, "Woerma yuangong jiti taoxin" (Walmart Workers Collectively Discuss Wages), *Sina News,* reprinted from *Nanfang Daoshi Bao* (Southern Metropolitan News), January 4, 2008, http://news.sina.com.cn/c/2008-01-04/092913195895s.shtml. Author's translation.

41. International Labor Rights Forum, "Wal-Mart Sweatshops Lawsuit Filed," September 1, 2005, http://www.laborrights.org/creating-a-sweatfree-world/wal-mart-campaign/resources/10673.

42. J. Spencer and J. Ye, "Toxic Factories Take Toll on China's Labor Force," *Wall Street Journal,* January 15, 2008, http://online.wsj.com/article/SB119972343587572351. html.

43. Asia Network for the Rights of Occupational Accident Victims (AN-ROAV), *2009 Annual Report,* http://www.anroav.org/images/anroav%20con-ference%20re port%202009.pdf?PHPSESSID=67a81949d9d83121d2276abd977e 7d54, p.5.

44. Students and Scholars against Corporate Misbehavior (SACOM), "Wal-Mart's Sweatshop Monitoring Fails to Catch Violations: The Story of Toys Made in China for Wal-Mart," June 2007, http://sacom.hk/wp-content/uploads/2008/07/ walmart_reportsacomjun2007.pdf, 22–6.

45. E. Cody, "Short-Lived Strike Reflects Strength of Japan-China Ties," *Washington Post,* April 26, 2005, http://www.washingtonpost.com/ac2/wp-dyn/A16465-2005-Apr26?language=printer.

46. T. Lum, "Social Unrest in China," U.S. Congressional Research Service Reports and Issue Briefs, 2006, http://digitalcommons.ilr.cornell.edu/crs/19.

47. A. Tian, "Local Government Officials Give Green Light for Most Favored Nations to Wal-Mart and Other," Sina.com Finance website, March 6, 2009, http:// finance.sina.com.cn/roll/20090306/02025938155.shtml.

48. Author's interview with L. Xhuxi, vice chairman, Guangzhou Federation of Trade Unions, February 14, 2009; B. Shailor, "Skirting the Facts on China," *New Labor Forum* 14, no. 2 (2005): 105–8.

49. Shailor, "Skirting the Facts on China."

50. M. Fong and K. Maher, "U.S. Labor Leaders Aided China's Wal-Mart Coup," *Washington Post,* June 22, 2007, http://online.wsj.com/article/SB118245269561643754.html.

51. Change to Win, "Change To Win, China Trade Unions Sign First Formal Agreement," August 27, 2009, http://www.changetowin.org/no_cache/for-the-media/press-releases-and-statements/change-to-win-china-trade-unions-sign-first-formal-agreement.html?sword_list%5B%5D-china.

NOTES ON CONTRIBUTORS

Diana Beaumont until recently worked at the Textile Clothing Footwear Union of Australia, and prior to that she worked at the Asia Monitor Resource Centre in Hong Kong where she conducted research on Chinese labor and contributed to the journal *Asian Labour Update*. She also spent a year working in Shenzhen, China, for a Chinese labor NGO. With Anita Chan, Beaumont coedits a Web-based journal, *China Labor News Translations*.

Anita Chan is research professor at the China Research Centre of the University of Technology, Sydney. She has published widely on Chinese industry, labor issues, rural China, and Chinese youth, and was coeditor of the *China Journal* from 1989 through 2005. The most recent of her ten books are, as coauthor, *Chen Village: Revolution to Globalization* (2009), and as editor, *Labor in Vietnam* (2011).

David J. Davies is associate professor of anthropology and director of the East Asian studies program at Hamline University in Saint Paul, Minnesota. His current research examines the sociocultural construction of success in contemporary urban China, and his work on management culture at Walmart in China has been part of this larger project. Davies has published on nostalgia and social memory of the Cultural Revolution, and Chinese celebrity entrepreneurs.

Nelson Lichtenstein is MacArthur Foundation Professor of History and director of the Center for the Study of Work, Labor, and Democracy at the

University of California, Santa Barbara. He is the author, most recently, of *The Retail Revolution: How Wal-Mart Created a Brave New World of Business* (2009) and editor of *American Capitalism: Social Thought and Political Economy in the Twentieth Century* (2006).

Scott E. Myers is visiting professor of Chinese translation and interpretation at the Monterey Institute of International Studies. A former union organizer, he holds master's degrees in comparative literature from New York University and Chinese translation from the Monterey Institute of International Studies. Myers recently completed an English translation of *Beijing Comrades*, a contemporary novel by Bei Tong.

Eileen M. Otis is assistant professor of sociology at the University of Oregon, and she is the author of *Markets and Bodies: Women, Service Work and the Making of Inequality in China* (2011). Otis held an An Wang Postdoctoral Fellowship at Harvard University's Fairbank Center. She has conducted research on China's retail sector and has published in *American Sociological Review, American Behavioral Scientist, Qualitative Sociology,* and *Politics and Society*.

Pun Ngai is deputy director of the Peking University-HK Polytechnic University Social Service Research Center and associate professor at Hong Kong Polytechnic University. Her book *Made in China: Women Factory Workers in a Global Workplace* (2005) won the C. Wright Mills Award as the best sociological work on a contemporary public issue. She has published widely on industrial, labor, and gender issues in the *China Journal, China Quarterly, Modern China,* and other journals.

Katie Quan is associate chair of the University of California, Berkeley, Center for Labor Research and Education, and codirector of the International Center for Joint Labor Research at Sun Yat-sen University in Guangzhou, China. Formerly a garment worker and union organizer, she now specializes in labor strategies in the global economy. Quan has recently published in *Amerasia Journal*, Charles Whalen's *The Global Evolution of Industrial Relations,* Dorothy Sue Cobble's *The Sex of Class,* and Michael Zweig's *What's Class Got to Do with It?*

Taylor Seeman is a former student of David J. Davies at Hamline University in Saint Paul, Minnesota. In 2008 she was awarded a collaborative research fellowship to conduct research on Walmart management in China. In 2009 she returned to China on a Critical Language Scholarship from the U.S. Department of State. Seeman currently is a Teach for America Corps member, after which she plans to study international law.

Kaxton Siu is a doctoral candidate at the Australian National University conducting comparative research on the garment industry in China and Vietnam. He has published on labor issues in China, Vietnam, and Hong Kong and is presently coediting a special journal issue on the "Resurgence of Class Analysis."

Jonathan Unger is a sociologist at the Australian National University. He has published more than a dozen books about China, including *Chen Village: Revolution to Globalization* (2009, coauthored). From 1987 through 2005 he edited the *China Journal,* one of the two major journals in the field.

Xue Hong is a lecturer in the Department of Sociology at East China Normal University. She received her Ph.D. in sociology from the Chinese University of Hong Kong in 2009. Her doctoral dissertation, "Manufacturing Uncertainty: The Politics of Flexible Production in China's High-Tech Electronics Industry in the Age of Globalization," was awarded the biannual Best Thesis Award by the Hong Kong Sociological Association. Xue's research has appeared in *International Labor and Working Class History* and other Chinese journals.

Yu Xiaomin is associate professor of the School of Social Development and Public Policy at Beijing Normal University. She obtained her doctoral degree in social sciences from the Hong Kong University of Science and Technology. Her primary research interests include industrial relations, corporate social responsibility, and civil society. Yu's publications have appeared in a variety of academic journals, including *Journal of Business Ethics, Economic and Industrial Democracy,* and *Social Enterprise Journal.*

INDEX

Page numbers in *italics* indicate figures or tables.

factory inspections, impact of, 67–68
full-time workers, 178–79, 219–20, *220,
221
garment workers, 73, 79–81, *80, 82,*
88–89
hourly *vs.* monthly expression of, 87–89,
92–93
migrant workers, 75–76, *76,* 78–81, *80*
sales representatives, 222–23
toy workers, 79–81, *80, 82,* 88–89
urban residents, 75–76, *76*
wages, desired
migrant workers, 85–87, *86*
Wake-Up Wal-Mart, 253n6
Wallerstein, Emmanuel, 17
Walmart, 32–33, 70, 239
China, expansion into, 1, 97, 176, 177
Chinese Walmart stores, comparison
to, 6–7, 173–74, 180
code monitoring, 62, 63–64, 64–69
code of conduct (*See* Ethical Standards
program)
cultural paraphernalia, display of, 8
disciplinary system, 133, 184, 185, 273n25
economic power, 1, 16, 253n1
employee turnover rates, 8, 199, 223,
234
Gifts and Gratuity Policy, 50, 114–15,
127, 139, 183
labor law violations, 179, 241–42, 247
labor practices, 30–32, 55
lawsuits against, 32, 241–42, 247
logistics technology, 5, 21–25
organizing efforts against, 240–45,
249–51
rural origins, 18–21
toy retailing, 4, 57, *58,* 58–59
union avoidance, 2, 19, 199, 215
working conditions, 241–43
See also Walmart China
Walmart, corporate culture, 7–8, 19–21,
99, 107–10
beliefs and values, 107–8
Christian ethos, 20

coercive nature of, 117–19, 127–28, 129
communitarian ethos, 19–20
deployment of, 108–10, 128
See also Walmart China, corporate
culture
Walmart cheer, 8, 109–10, 182
Walmart China
American image, promotion of, 177
anti-union tactics, 203, 210
collective bargaining, 211–14, 235–37
cultural paraphernalia, display of, 8
employee rankings, 103–4
English naming practice, 103, 177,
269n4
management structure, 102–6,
160–61
organizing efforts against, 246–51
technological control of workers,
174–75
trade unions, undermining of, 226–27,
233
unionization of, 8–9, 143–48
U.S. stores, comparison to, 6–7, 173–74,
180
wage package, manipulation of, 219–20,
222
working conditions, 218–23, 222,
262n56
See also Walmart; *specific Walmart
China stores*
Walmart China, corporate culture,
110–29
cooperative spirit, 119–20, *120*
customer satisfaction, *124,* 124–25
display of, 110–17, *112*
egalitarianism, 120–21, 182–83
feedback mechanisms, 121–25
"open door policy," 120
refinement of, 128–29
transformative value of core principles,
115
variety in representation, 111, 116–17
yellow "smileys," 115–16
See also Walmart, corporate culture

Walmartization, 1–2
    global supply chain, 3–6
    Walmart China stores, 7–8
"Walmart people," 125–26
Walmart suppliers. *See* suppliers
Walmart Watch, 253n6
The Walmart Way (Soderquist), 20
"Wal-quotes," 111–13
Walton, Sam, 18–20, 259n13
    Mao and, 268–69n17
    middlemen, hostility to, 22–23
    mythic persona, 7, 107
Wang, Mr. (toy factory employer), 43
Wang Zhaoguo, 202
"war room," 253n6
Washington Post, 45
Webb, Sidney and Beatrice, 72
Williams, Tom, 64
Wong, Charles, 27
work hours
    export-industry workers, 79–81, *80, 81,*
        84, 84
    factory inspections, impact of, 66–67
    See also overtime
working conditions
    export-industry workers, 5

factory inspections, impact of, 66–69
Walmart China, 218–23
See also code monitoring; codes of
        conduct; wages; work hours
work-study program, 178
Wu, Tiger, 32

Xiao Wei, 135–36, 150
Xixiang Walmart, 218
    trade union, 223–25, 226
    wages, 219, 220, *220*
Xuanwu District Trade Union, 229–30,
        232–33, *233*
Xuanwumen Walmart trade union, 232, 234
    worker perception of, 231
Xu Mingde, 213, 214

Yantian International Container Terminal, 15
yellow "smileys," 115–16
Yeung, C. K., 60
Yu Yuan factory complex, 15, 32
Yuxi City, Yunnan Province, 177

Zhichun Road Walmart trade union, 231,
        232, 234
    worker perception of, 231